I0810543

IMAGES
of America

WAYNESBURG

On the Cover: Jimmie's Lunch on the southwest corner of High and Morris Streets was famous throughout the area for its hot dogs available with a variety of optional toppings. The most popular customer request was "please run my dog through the garden." (Courtesy of the Greene County Historical Society.)

IMAGES
of America

WAYNESBURG

Glenn J.R.T. Toothman III
and Candice L. Buchanan

ARCADIA
PUBLISHING

Copyright © 2015 by Glenn J.R.T. Toothman III and Candice L. Buchanan
ISBN 978-1-4671-2278-8

Published by Arcadia Publishing
Charleston, South Carolina

Printed in the United States of America

Library of Congress Control Number: 2014943657

For all general information, please contact Arcadia Publishing:
Telephone 843-853-2070
Fax 843-853-0044
E-mail sales@arcadiapublishing.com
For customer service and orders:
Toll-Free 1-888-313-2665

Visit us on the Internet at www.arcadiapublishing.com

In honor of Fred High, Dr. G. Wayne Smith, and James "Fuzzy" Randolph, whose inspired preservation of Waynesburg's history has made all the difference

Contents

ACKNOWLEDGMENTS

As you turn the pages of this tribute to hometown history, we hope that you will be thinking of the precious images in your own family and local collections. This book has been made possible thanks to individuals, families, and organizations that have allowed their pictures to be made available to the community through the Greene Connections: Greene County, Pennsylvania Photo Archives Project. Whether it shared one photograph or a thousand, each collection has added to the captivating assortment now available to relatives, researchers, and all those who harbor a fondness for this little piece of southwestern Pennsylvania. We express our deepest gratitude to every contributor credited throughout this work and also to each of you who has shared photographs with the overall Greene Connections project.

Photograph research requires finding images and accurately identifying them. A special thank-you goes to each person who has provided evidence and commentary on the Greene Connections website (www.GreeneConnections.com) to help us work together to determine dates, put names to faces, pinpoint places, identify events, and add caption details to the captured moment.

In addition to the bibliography of excellent resources to identify images, we would like to thank researchers who shared their expertise and repositories which opened their doors: George Blystone, Matthew Cumberledge, David Kent Fonner, Mary Beth Pastorius, James "Fuzzy" Randolph, the late Dr. G. Wayne Smith, and James Weinschenker, as well as the amazing volunteers and staff at the Cornerstone Genealogical Society, the Greene County Historical Society, the Waynesburg Borough office, and the Waynesburg University Museum. A thank-you goes to our Arcadia acquisitions editor, Abby Walker, for her prompt, consistent, and helpful guidance in this endeavor. We love the pictures of our past, and that is both the focus and the format of this book—to display pictures more than text. Yet, we do love the stories of our community as well and will look to follow this book with one that focuses more on them.

Finally, a thank-you is extended to Donna and Joshua Buchanan for the time devoted to assisting with the scanning and organization of the archival images.

INTRODUCTION

The opportunity to be an active participant in the romantic fantasy of time travel has been the subject of many a good book. Even the person who has no inclination towards history often can be easily persuaded to take a second look at a display of "how things used to be," especially if it involves something in proximity to their world. This book shares a range of images that should be of interest to those from the casual historian all the way to the obsessed student of history. Anyone who has grown up in this community, enjoyed the nurture and embrace of its people and places, or has had an occasion to call this place home at some point in his or her life should find flipping through these pages an enjoyable small act of time travel.

This town sprang into existence at a time (1796) and location close to events that formed our nation. As the result, it has a genuine place in regional history that, in turn, has had a significant standing in the national picture, such that there are threads of the national tapestry that are woven right down its streets. Also, the town's founding of one of the nation's earliest coeducational institutions of higher learning, Waynesburg College (1849), has served to be an important, consistent, not-so-subtle ambassadorship of this town to the world's stage. The sons and daughters of this community for nearly two centuries, whether born and reared here or adopting this home to secure higher education, have actively engaged in the fundamental struggles of the birthing and evolution of this dear old United States—its conflicts, its industry, its religion, its expansion. Displayed within the pictures of this book one will find the backdrop of buildings, streets, landscapes, and faces that have been the product of these generations of active sons and daughters, herein pushed through a kaleidoscope of time and offering readers opportunities to see change and also to see no change.

At one time, Waynesburg had most all of the necessary elements for facilitating strong development and economic growth, such as a college; industries focused in oil, gas, wool and manufacturing; a public railroad allowing travel access to the world; and a physical appeal with its charming parks and gentle rolling hills mixed in and among its residential and business areas. The land that makes up this town was originally a portion of a land patent obtained by an early settler, Thomas Slater, and by his patent, he named this land Eden. Given the lush green grass of the area's featured parks, the flowers of spring and summer, its rolling hills, and the small streams within its dimension, this original name may have been an appropriate beginning to this small, special town. Waynesburg originally was created to be, and has always been, the center for legal business to be conducted for any and all matters pertaining to property or persons residing in Greene County. As a result, it has always had a prominently featured courthouse and the supporting infrastructure for the legal system, such as a jail, hotels, attorney's offices, and several newspaper publishers, for keeping the people informed of the court's activities. From this core legal function that continues to this day, Waynesburg has, over the years, found it possible to attract and maintain people and businesses. Since its early days, Waynesburg's managers have taken responsibility to develop public utility systems such as water, roads, electric, telephone, and sewers that have allowed for construction and expansion to varying degrees in both its residential and business areas. However, this expansion has never been to a level that has, to date, forced Waynesburg to give up the look and ambiance of an attractive, quintessential American small town. Yet, even with Waynesburg's small-town charm, a close look at some of the photographs displayed in this book will show how oil and gas wells were a common fixture mixed in and among both its houses and stores at one time. This part of its past landscape is certainly something that would not be much tolerated today. Many things have changed over the years as to how this town's economy is supported. Gone are the thousands of sheep from the neighboring hills and the robust wool economy of the late 1800s and early 1900s. Gone is the access to a public railroad that allowed the people of Waynesburg to jump on a train and head anywhere. The trains, now traveling *through* the town for the most part, exclusively carry area coal to the ports of the Atlantic for export. The oil and gas wells of 120 years ago and the economy of the community that they generated had all but vanished by the year 2000. Yet, now, due to new developments in drilling technology, it is undeniably evident that this town is experiencing a phenomenal rebirth of this industry and will most certainly face challenges of growth and change accordingly. Given the current emerging, powerful force of the area's oil and gas boom, one hopes that local images 100 years from now will continue to reveal—as is the theme of this book—that the town has a capacity to endure, embracing change yet holding on to a significant special character of charm and appeal.

One

A Bird's-Eye View

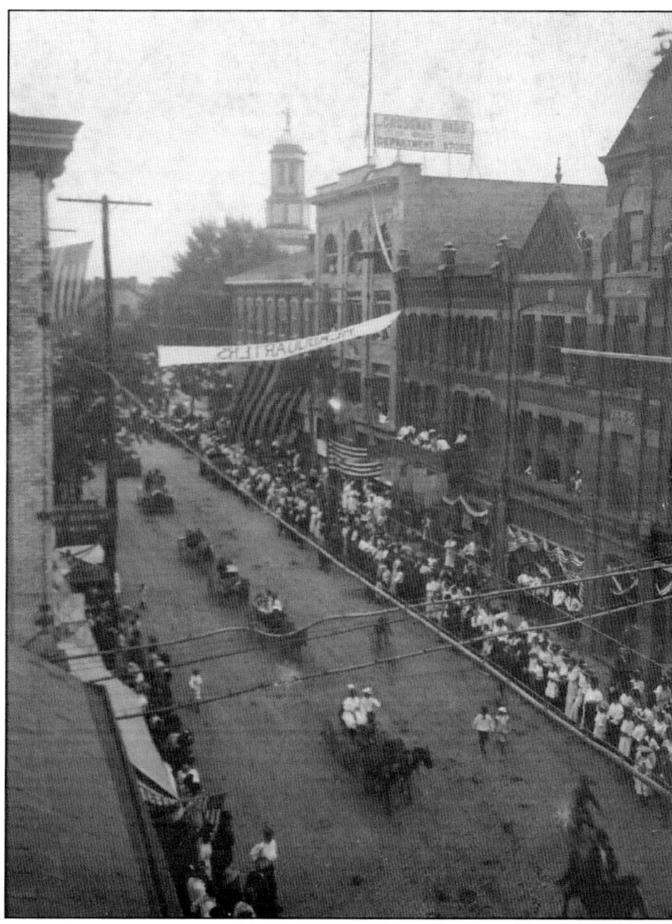

It is certainly often common for a town to celebrate an important community event with a parade; so then begins this book in parade fashion to help set up the celebration of Waynesburg's passing of time. This c. 1900 stereograph image, with a view looking east toward Washington Street, features a parade on High Street. Notice that the road is not yet paved. The buildings on the southern side are, from left to right, the Greene County Courthouse, Downey House, Grossman Building, Silveus Building, and Wisecarver Building. (Courtesy of the Greene County Historical Society.)

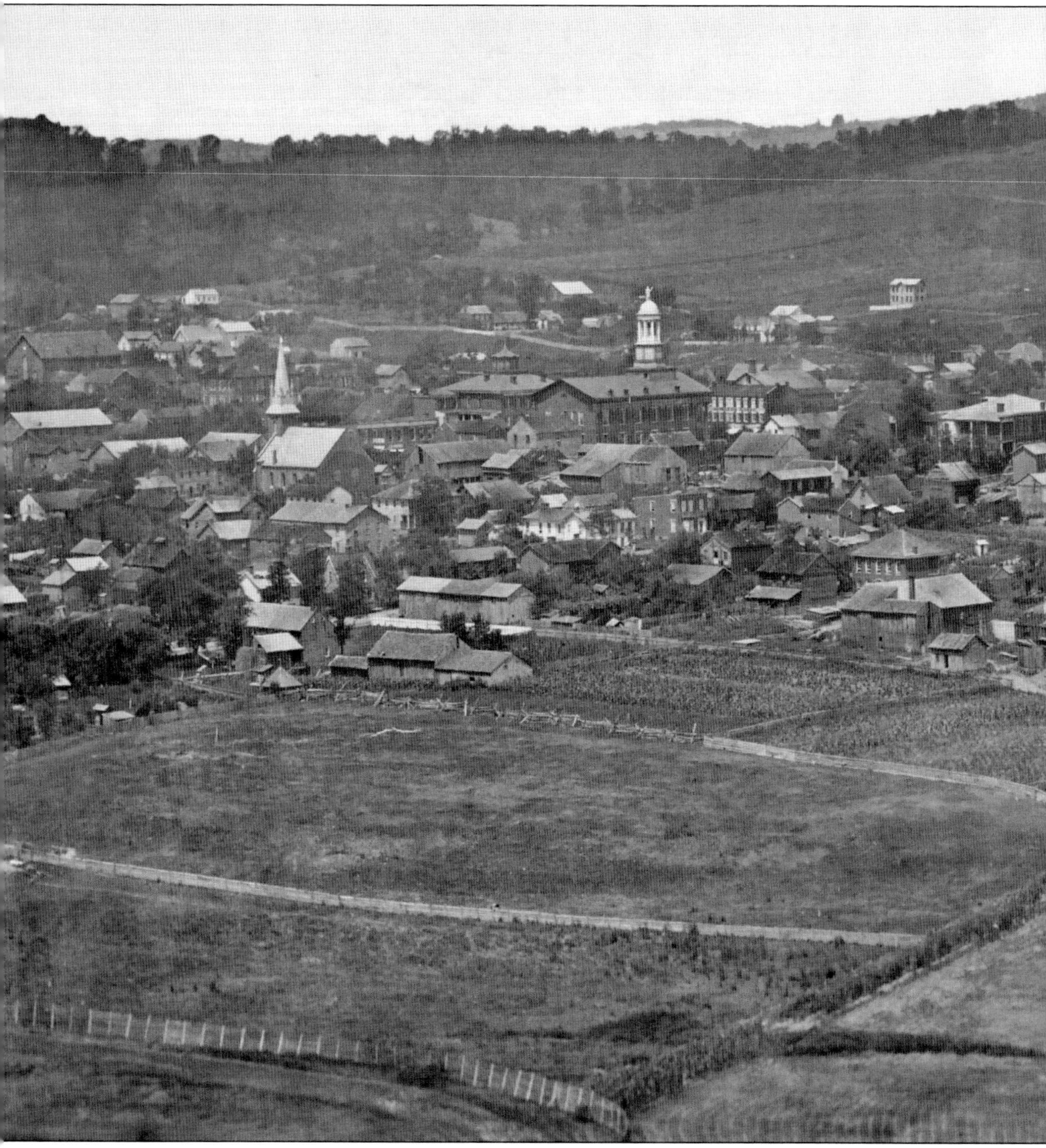

The view in this c. 1876 photograph looks north from the south high ground. Points of interest include Cumberland Presbyterian Church (first large building to appear at upper far-left edge), built in 1868 on High Street, and old Methodist Episcopal church (further right with pointed steeple) on Washington Street, constructed in 1876. Near the center, from left to right, are the Downey House (short cupola), Greene County Courthouse (domed cupola topped by statue of Gen. Nathanael Greene), and newly titled Messenger Building (whitewashed front, across from courthouse). Further right are Commons Cemetery (at current Monument Park) and Union School (later known as North Ward). To its right, more tombstones represent St. Ann Roman Catholic

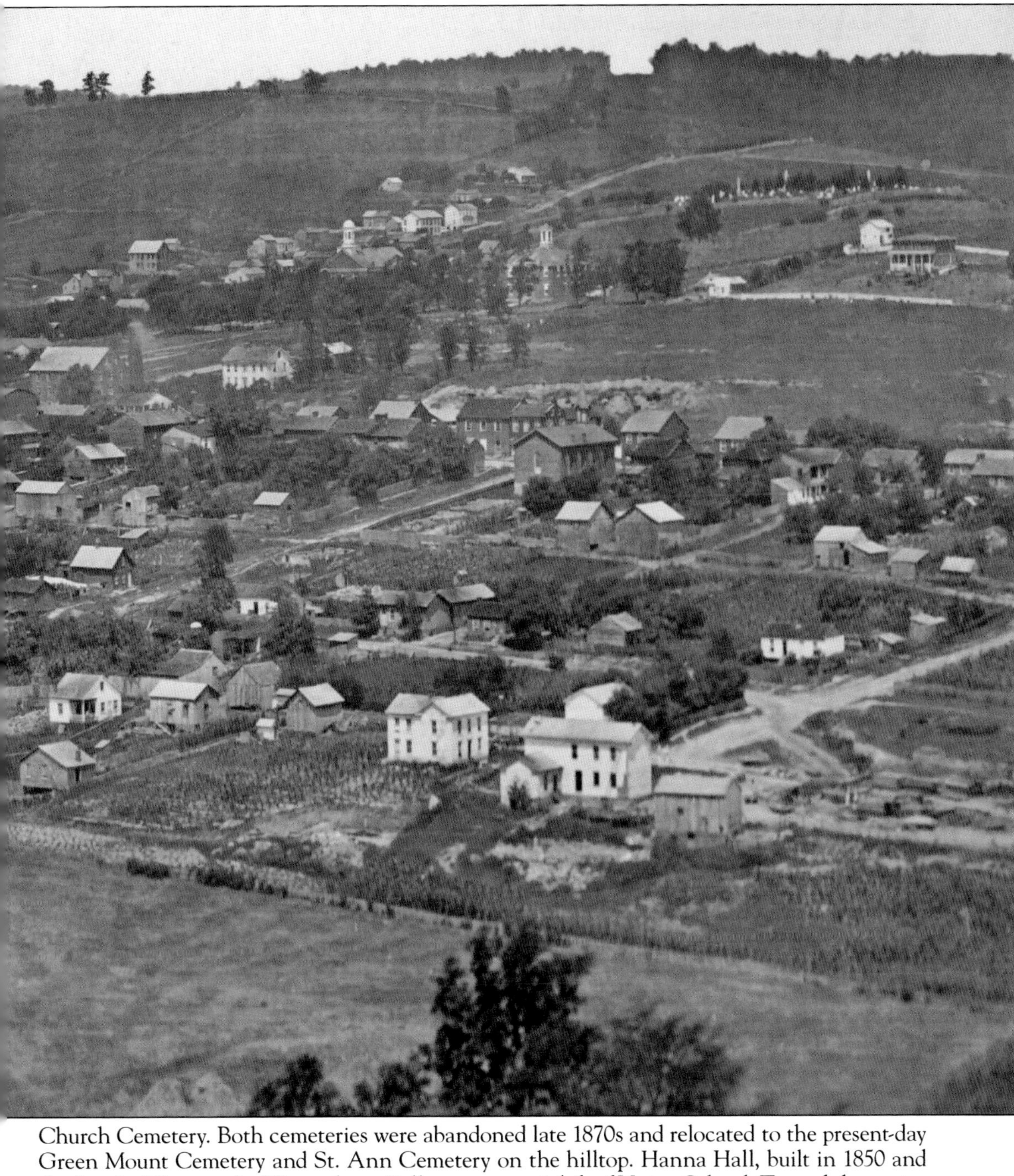

Church Cemetery. Both cemeteries were abandoned late 1870s and relocated to the present-day Green Mount Cemetery and St. Ann Cemetery on the hilltop. Hanna Hall, built in 1850 and the first building on the Waynesburg College campus, is left of Union School. Toward the center of the photograph (on page 10) along the top border of the fields, is a small log structure across from a larger brick building that has five windows in a row. This log cabin is the first Greene County Courthouse, built in 1797 and still standing, now home to the Cornerstone Genealogical Society. (Photograph from the Helen Mae [Jacobs] Fonner Collection, courtesy of George and Anna [Fonner] Blystone.)

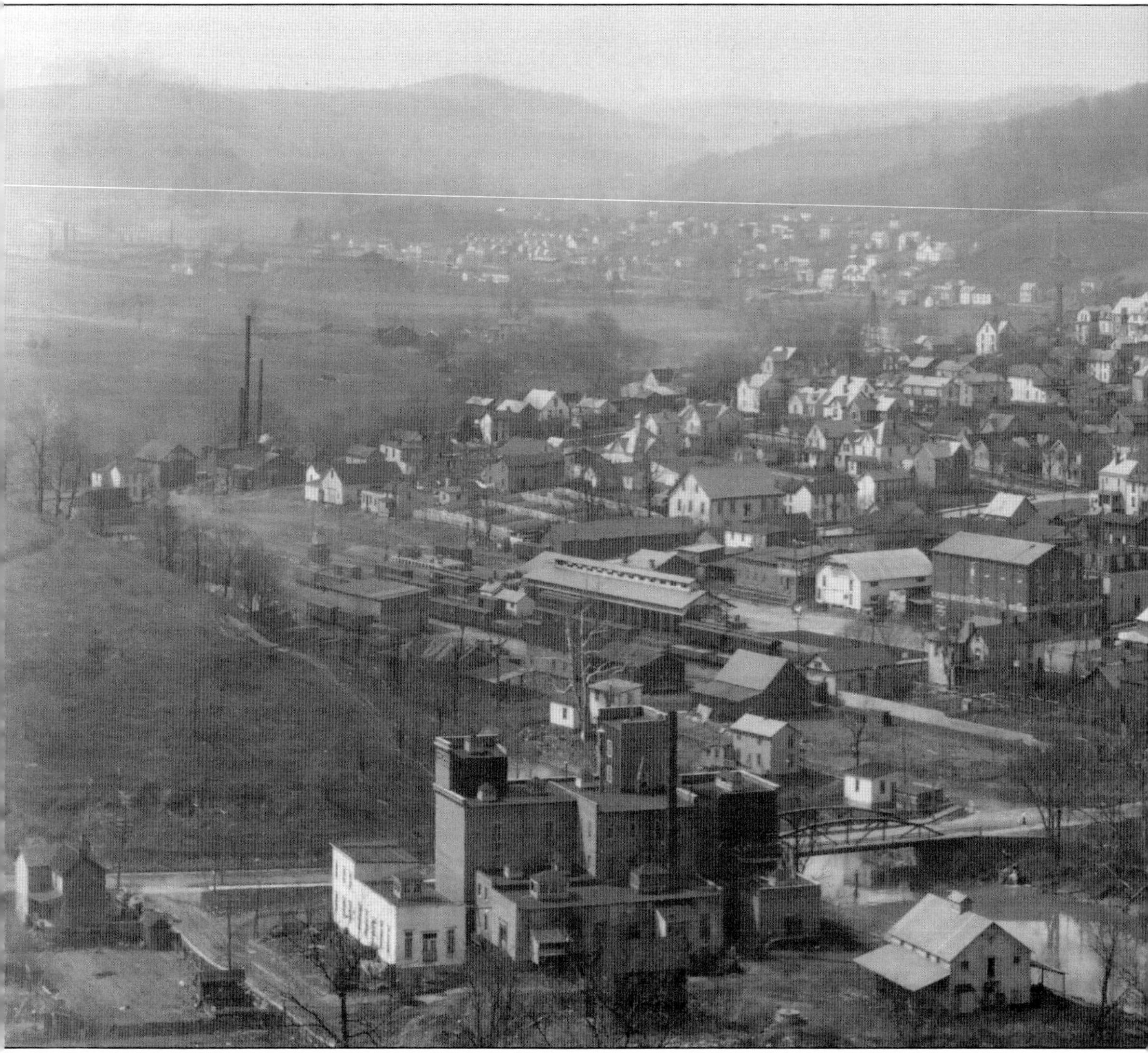

In this c. 1905 photograph with a view looking northwest over Waynesburg, highlights include a brewery (lower left), Waynesburg & Washington Railroad station (just above the brewery),

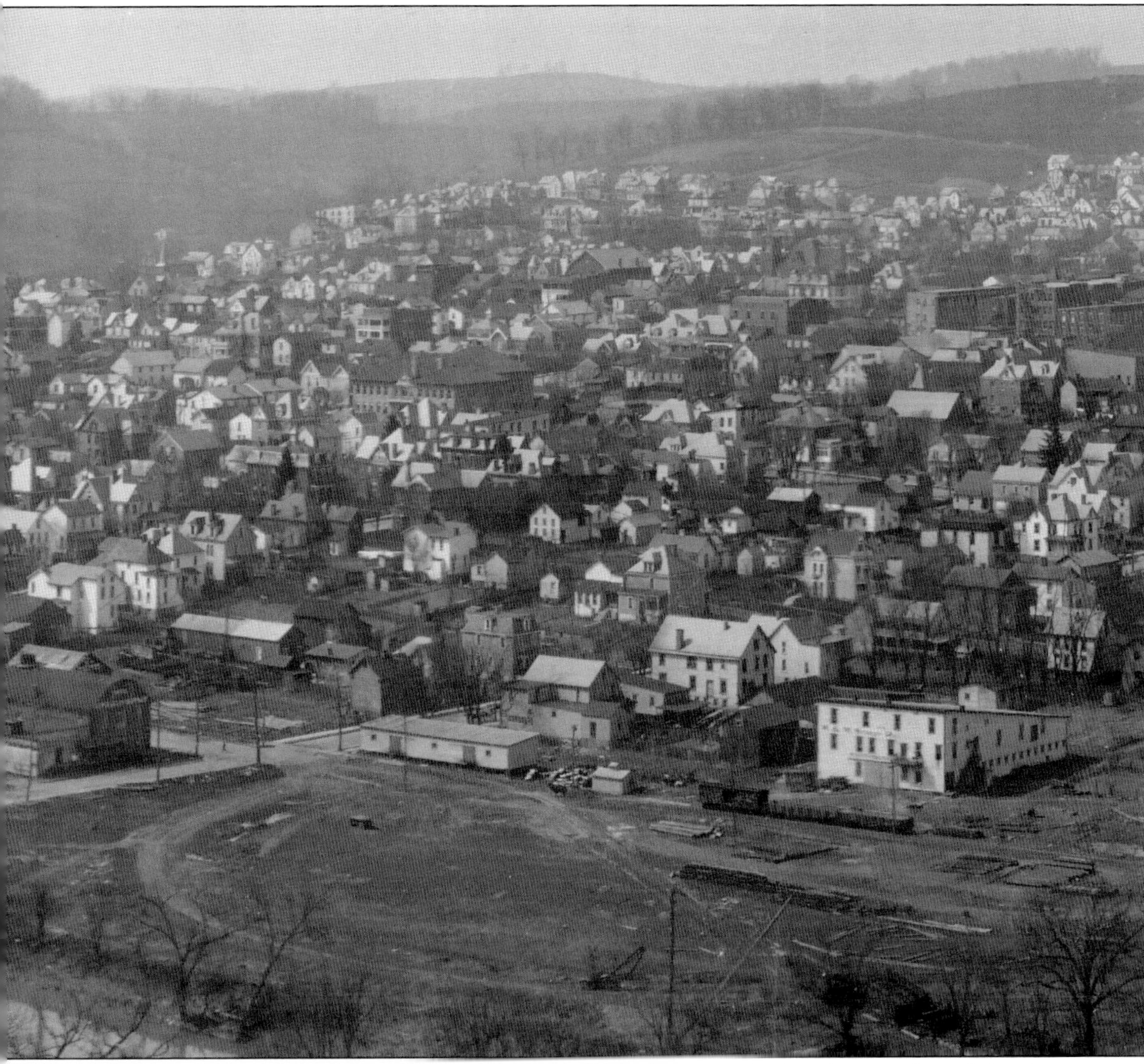

Waynesburg Milling (across from the Waynesburg & Washington Railroad station), and South Ward School (toward the right center). (Courtesy of the Greene County Historical Society.)

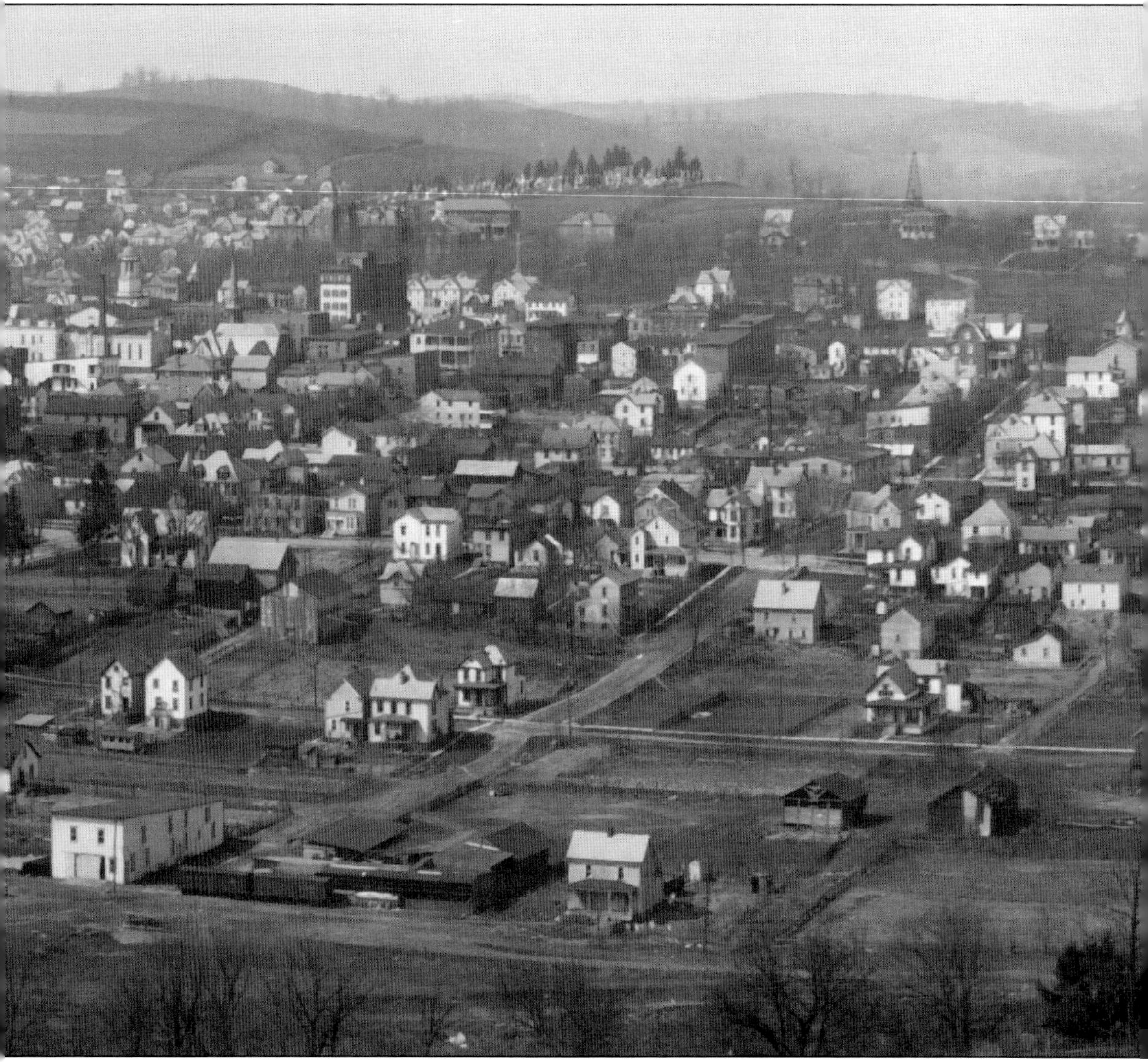

In this view continuing northwest over Waynesburg around 1905, one can see the community baseball field (lower right) in the area that was once the fairgrounds and became the Waynesburg University athletic field. The two prominent streets running from left to right in the center of the

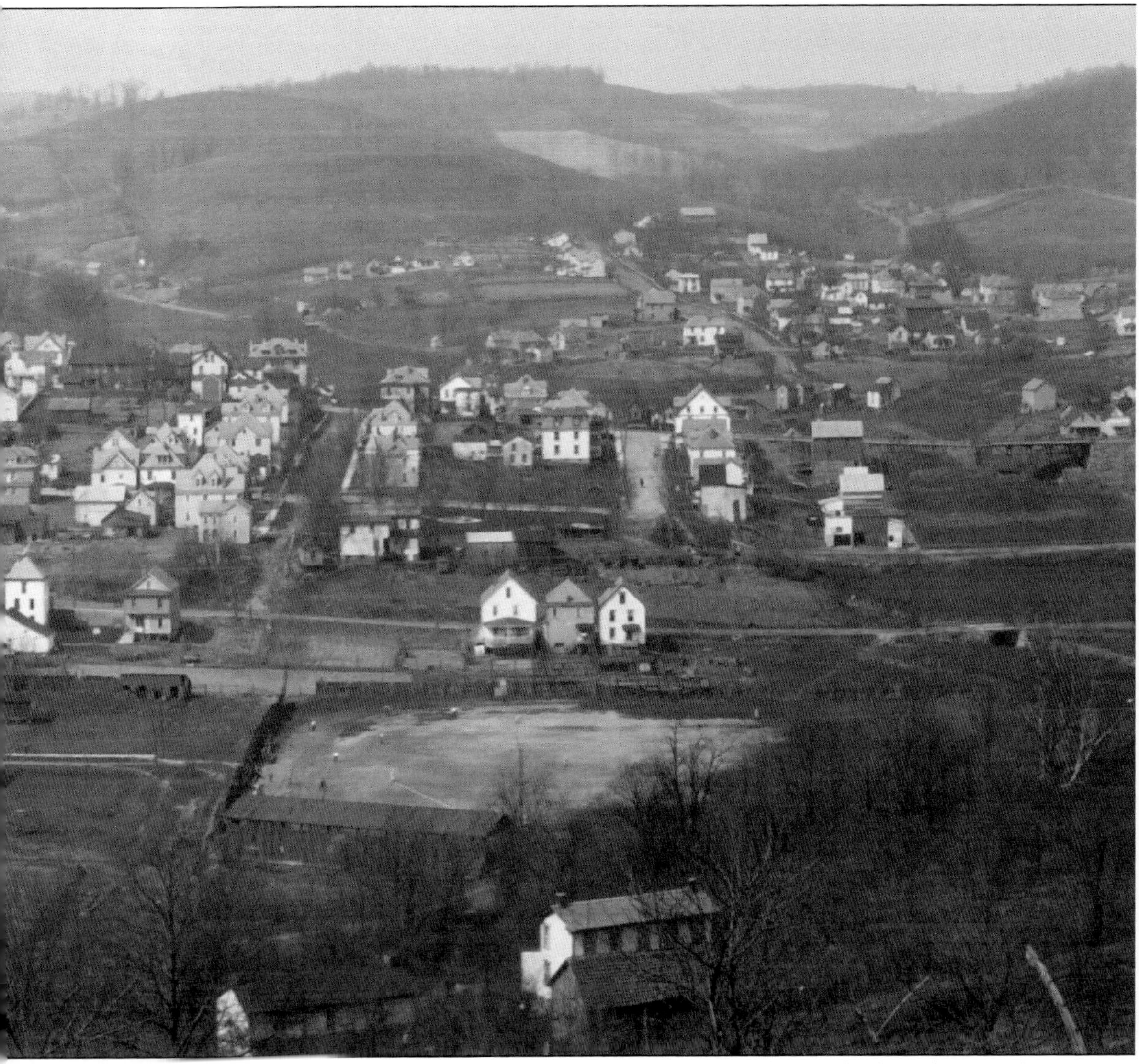

photograph are High Street (above) and Greene Street (below). The bridge on the far right toward the center is on High Street, which is in an area that became the playground. An oil derrick is visible in the upper center background. (Courtesy of the Greene County Historical Society.)

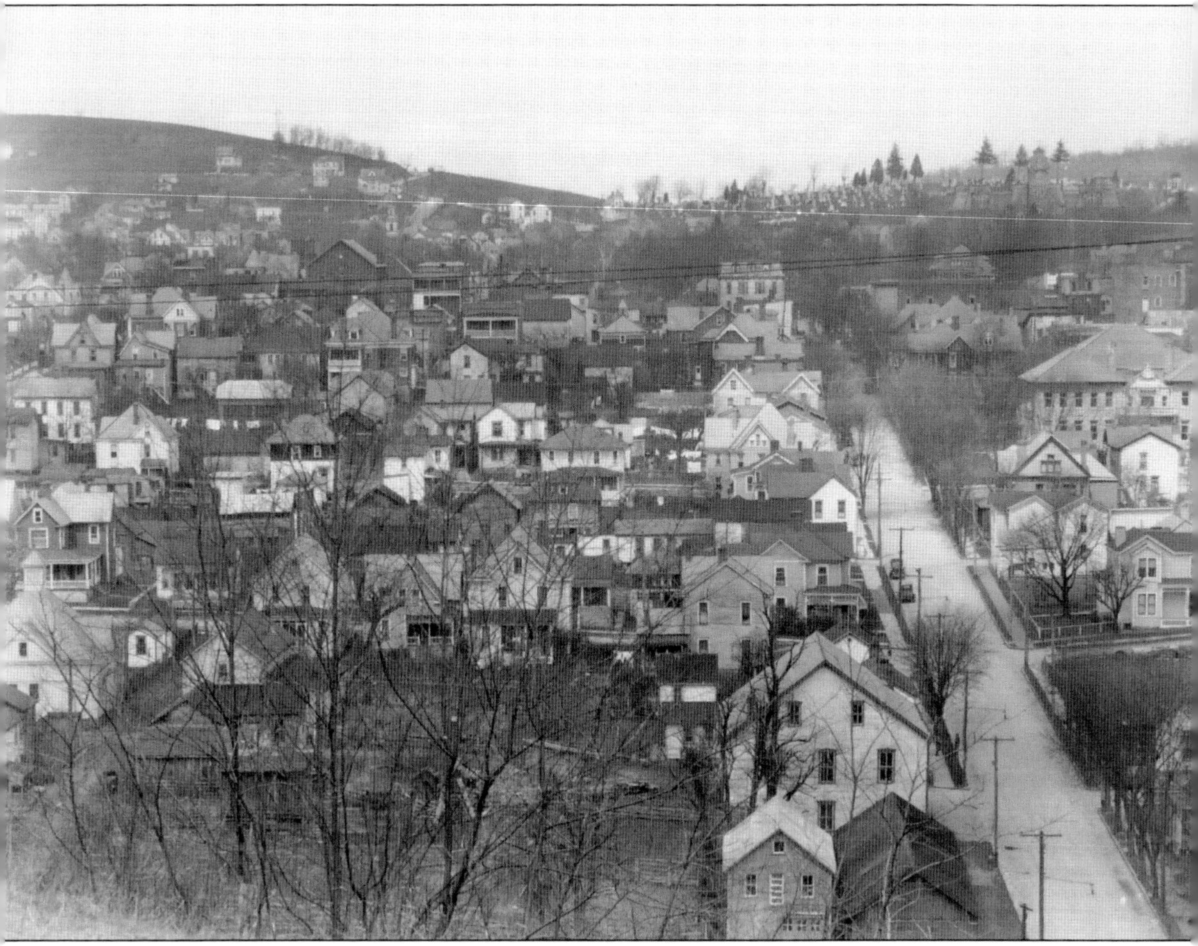

In this c. 1930 view of town, looking north over Waynesburg, South Ward School is the largest building at the right-center of the image. To the north, just before Green Mount Cemetery fills the hilltop, the unique outline of Miller Hall and the domed cupola of Hanna Hall can be seen on the Waynesburg College campus. (Courtesy of the Greene County Historical Society.)

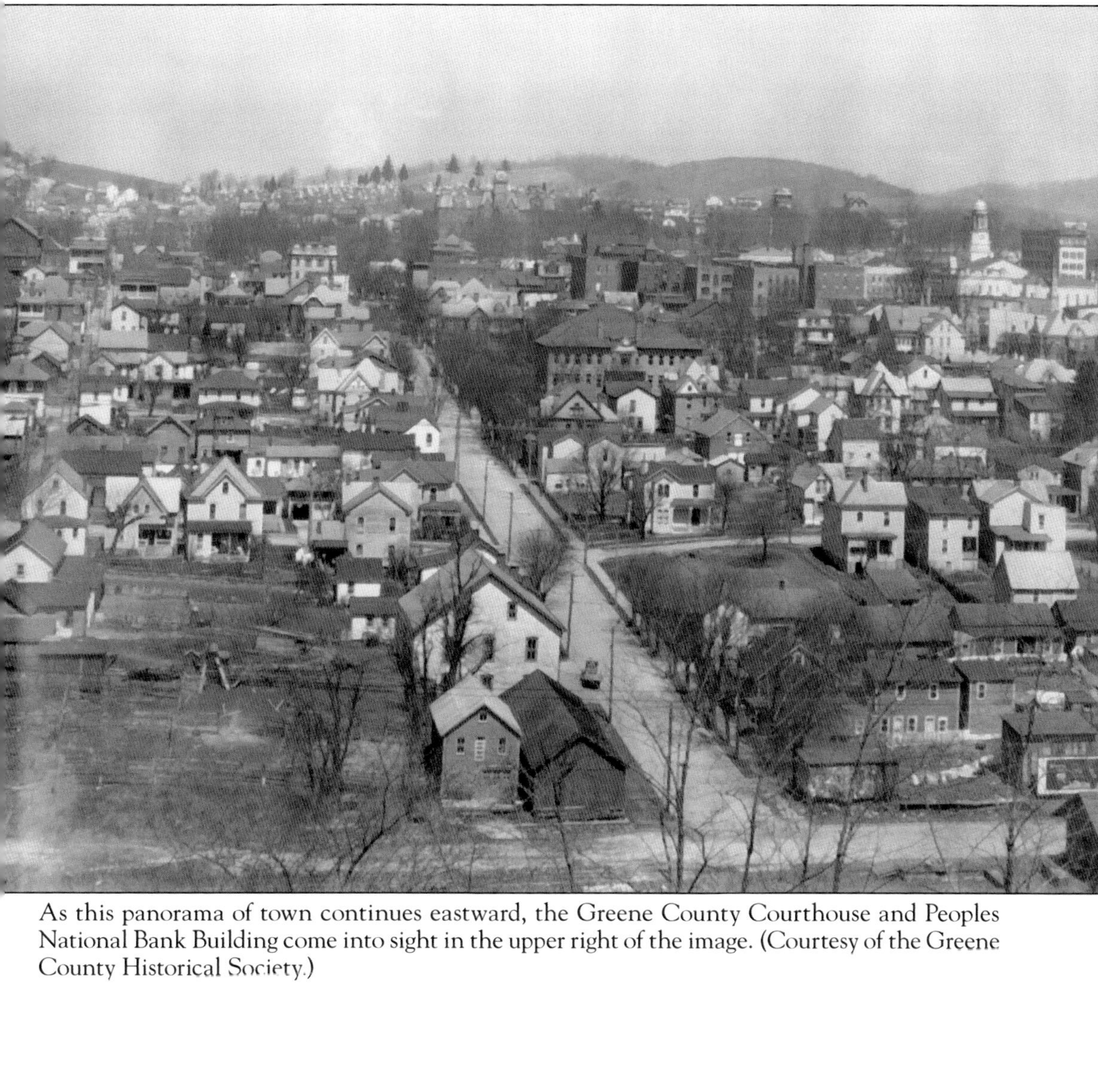

As this panorama of town continues eastward, the Greene County Courthouse and Peoples National Bank Building come into sight in the upper right of the image. (Courtesy of the Greene County Historical Society.)

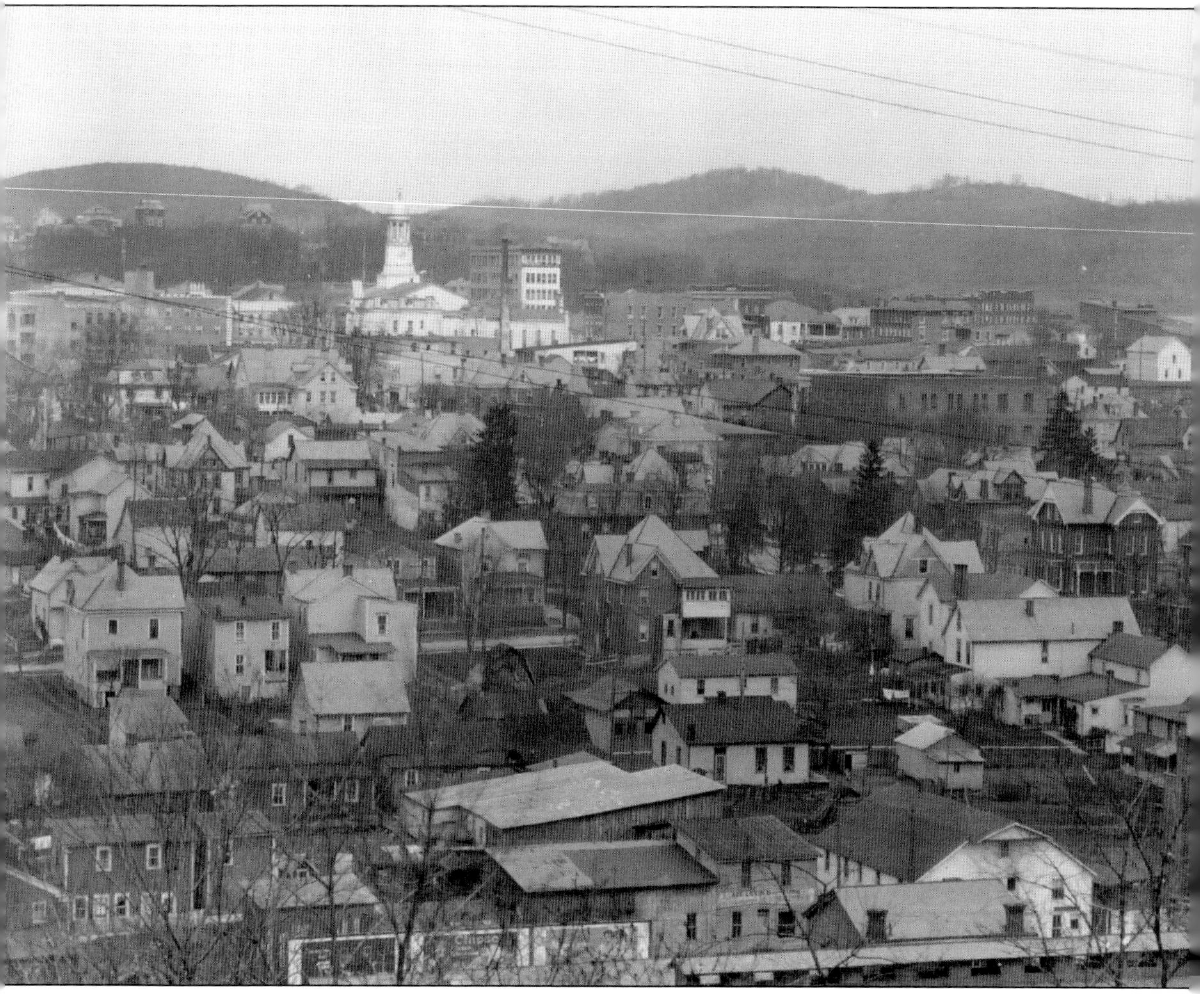

This angle shows the Fort Jackson Hotel, which replaced the Downey House on the southwest corner of High and Washington Streets in 1926. (Courtesy of the Greene County Historical Society.)

Two

Time Takes a Walk through Town

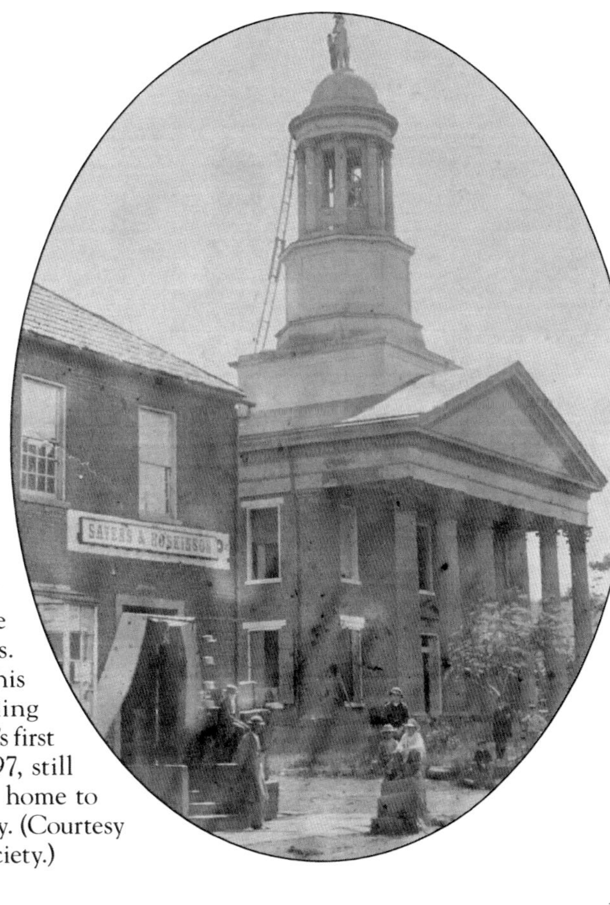

This is an early view of Sayers Corner and the present Greene County Courthouse (built 1850–1851) on the corner of Church and High Streets. This courthouse was the second at this location. It replaced a brick building constructed around 1800. The county's first courthouse, a log cabin built in 1797, still stands on Greene Street, serving as home to the Cornerstone Genealogical Society. (Courtesy of the Greene County Historical Society.)

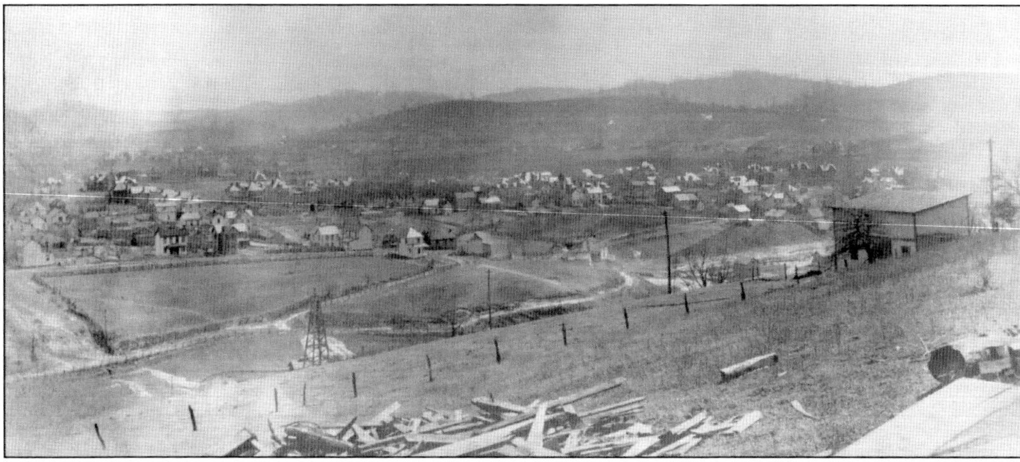

This is a view of East Waynesburg from the hilltop of Green Mount Cemetery. The East Ward school building can be seen left of center in the image. Close inspection reveals several oil derricks spread throughout the view. (Courtesy of Waynesburg Borough.)

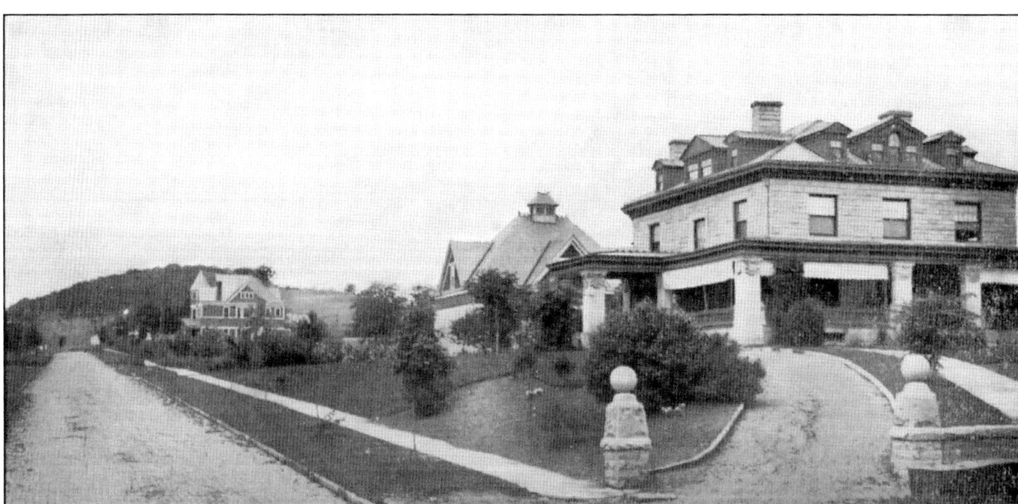

This palatial home on High Street was built by James B.F. Rinehart, infamous cashier and vice president of the Farmers & Drovers Bank when it crashed in 1906. Rinehart was the only person associated with the bank to be criminally charged for its failure. President Taft pardoned him in 1912. (From the Walter "Blackie" Markiewich Postcard Collection, courtesy of Brice and Linda Rush.)

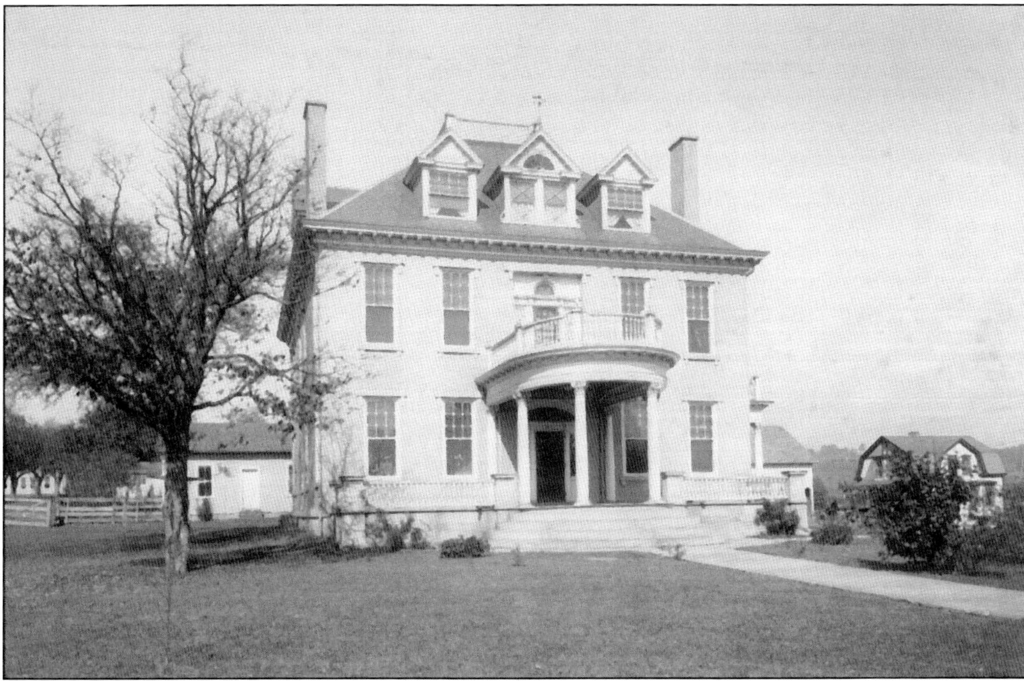

The Timothy Ross family home on East High Street later became the site of the Dairy Mart, State Liquor Store, and Wade's Autobody Shop. A Jacobs birdhouse is at the far left of the photograph below. (Above, courtesy of Waynesburg Borough; below, courtesy of the Greene County Historical Society.)

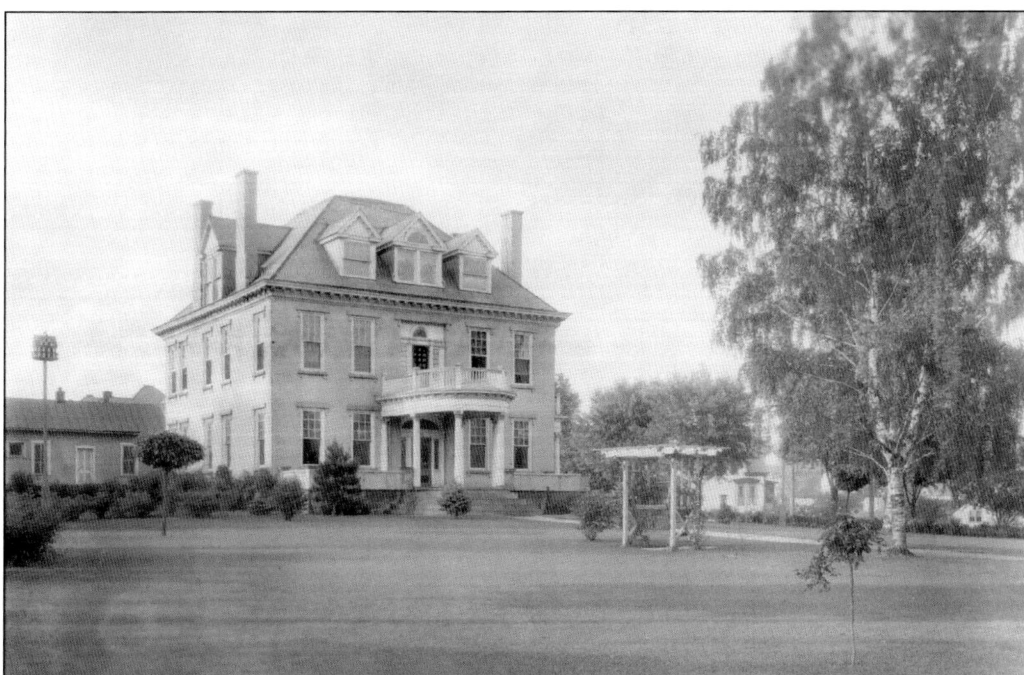

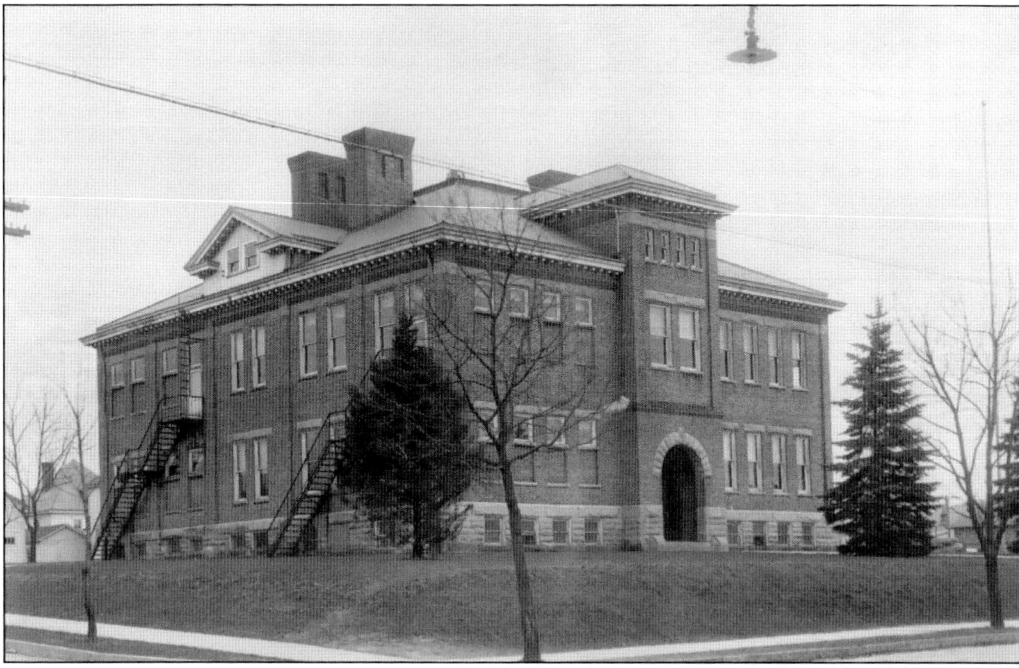

Mischievous students pose in front of the East Ward Elementary School on Porter Street. (Above, courtesy of the Greene County Historical Society; below, courtesy of Waynesburg Borough.)

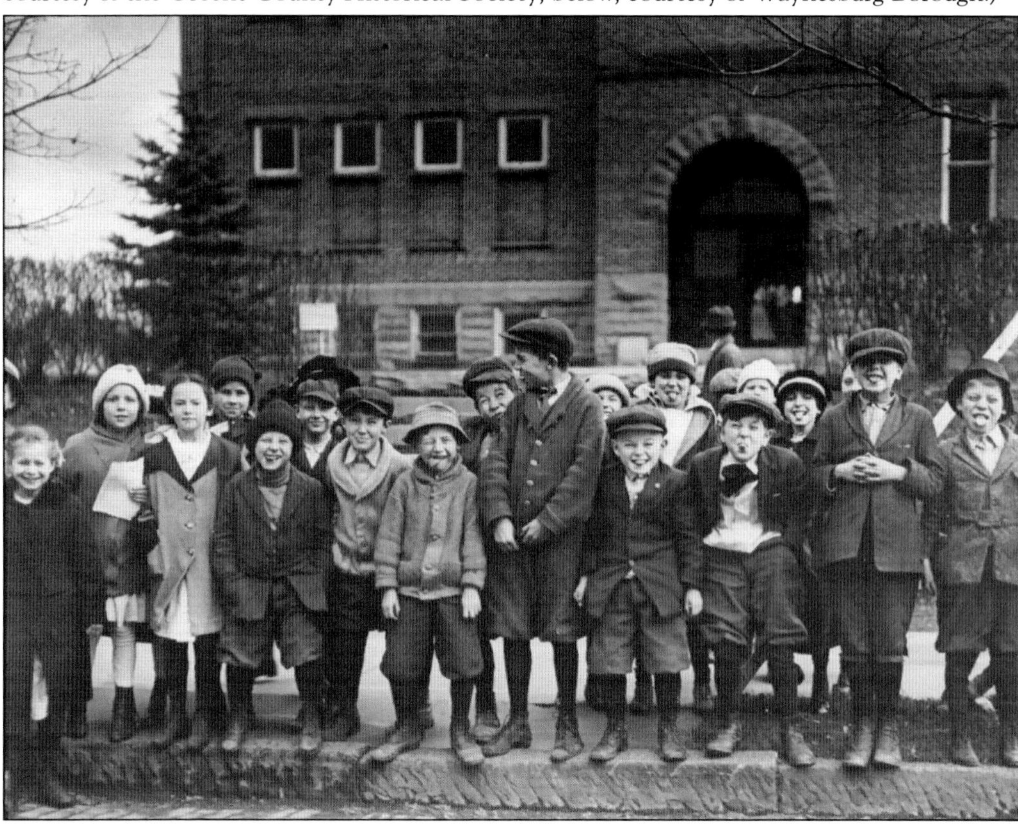

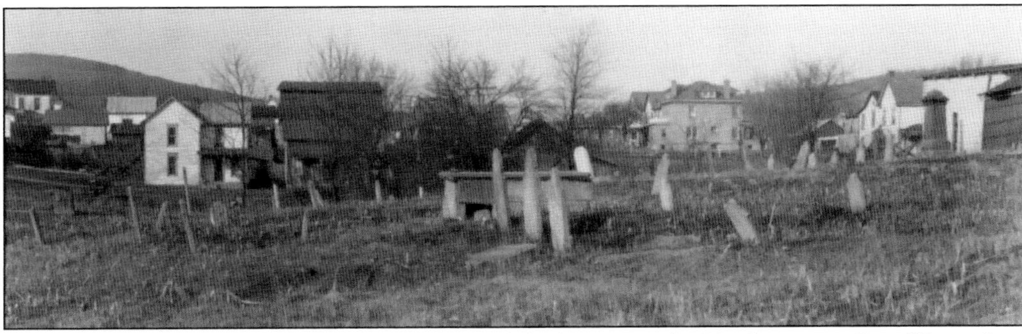

The old Methodist Episcopal Church Cemetery (also known as the Hookstown or East Waynesburg Cemetery) was located on Liberty Street where housing units stand today. The cemetery was abandoned in the early 1960s. A memorial to those known to have been buried here was placed in Section P, Lot 99 of Green Mount Cemetery. (From the William Francis Jacobs Collection, courtesy of David Kent Jacobs.)

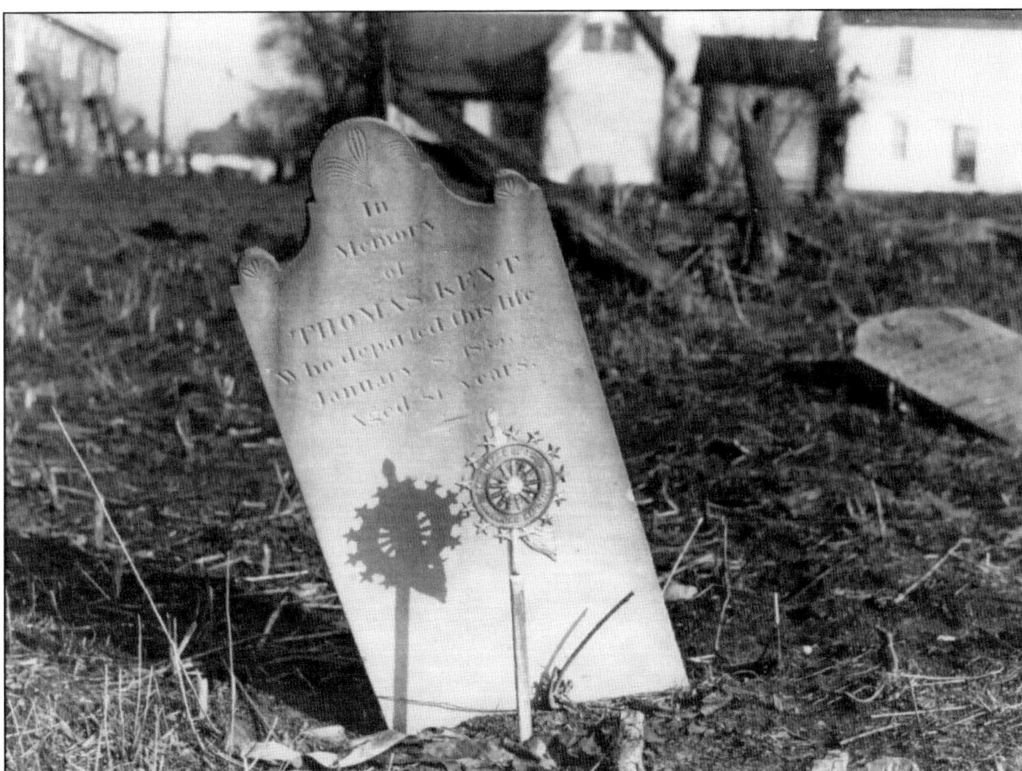

The tombstone of Thomas Kent, veteran of the American Revolution, reads, "In / Memory / of / Thomas Kent / Who departed this life / January 8, 1835 / Aged 81 years." Kent and his wife, Ann (Ralston) Kent, were removed from the old Methodist Cemetery on September 18, 1934, and reinterred at Greene County Memorial Park. (From the William Francis Jacobs Collection, courtesy of David Kent Jacobs.)

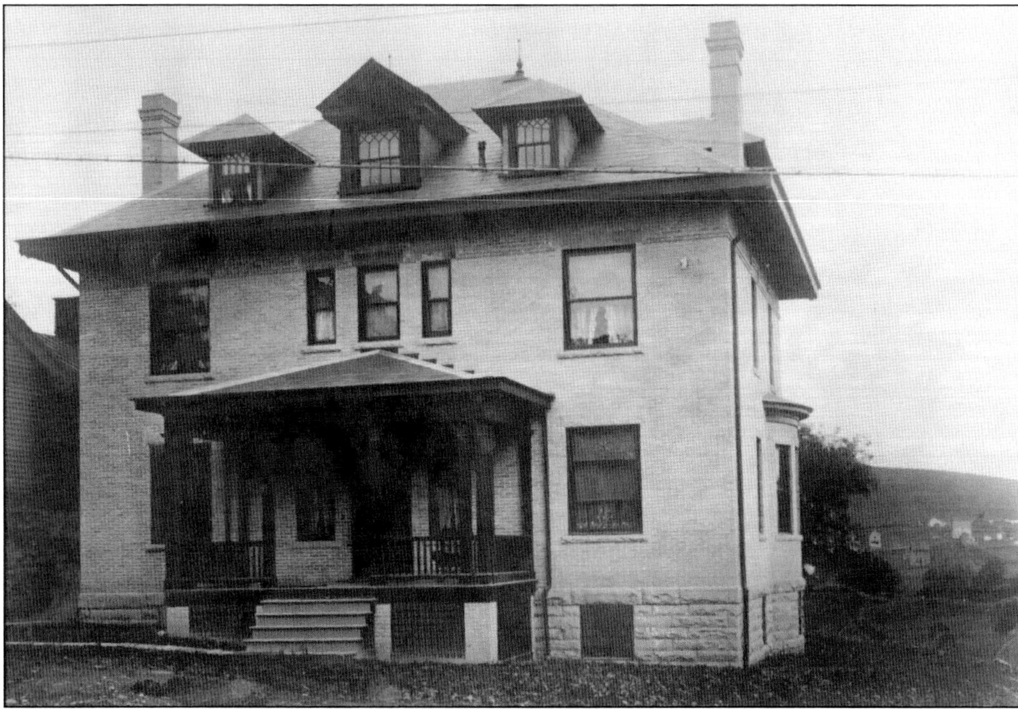

The Haman C. and Samilda (Denny) Staggers family home still stands on the corner of High and East Streets. (Courtesy of the Greene County Historical Society.)

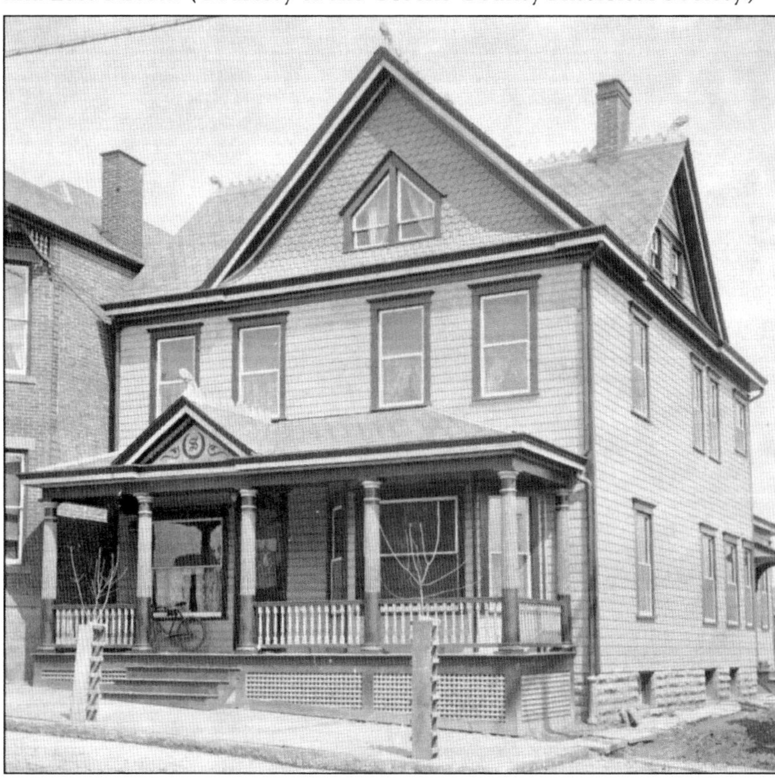

The Samuel M. and Elizabeth (Moredock) Smith family home remains in use today on High Street, next to Findley Alley. (Courtesy of the Greene County Historical Society.)

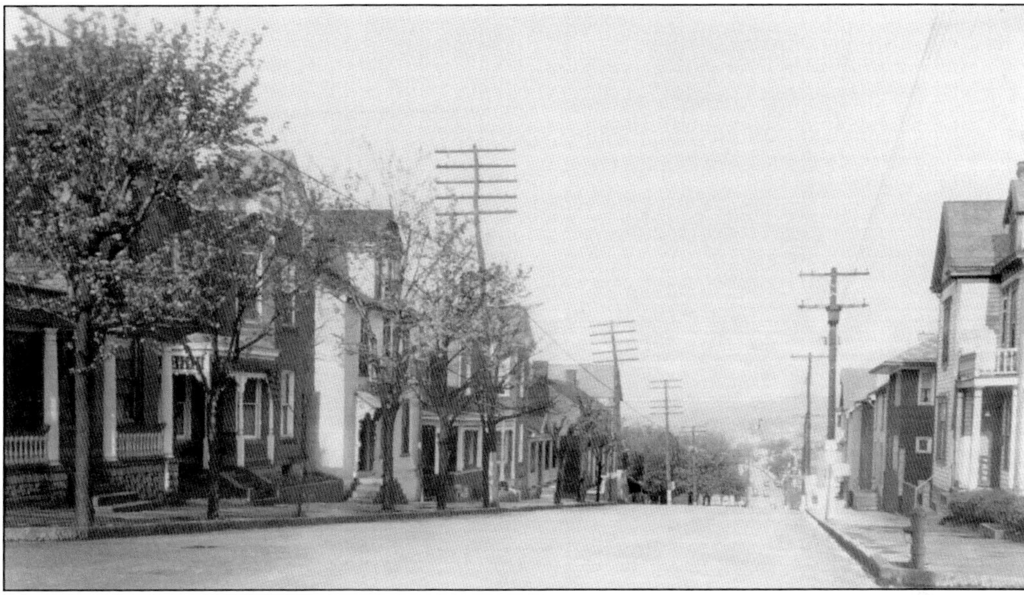

The view in this image looks east from Cumberland Street down High Street's brick-paved hill. St. Ann Roman Catholic Church is just out of view to the right. (Photograph by William E.S. Fletcher, courtesy of the Cornerstone Genealogical Society.)

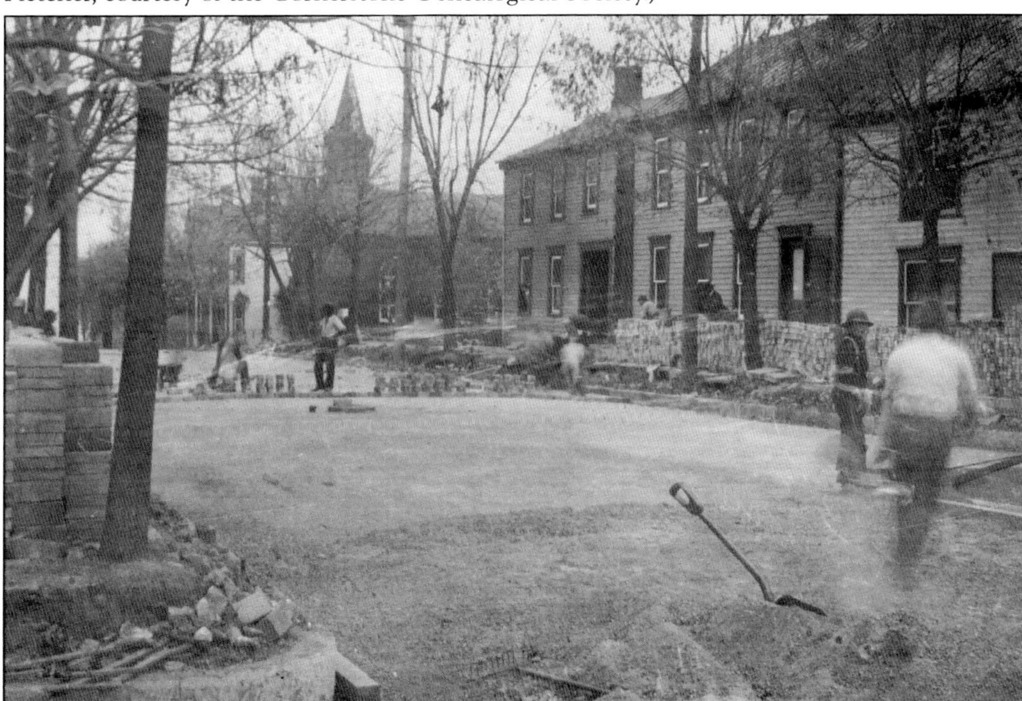

High Street received major renovation in 1903. George David Jenkins was appointed Waynesburg borough engineer in 1900 and oversaw the installation of sewer systems and the very first brick-paving of roads throughout town. Located toward the corner of Cumberland and High Streets, St. Ann Catholic Church and neighboring homes benefitted from the upgrade of the old dirt road. (Photograph by A.P. Smith, courtesy of the Greene County Historical Society.)

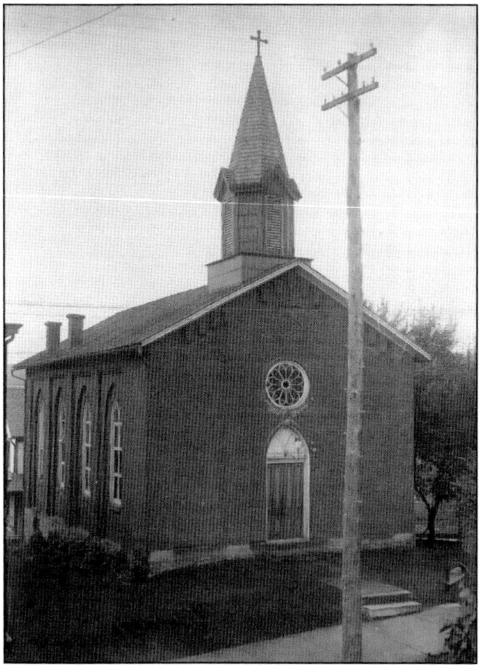

The St. Ann Roman Catholic Church building on High Street was constructed in 1871. This location has the distinction of being the only property in continuous ownership from the original sale of lots at the creation of the town. Father Patrick Lonergan, a missionary priest from Ireland, bought five lots in 1799, one of which—Lot 136 of the original plan of Waynesburg—is where this church was constructed. (Photograph by W.T. Hays, courtesy of Waynesburg Borough.)

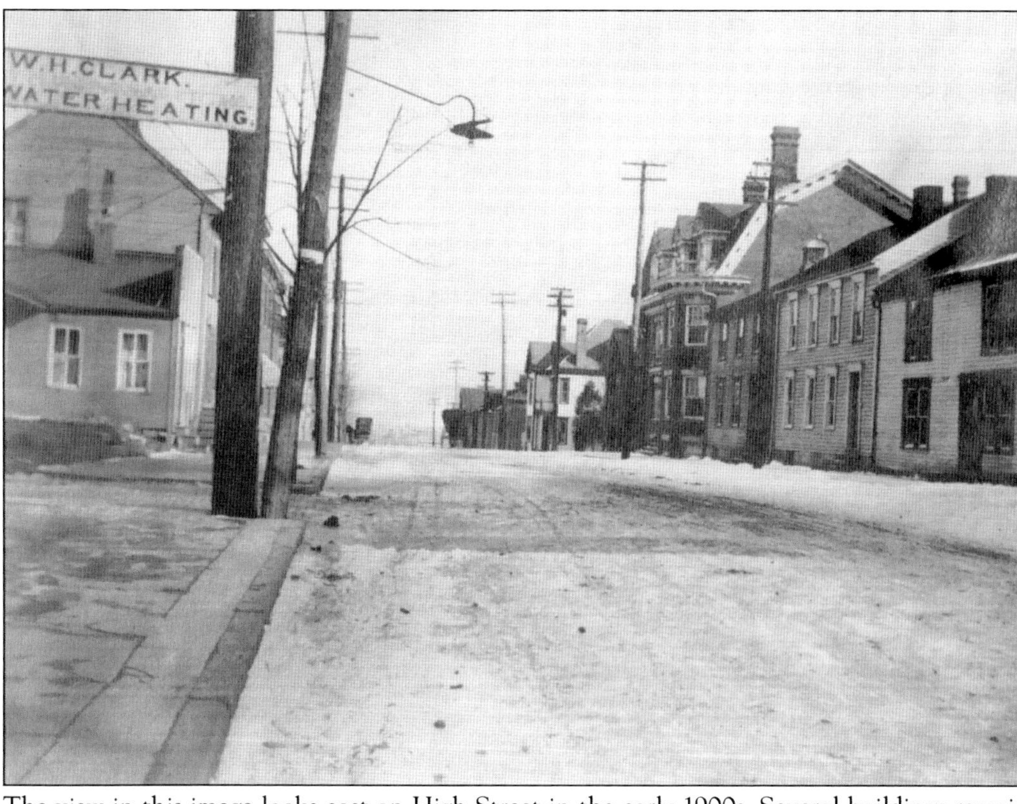

The view in this image looks east on High Street in the early 1900s. Several buildings remain standing to this day. (From the George David Jenkins Collection, courtesy of the Greene County Historical Society.)

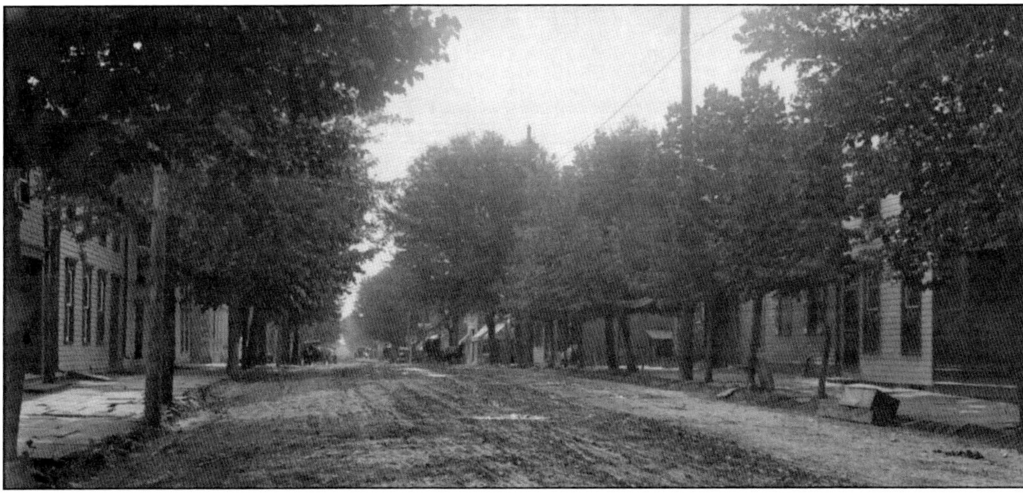

Above is a late-1800s westward view of High Street; the image was taken near Cumberland Street and the view looks toward Morgan Street. Below is the same view during the World War I era. On the left, the first two frame houses were in place by the Civil War, though they likely date to much earlier. The one closest to Wood Street (formerly Whiskey Alley) sits on what was known as the Potters Lot, where bricks for the first buildings on High Street were manufactured. The tall Ganiear Building was constructed in three sections beginning in the 1890s. Next door, the western section of the Ganiear House was built during a period around 1808–1814; the eastern half was added around 1847. The next frame house was James Andrew Jackson Buchanan's in-town home and later belonged to his daughter's family, Daniel Spindler and Mollie (Buchanan) Walton. (Above, courtesy of Waynesburg Borough; below, courtesy of Scott and Teresa [Crouse] Roberts.)

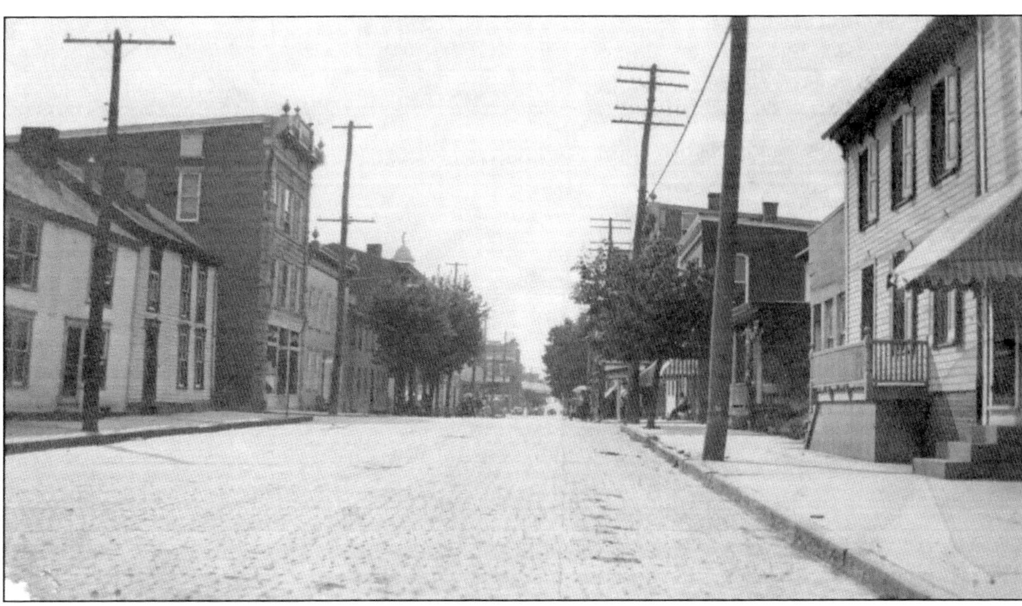

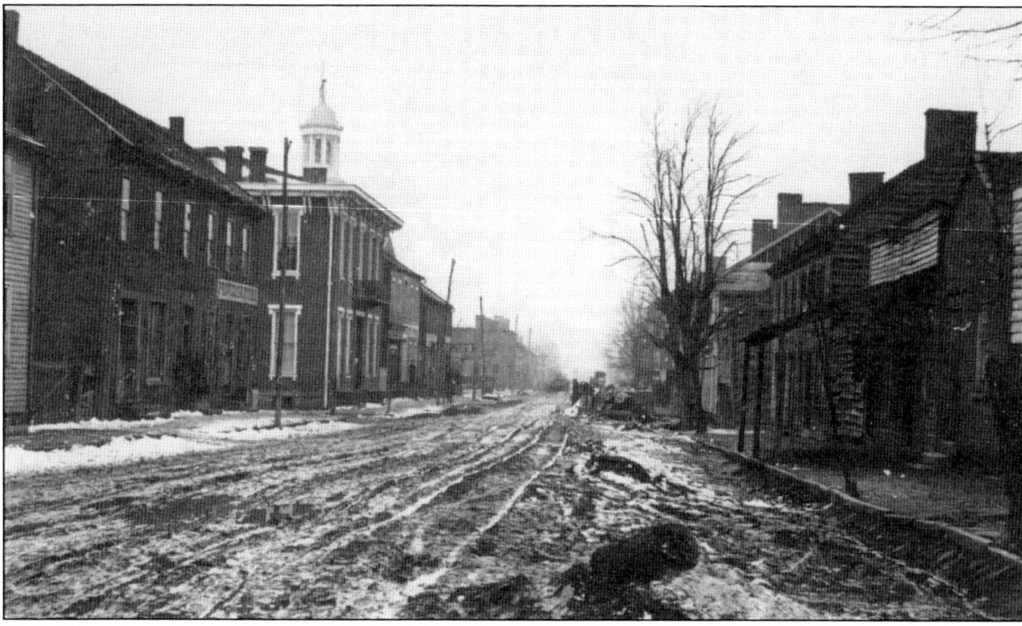

Probably taken during the Civil War, this early image of High Street shows the Farmers & Drovers Bank prominently on the southwest corner of Morgan Street. Across Morgan Street is the brick Crawford Mansion that was replaced in 1870 by John T. Hook. Catty-corner to the bank stands the frame house of one of its founders, Andrew Buchanan, who also served as the area's US congressman from 1835 to 1839. (Courtesy of Waynesburg Borough.)

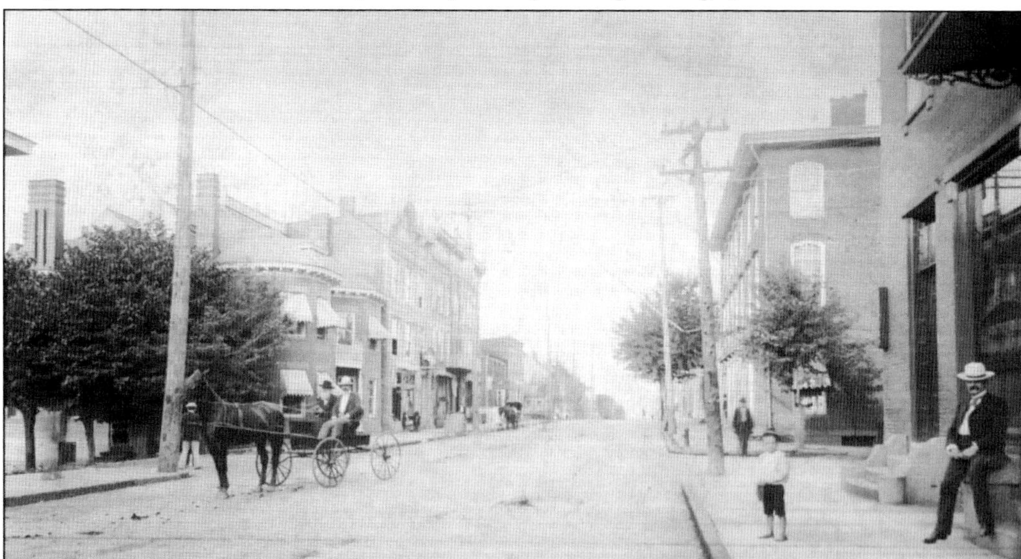

With a view looking east on High Street from the Green House in 1903, this image shows the brick home of Dr. Rufus Edward Brock, which replaced the old Buchanan wood-frame structure on the northeast corner of Morgan Street. Continuing east down the street are the Spragg & Wood and W.F. Blair buildings; in the right foreground is the Farmers & Drovers Bank, and across Morgan Street is the Hook Building. (Photograph by *Waynesburg Semi-Weekly Messenger*, courtesy of Matt W. Cumberledge.)

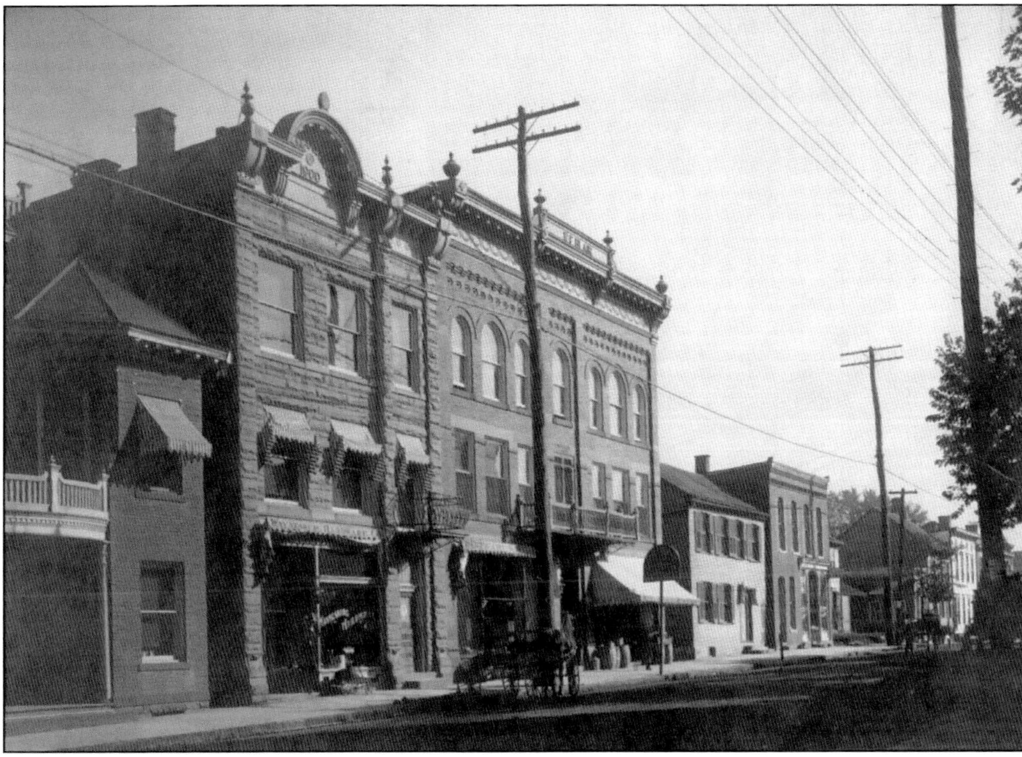

At the time of this c. 1905 photograph, with a view looking northeast from Morgan Street, buildings on High Street included the Dr. Rufus Edward Brock residence, Spragg & Wood building, W.F. Blair building, the Mary (Dickerson) Cosgray residence, and Corbly Orndoff residence. (Courtesy of Waynesburg Borough.)

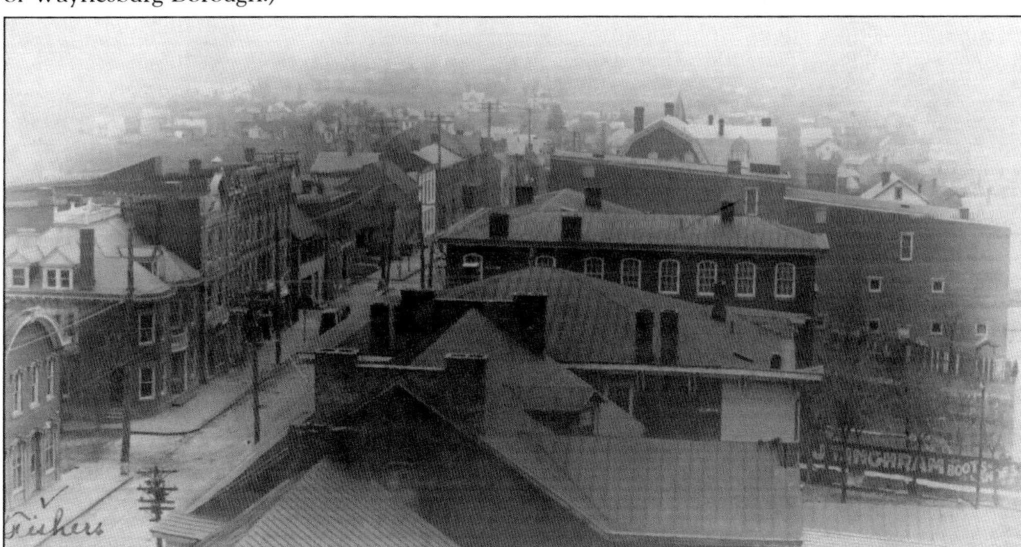

Probably photographed from the courthouse cupola, this northeastern view of High Street features the blocks between Morgan and Cumberland Streets. The Brocks' house at the corner of High and Morgan Streets has a widow's walk. (Courtesy of Waynesburg Borough.)

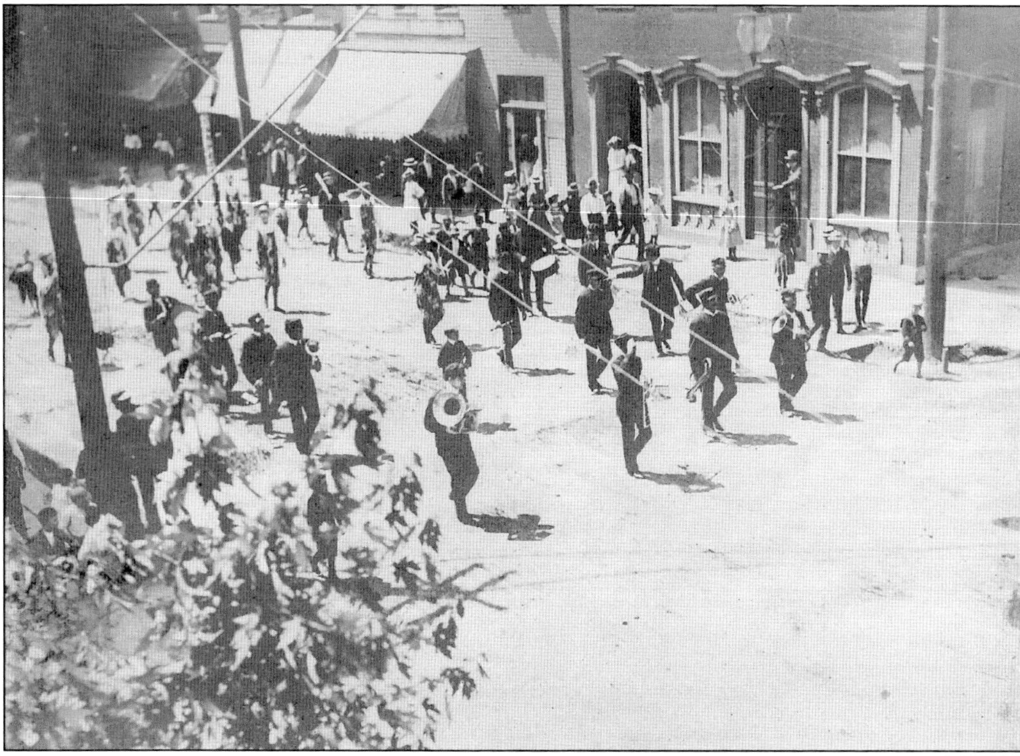

Pictured at the northwest corner of High and Morgan Streets around 1895, the annual Fourth of July baseball game began with a parade. Townspeople followed local athletes to the baseball diamond at the old fairgrounds, where the Waynesburg University athletic field is today. The teams, made up of local businessman, were affectionately named the Fats and the Leans. The event was put on to raise money for the improvement of the four parks that had recently replaced the Waynesburg Commons. (Courtesy of the Greene County Historical Society.)

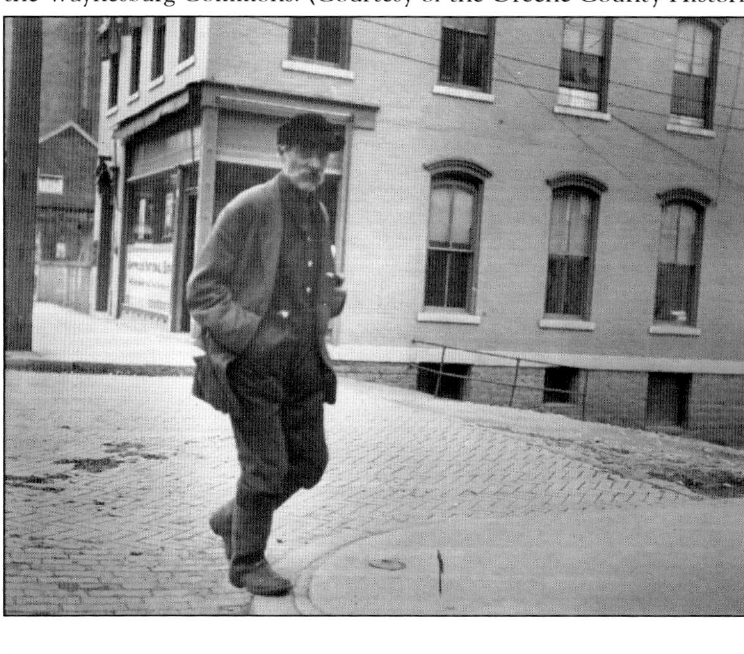

Barnet Ellsworth "Barney" Smith was photographed around 1915 as he crossed to the northeast corner of High and Morgan Streets. Behind him, the American National Bank building and the adjoining lot were later replaced by the Long Building. (Courtesy of Waynesburg Borough.)

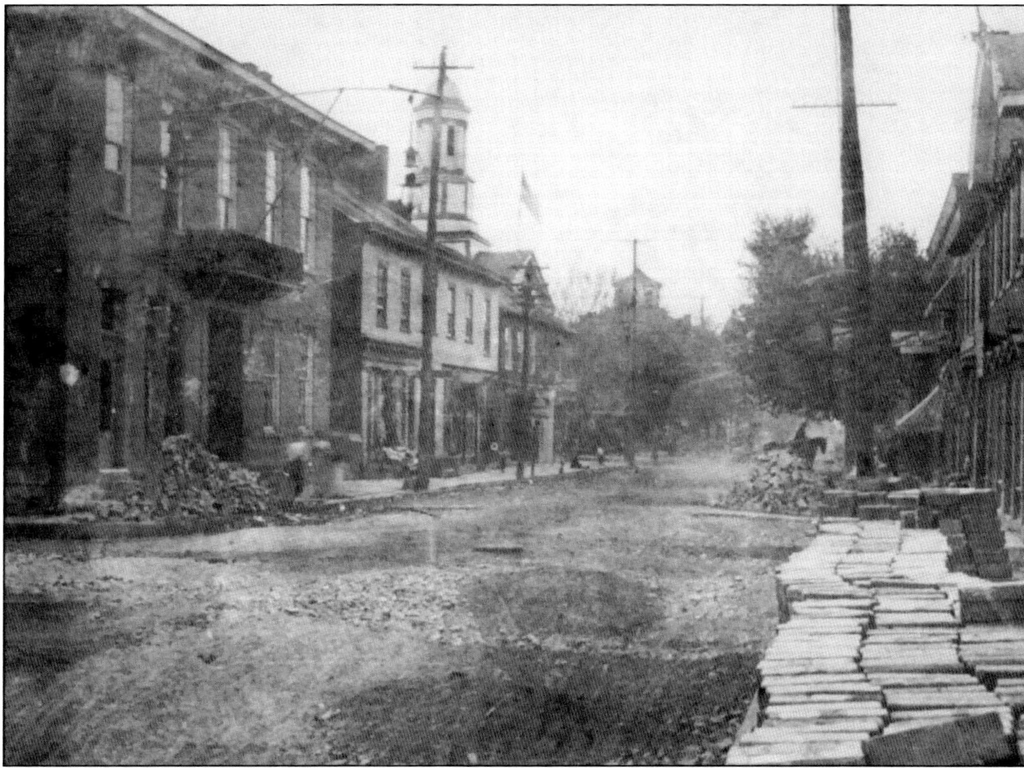

Brick pavers line the road in 1903 as George David Jenkins prepares to bring his team through the heart of town. (Courtesy of the Greene County Historical Society.)

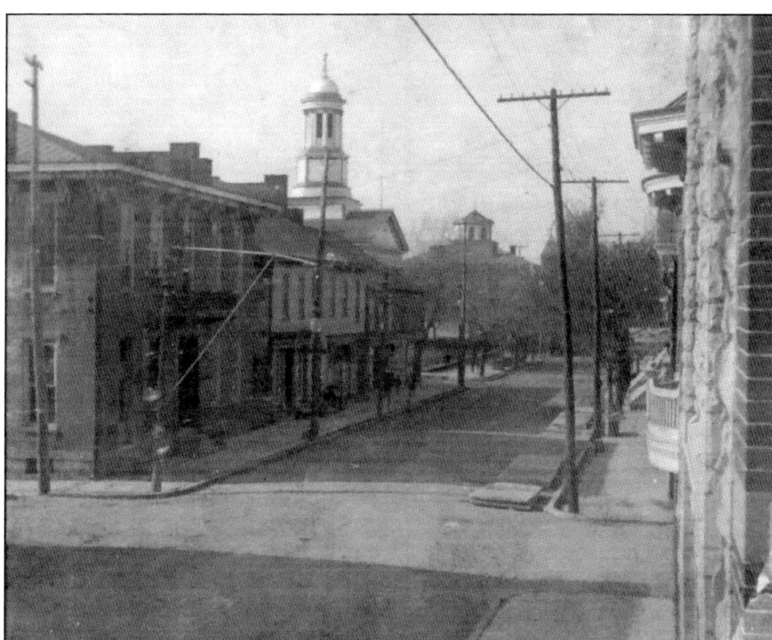

The first brick paving of High Street provided a stately look to the booming town. To the west from Morgan Street are, from left to right, the Farmers & Drovers Bank, Green House, Sayers Corner, Greene County Courthouse and Downey House. (Photograph by A.P. Smith, courtesy of the Greene County Historical Society.)

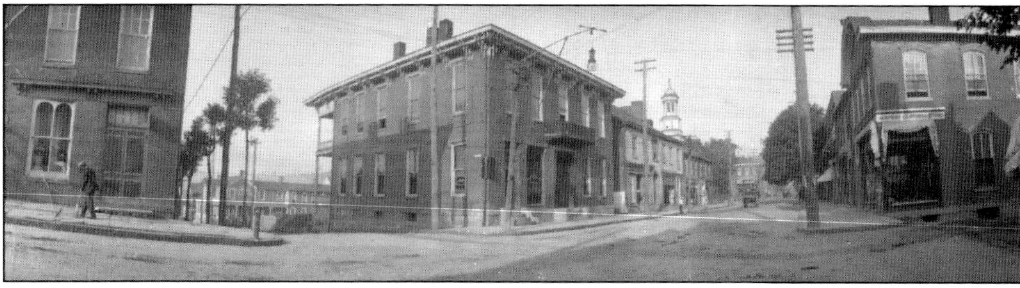

The intersection of High and Morgan Streets saw a lot of activity in the early 1900s. The Farmers & Drovers Bank, featured prominently in this photograph, was the center of a much-publicized financial scandal that drastically negatively influenced the business future of Waynesburg and Greene County. Farmers & Drovers was organized as a state bank in 1835 and as a national bank in 1865, but closed its doors as a failure in 1906. Repurposed as the Borough Building, the structure still stands and currently houses the Borough Police Station. The building to the right across the street was known as the Fisher Building, ultimately being the location of the American National Bank of Waynesburg, with offices opening in April 1906. The Long Building is now located at this site. (Courtesy of the Greene County Historical Society.)

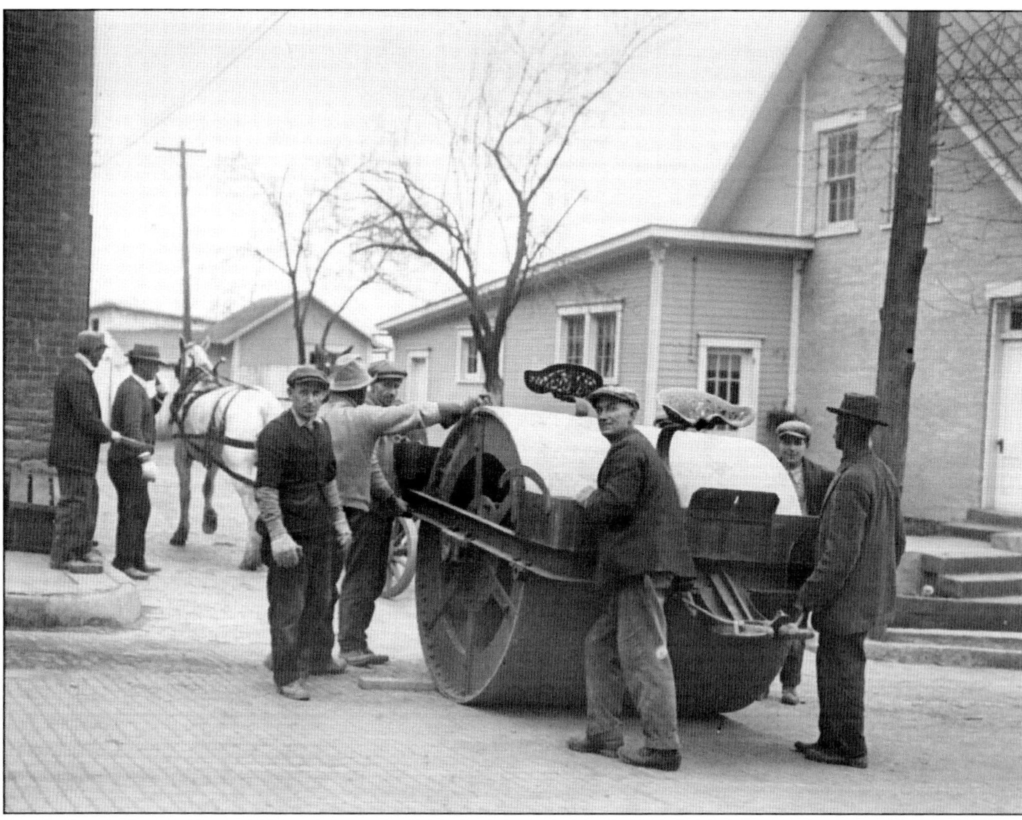

At the corner of Morgan Street and Cherry Alley, a street maintenance crew uses a horse-drawn roller with seats mounted at both ends so that the team could be redirected without having to drag the equipment in a circle. (Courtesy of Waynesburg Borough.)

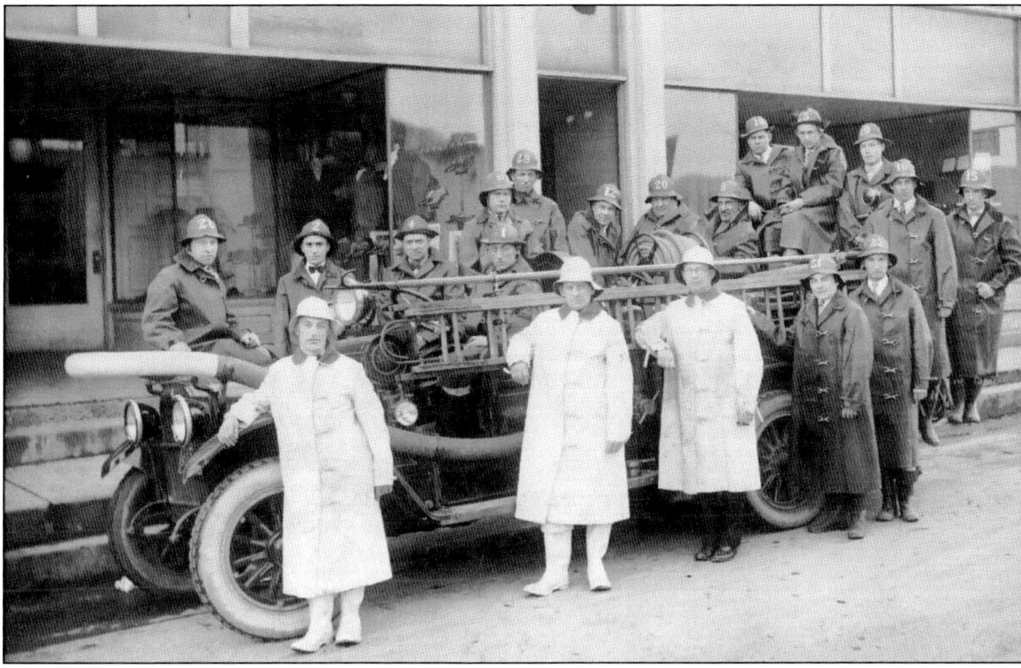

Waynesburg's call for help during the disastrous Downey House fire on December 23, 1925, was answered by many area fire companies. The image above, dated October 1928 and taken in Waynesburg, includes members of the Rices Landing Fire Company, one of those companies that came. The Waynesburg Volunteer Fire Company was officially incorporated in 1926 as a direct result of this devastating fire. Both of these photographs were taken near its original headquarters on High Street. The picture below shows a 1902 horse-drawn American Steam Fire Engine; behind is a sign above the alley between the Borough Building and the Green House that reads, "Waynesburg Volunteer Fire Company." (Above, courtesy of the Greene County Historical Society; below, photograph by William E.S. Fletcher, courtesy of the Cornerstone Genealogical Society.)

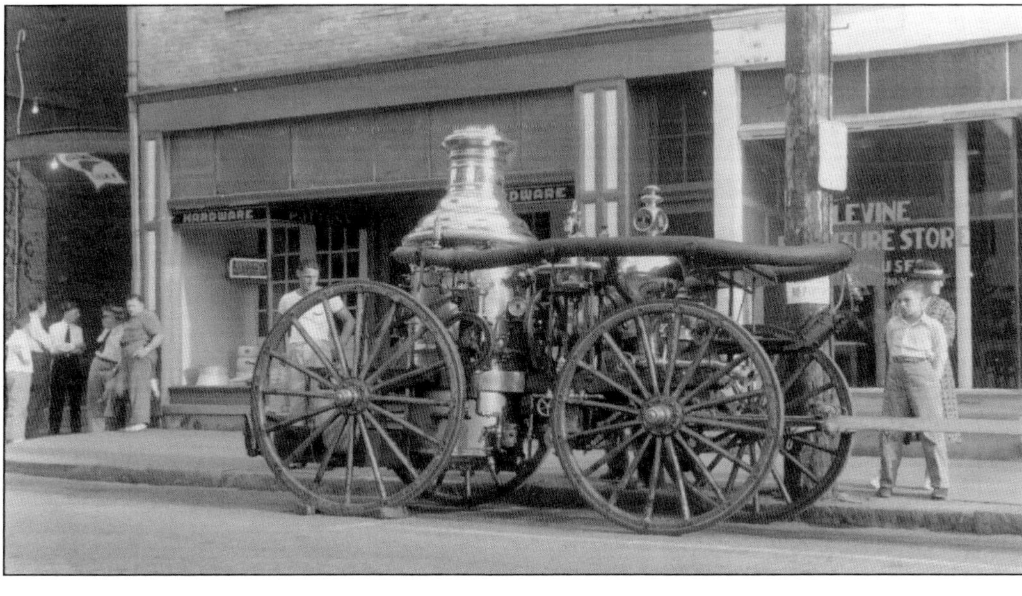

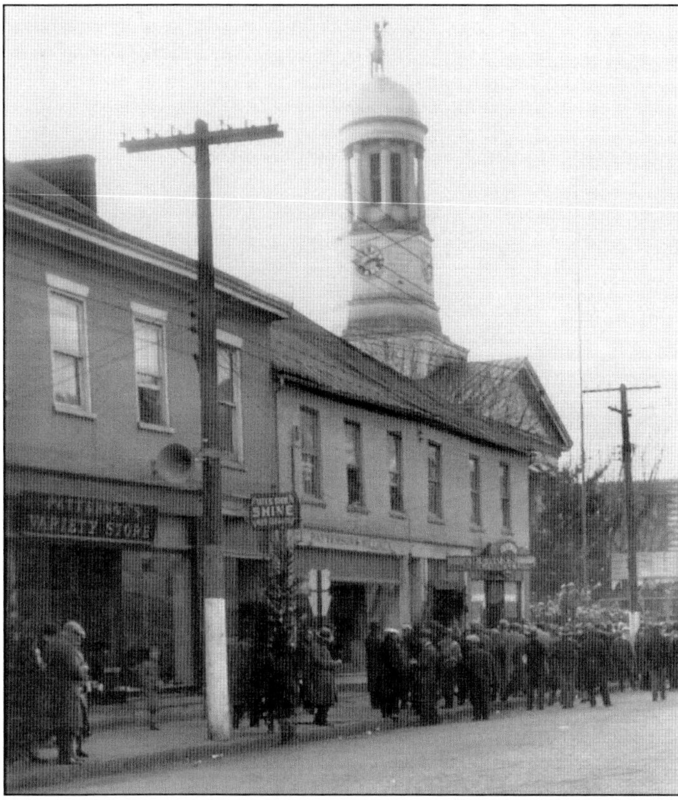

This view is looking west on High Street at the Sayers Corner building. The core of this building still incorporates what is believed to be the oldest stone structure in Waynesburg proper. Modified in 1810, the brick front addition allowed for use as a hotel. A variety of businesses have since occupied the building, such as a post office, law offices, a dry goods shop, millinery, gift shop, and today, Artbeat, an art retailer. (Photograph by William E.S. Fletcher, courtesy of the Cornerstone Genealogical Society.)

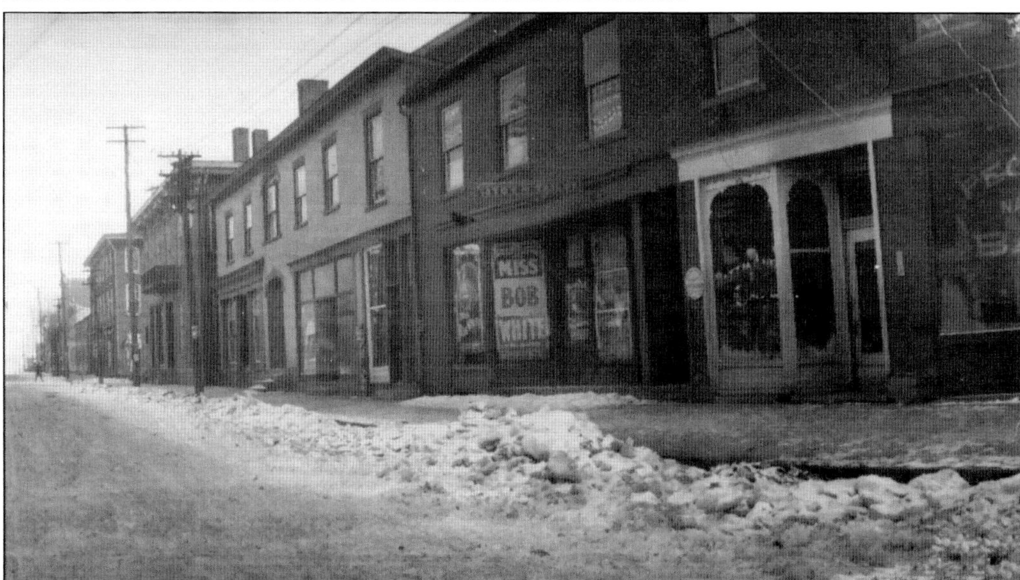

The view in this photograph looks east along the south side of High Street beginning at Church Street eastward towards the Farmer & Drovers Bank. On the right, the Peoples National Bank took a turn doing business out of this Sayers Corner building ahead of the construction of its seven floors of office space, which eventually occurred north across High Street. (Courtesy of the Greene County Historical Society.)

Church Street was named for the Presbyterian church that was built in 1880 facing the side of the courthouse and jail. It was the congregation's second home, the first having been a small building behind the Walton Hotel on Morris Street. In 1906, the congregation merged with the Cumberland Presbyterian Church on High Street to form the First Presbyterian Church. The members selected the Church Street building for Sunday services, using the High Street building for activities. It was during this period, probably around 1920, that the choir posed for this rare image inside what was by then the First Presbyterian Church. The Church Street building was destroyed after burning embers blew across the street during the Downey House fire on December 23, 1925. (Right, photograph by W.T. Hays, from the Walter "Blackie" Markiewich Postcard Collection, courtesy of Brice and Linda Rush; below, courtesy of Waynesburg Borough.)

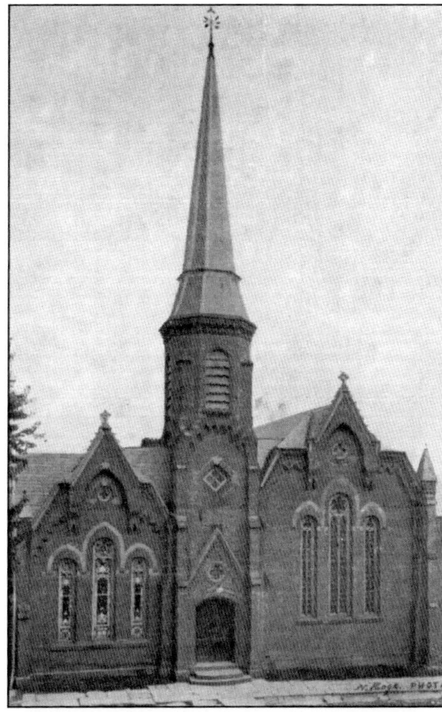

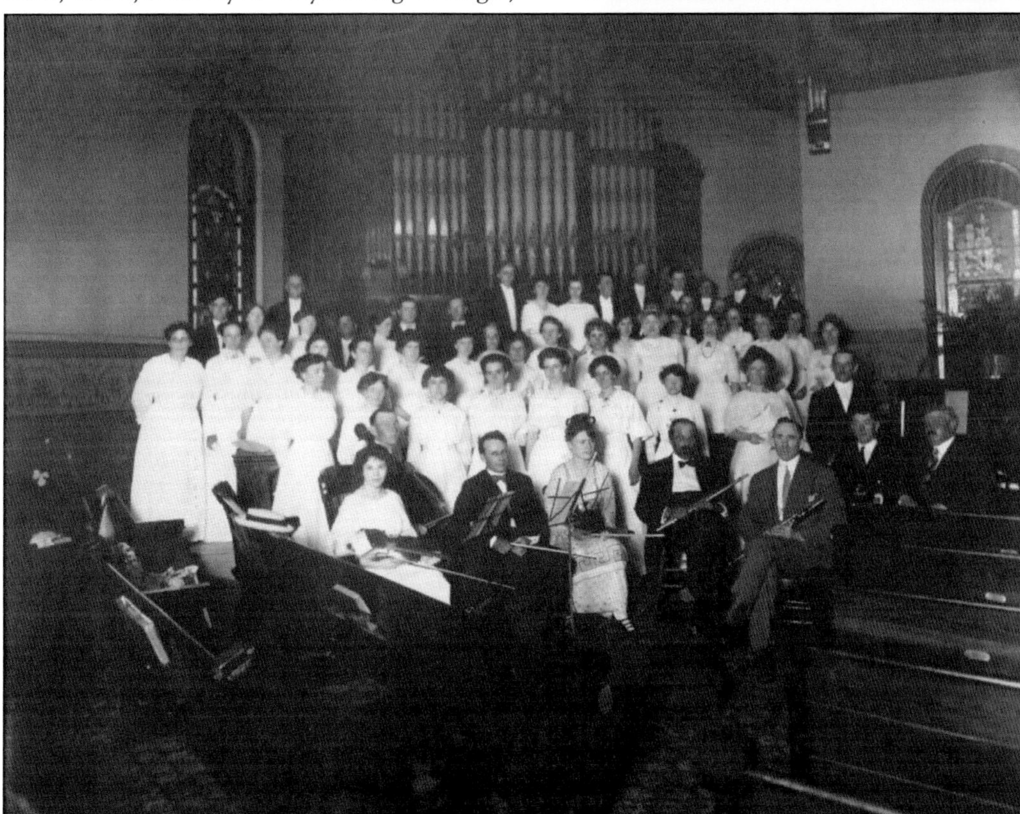

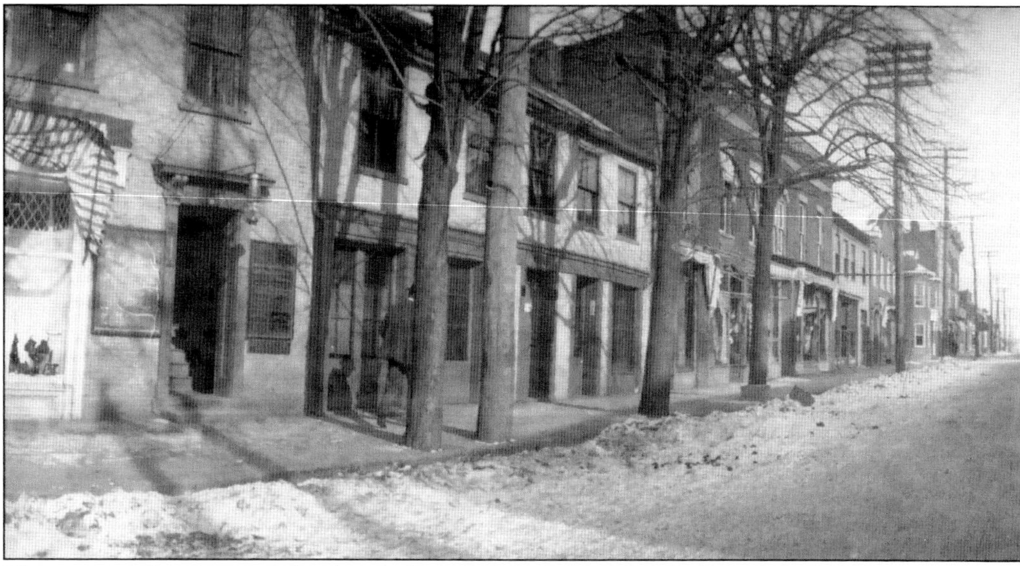

The view in this photograph taken before 1906 looks east on High Street, showing the buildings that existed at the time on its northern side between Church and Morgan Streets. (Courtesy of the Greene County Historical Society.)

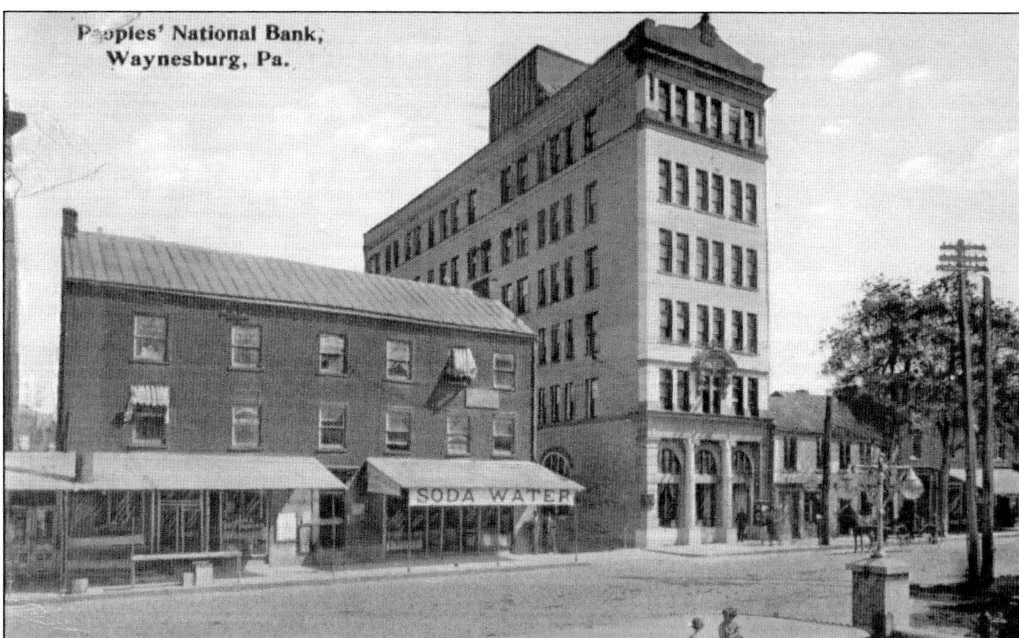

This postcard proudly featured Waynesburg's "skyscraper," the Peoples National Bank Building on High Street. To the left and right of the bank are the Allison Building and the Hooper Building, respectively. All three of these buildings have been razed, with Waynesburg's skyscraper being the most recent casualty in the summer of 2014. (From the Walter "Blackie" Markiewich Postcard Collection, courtesy of Brice and Linda Rush.).

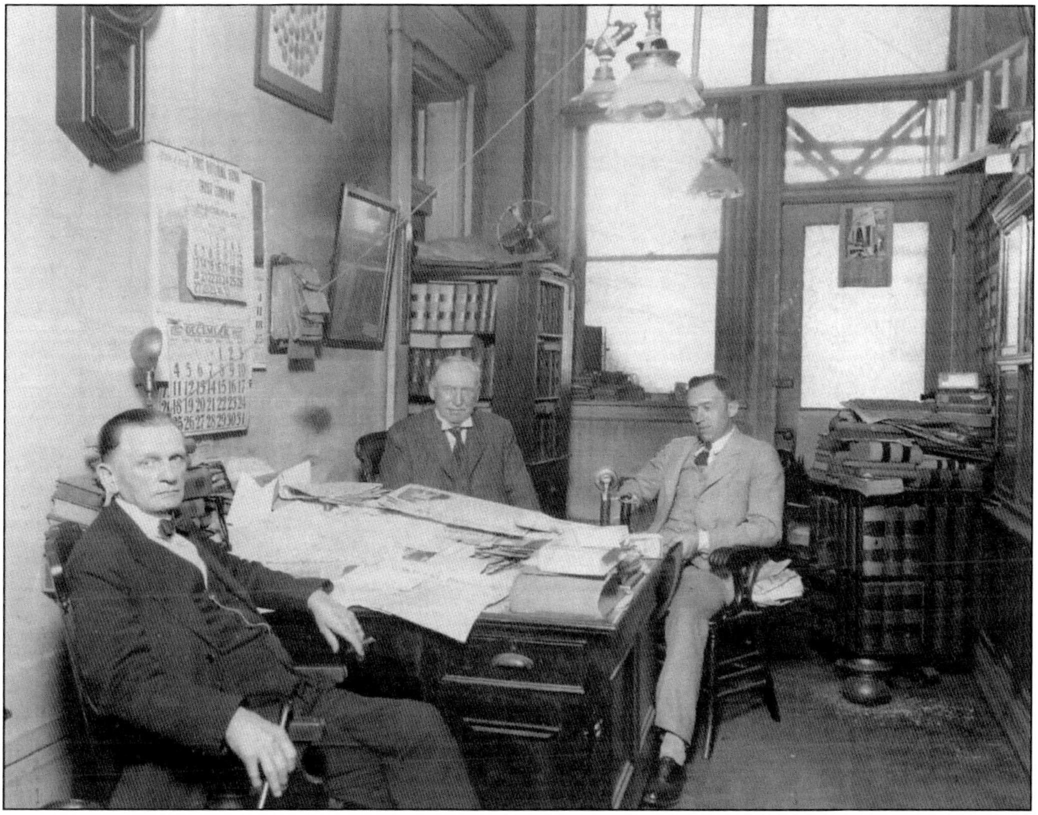

Daniel Spindler Walton, seated center, is pictured at his office inside the Peoples National Bank Building on High Street. His son Jack Buchanan Walton is seated at right. Daniel was a former Pennsylvania state senator and had been president of the Farmers & Drovers Bank when it crashed in 1906, an event that ended his promising political career. He continued to practice law in Waynesburg throughout his life. (Courtesy of Joanne Christina Walton.)

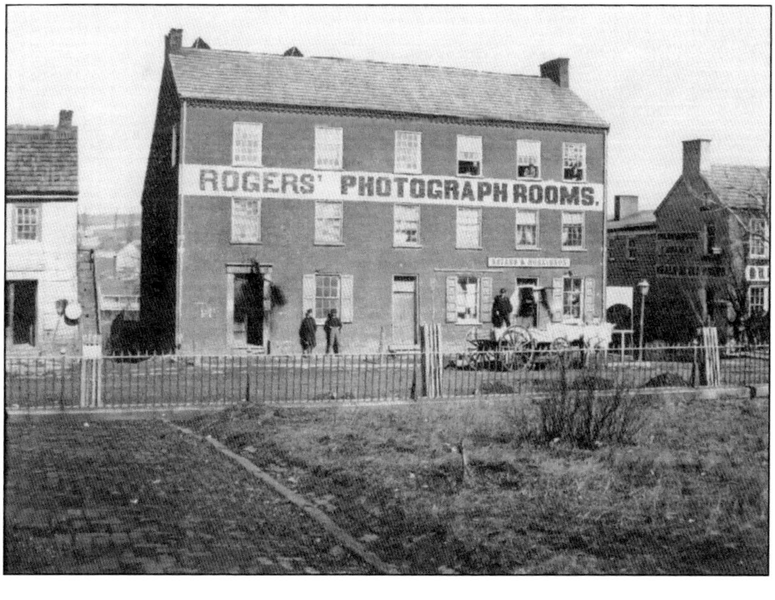

Pictured around 1885, across from the Greene County Courthouse, are, from left to right, the Ledwith Building, Allison Building, and Sherman House on High Street. (Courtesy of Waynesburg Borough.)

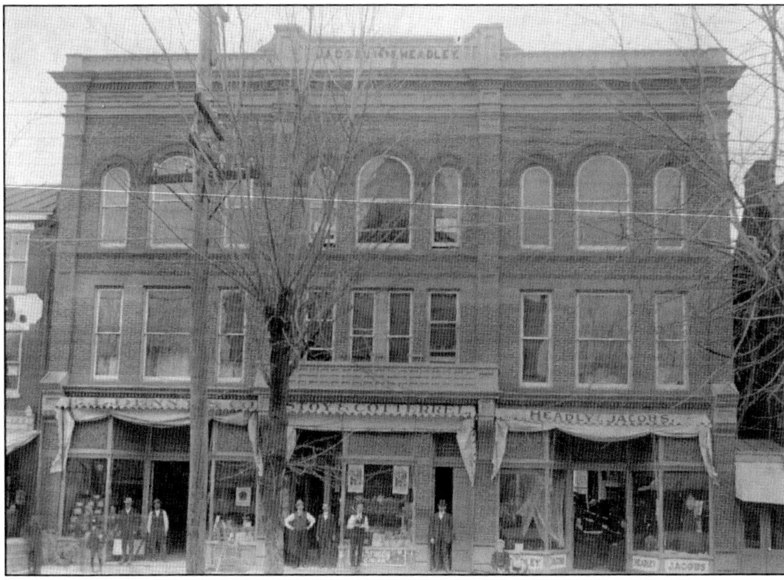

Posed for a formal photograph about 1900 are the occupants of the Jacobs & Headley Building, at the present location of First Federal Savings & Loan, on High Street. Built in 1895, this structure replaced the early log Ledwith Building. (Courtesy of the Greene County Historical Society.)

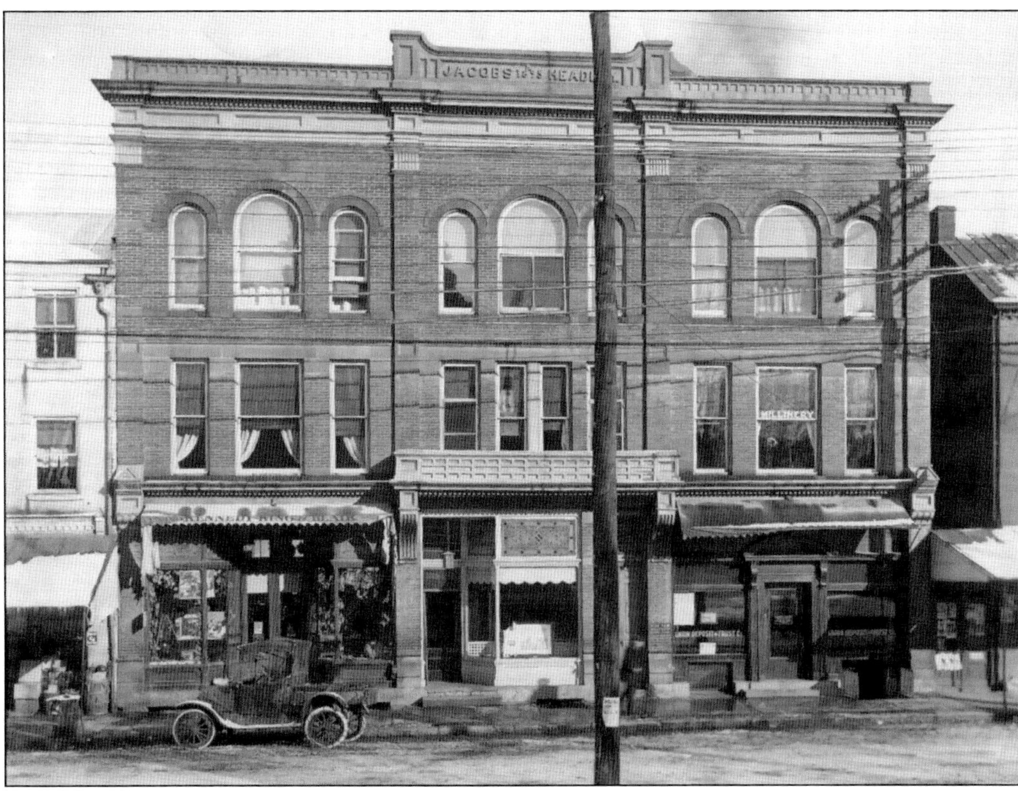

This building was renovated around 1906 to include the Union Deposit & Trust Co., as seen in the lower right of the image, and was refaced with Indiana limestone in the Italian Renaissance style in 1922. Union Deposit & Trust Co. later became First Federal Savings & Loan. (Courtesy of Greene County Historical Society.)

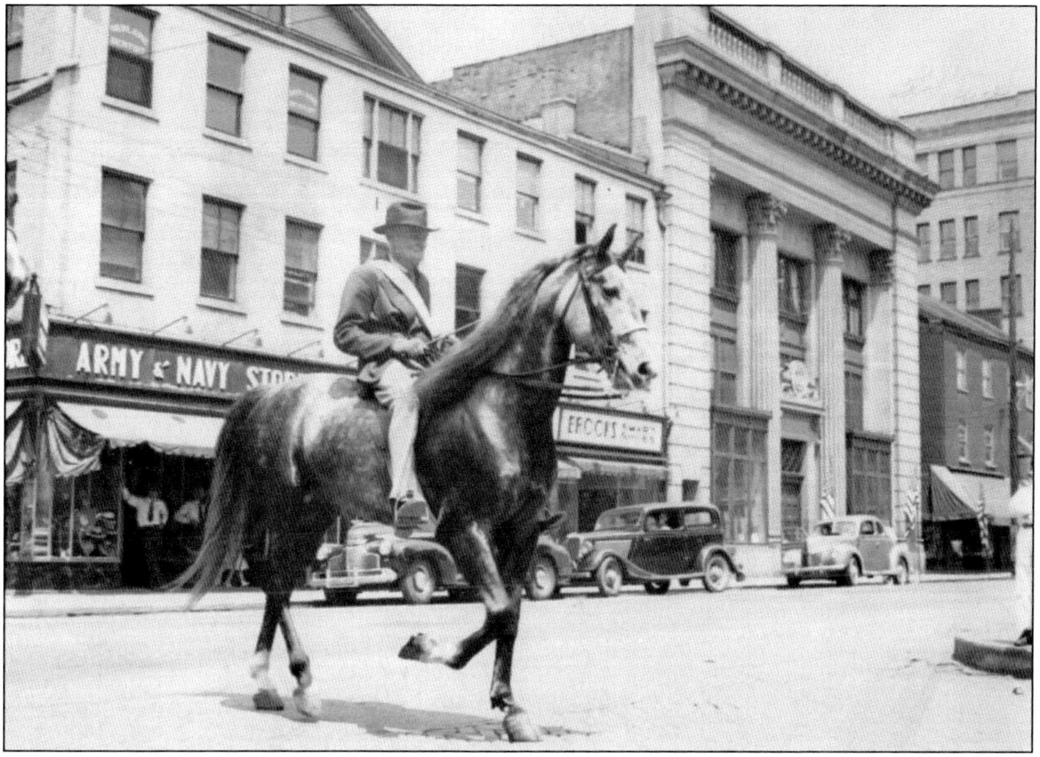

Dr. William A. Titus rides south through the intersection of Washington and High Streets. Behind him are the Messenger Building, Union Deposit & Trust Co. (later First Federal Savings & Loan), the Allison Building, and the Peoples National Bank. (Courtesy of the Greene County Historical Society.)

In 1903, new sewer lines were laid along High Street before the brick paving started. For the town to compete with other developing communities vying for new industry and residences, a major sewer and paving program was implemented. Many Italian workers were soon to become a part of the community as the primary labor force for this arduous task. (Courtesy of the Greene County Historical Society.)

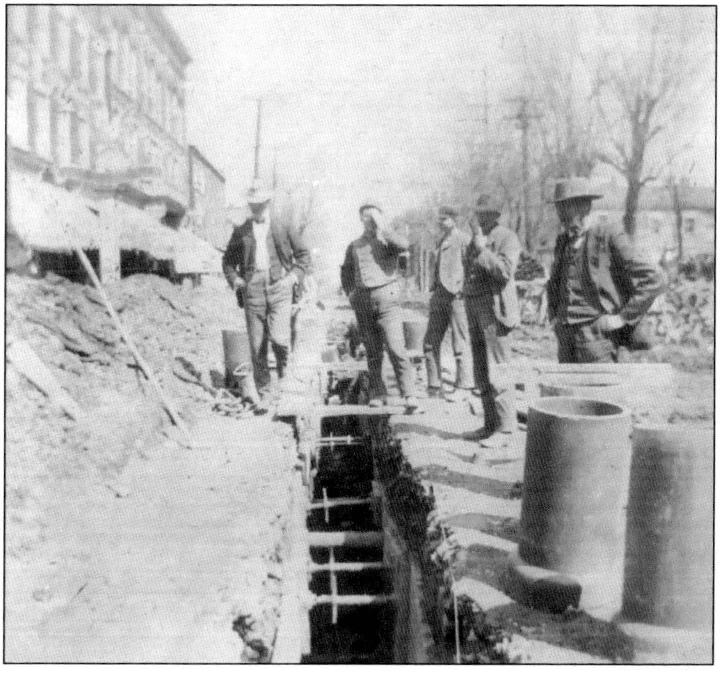

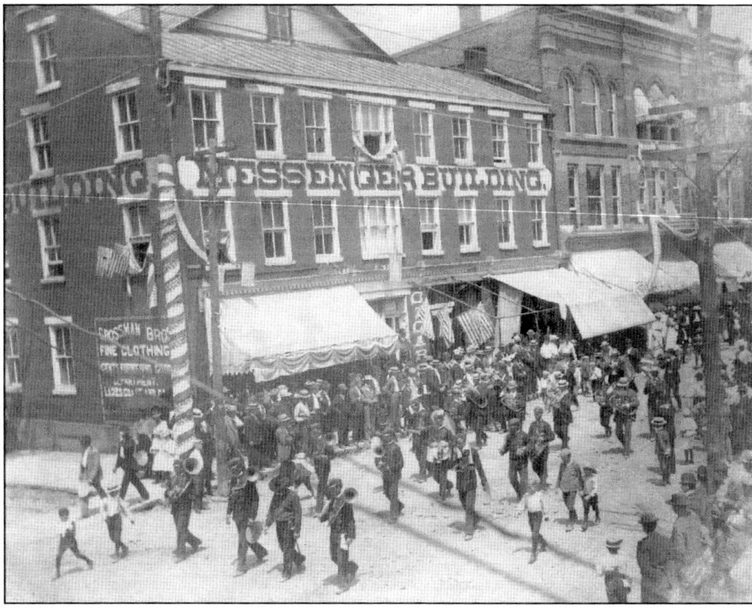

A parade passes the Messenger Building and Jacobs & Headley Building near the corner of High and Washington Streets. (Courtesy of Waynesburg Borough.)

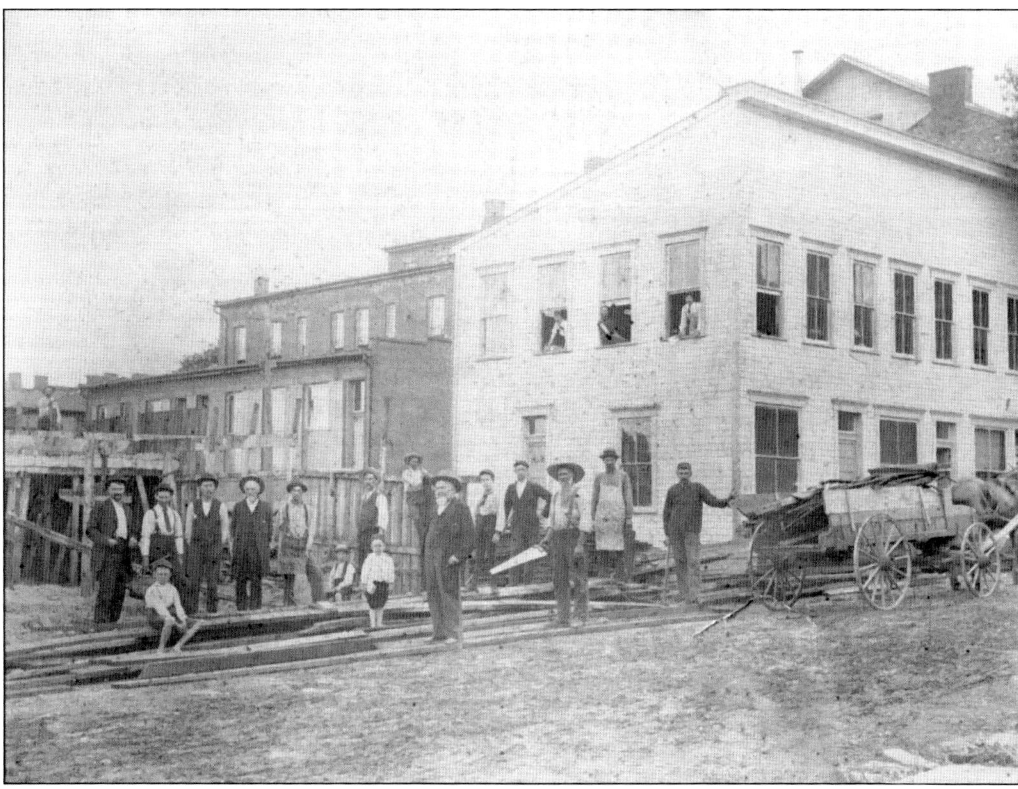

This is a view of the backside of the Messenger Building at the corner of High and Washington Streets. Toward the center of the crowd, sporting the short beard, is William Thompson Hays Pauley Sr., editor of the *Waynesburg Messenger*. This site was purported to be an after-hours location for finding something to quench a person's thirst during the years that Prohibitionists dominated local politics. (Courtesy of the Greene County Historical Society.)

The staff of the *Waynesburg Messenger* pose outside of the company's building. Pauley (second from the right), the editor-owner for 53 years, served in this capacity during the time that Prohibition politics divided the community between the "wets" and the "drys," wherein Pauley was known to favor the opportunity to share a splash of alcohol in good company. (From the Pauley-Thompson Collection, courtesy of the Cornerstone Genealogical Society.)

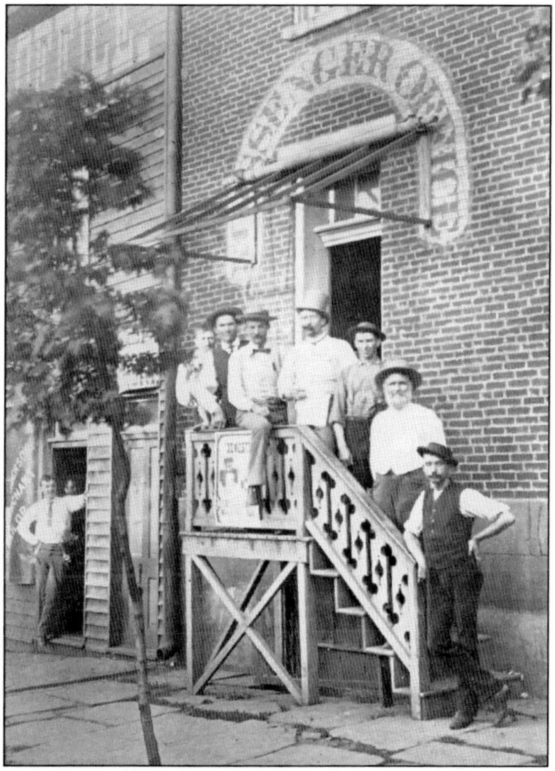

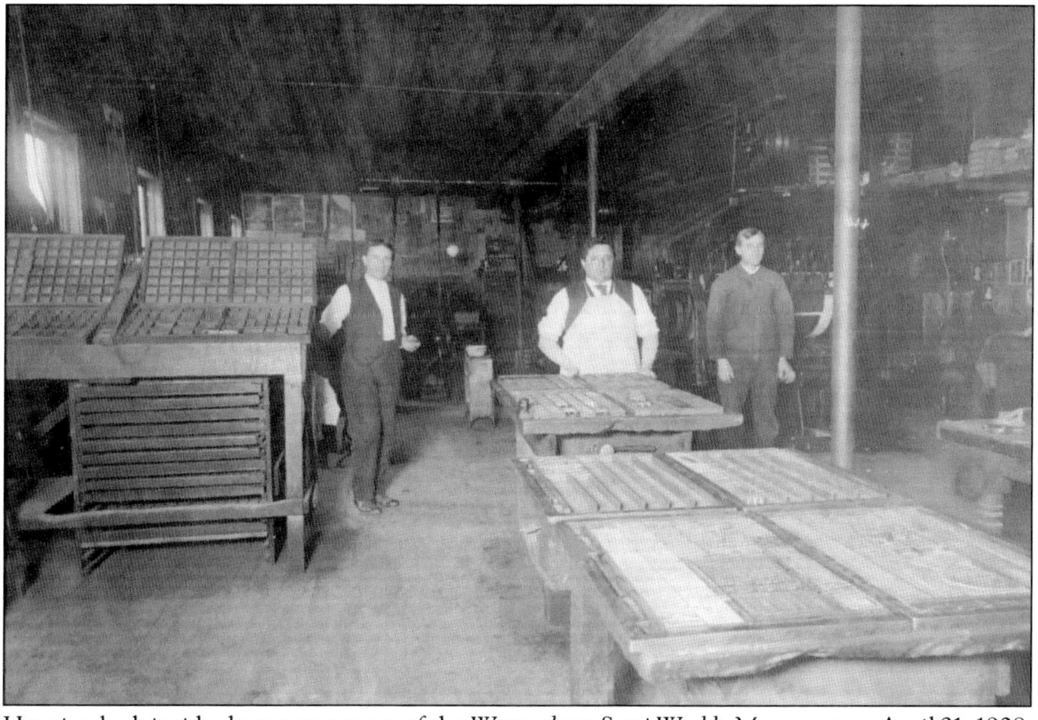

Here is a look inside the typeset room of the *Waynesburg Semi-Weekly Messenger* on April 21, 1908. (Photograph by *Waynesburg Semi-Weekly Messenger*, courtesy of Matt W. Cumberledge.)

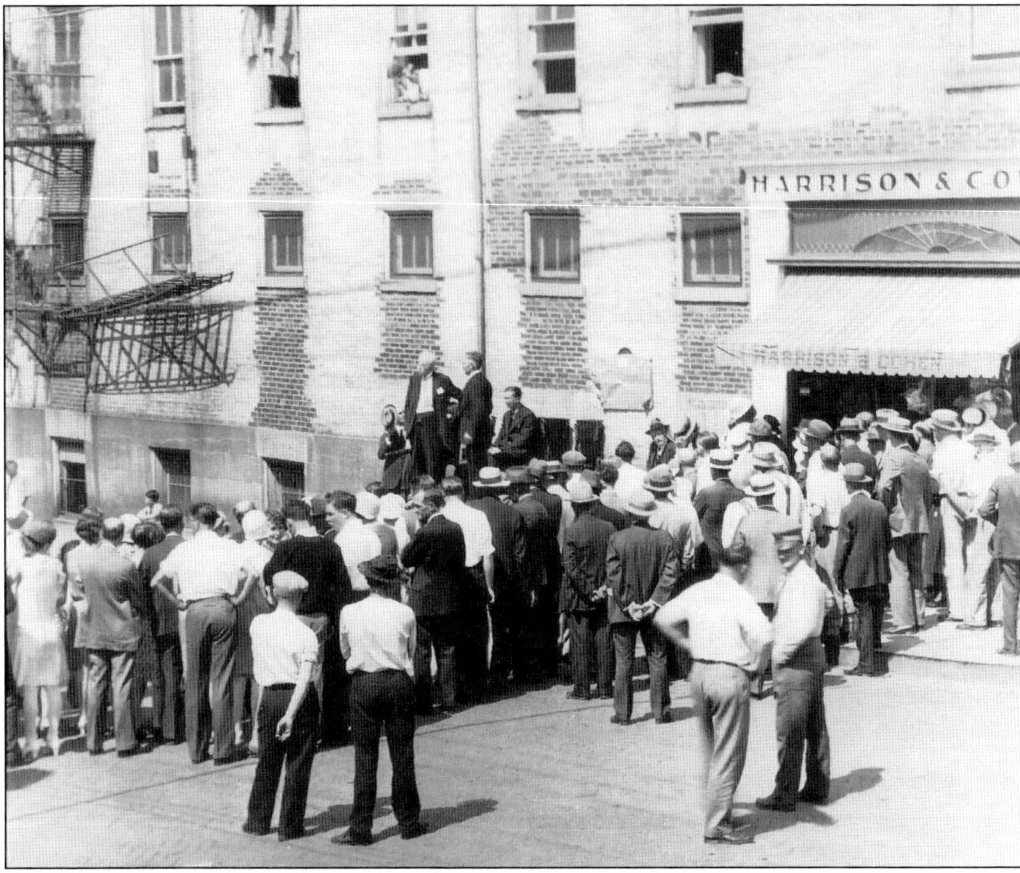

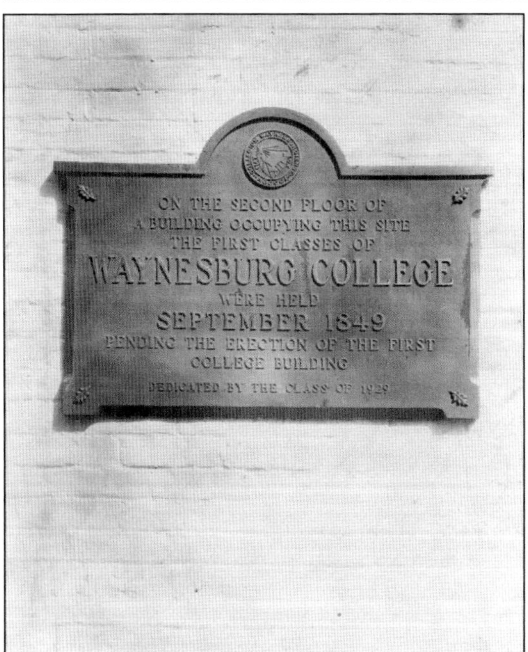

A crowd gathered for the Waynesburg College plaque dedication ceremony outside of the Messenger Building on the northeast corner of High and Washington Streets. The plaque, which has since disappeared, read: "On the second floor of / a building occupying this site / the first classes of / Waynesburg College / were held / September 1849 / pending the erection of the first / college building / Dedicated by the Class of 1929." (Both, courtesy of Waynesburg University.)

This view looks north on Washington Street from High Street around 1890. Given the bit of snow seen in the picture, a cold bath was probably easier to get than a hot one, and a place to kick the mud off one's shoes prior to entering any town location would have been essential. The large frame structure at the back right is a Civil War–era flour mill that was later torn down to make way for the construction of the Stewart Science Hall. (Courtesy of Waynesburg Borough.)

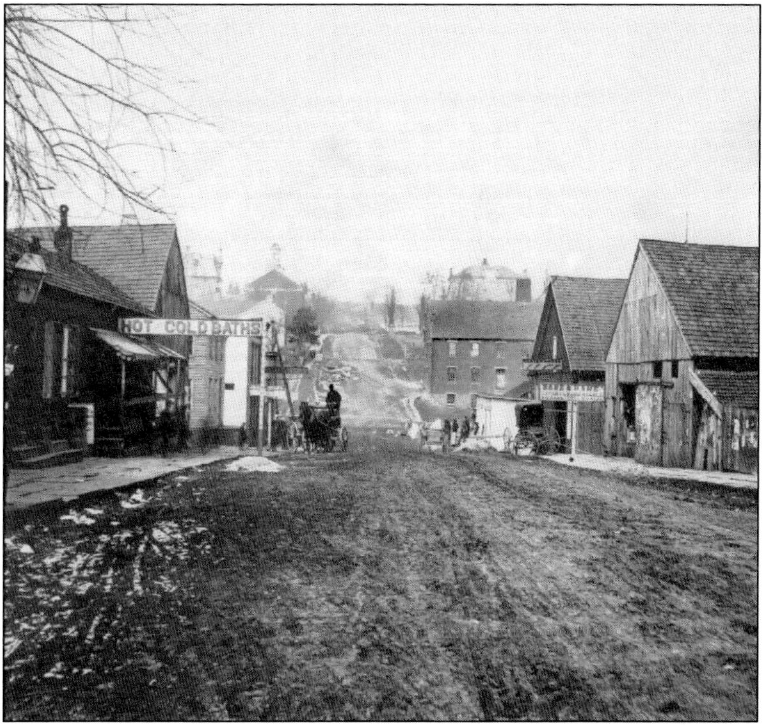

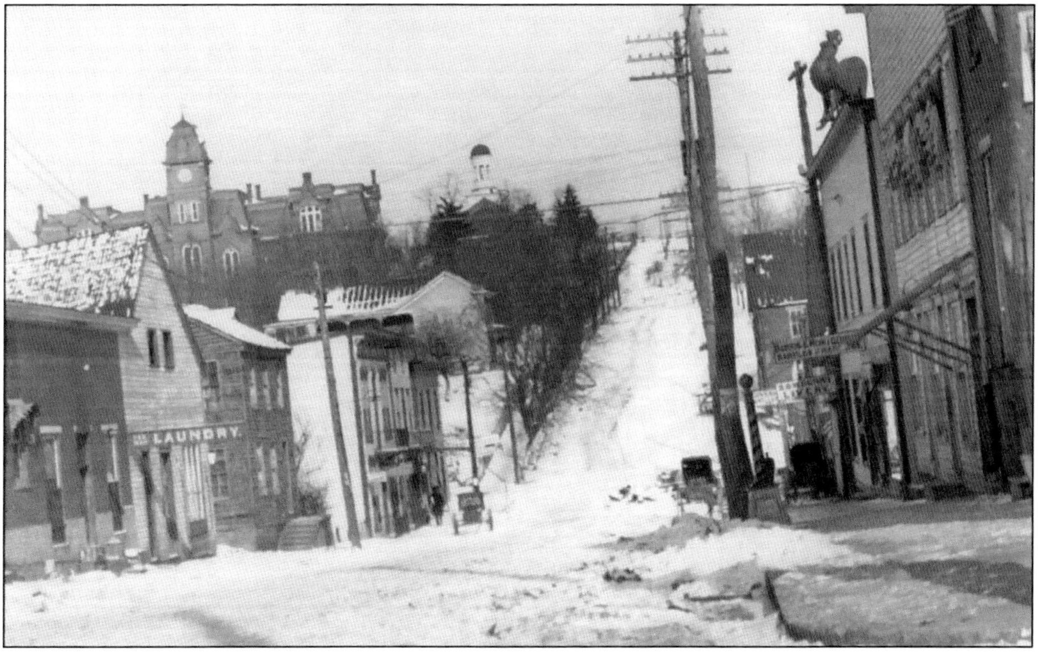

Years later, the street is paved with brick, and the public bathhouse has transitioned to a laundry. The large metal rooster atop the frame addition to the Messenger Building was the trademark of the *Waynesburg Messenger*. Signs advertise the Denny Livery and Burris & Montgomery Saddles. The building on the left was demolished in 1922 to make way for the new Citizens National Bank. (Courtesy of the Greene County Historical Society.)

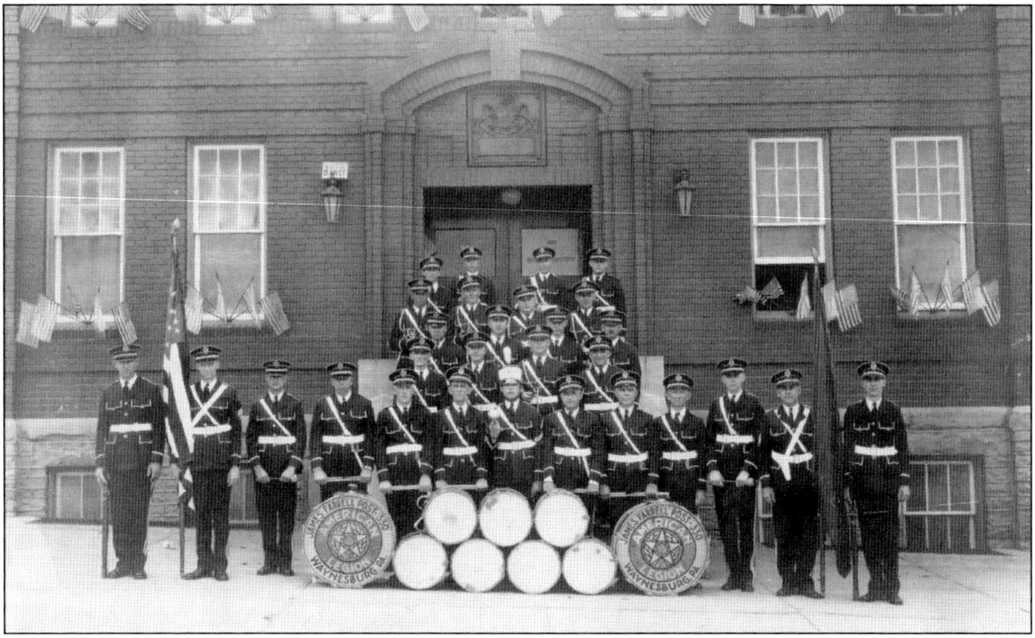

American Legion James Farrell Post No. 330 Drum and Bugle Corps poses in front of the armory on Washington Street around 1928. This building still stands and is now owned by Waynesburg University. From this armory, the boys of Company K headed out to World War I in 1917, marching to the Waynesburg & Washington Railroad station. (Photograph by Clarence F. Long of Community Art Shop, courtesy of Waynesburg Borough.)

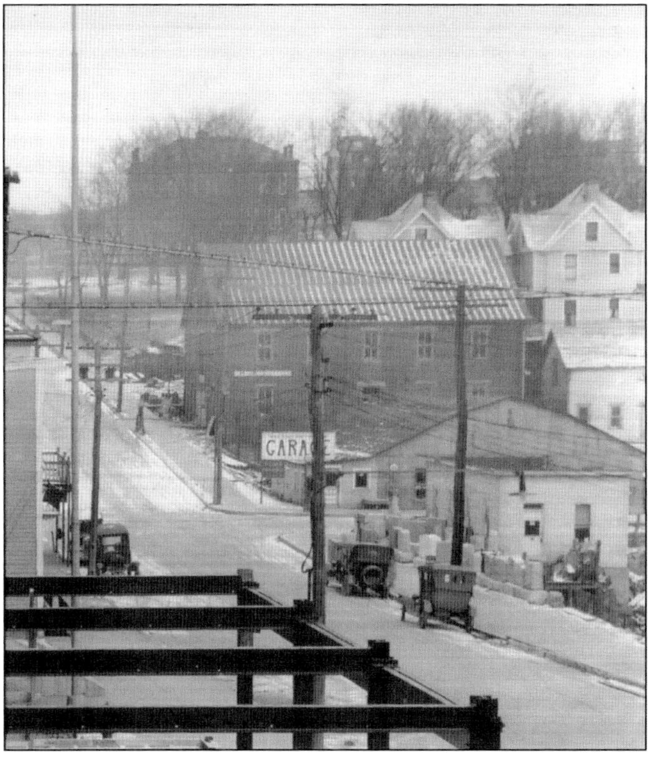

This northern view of Washington Street was taken during the construction of the new Citizens National Bank on the northwest corner of High and Washington Streets on January 17, 1923. The Summersgill Marble and Granite Works and the Walton Motor Garage are among the highlights. (Courtesy of the Greene County Historical Society.)

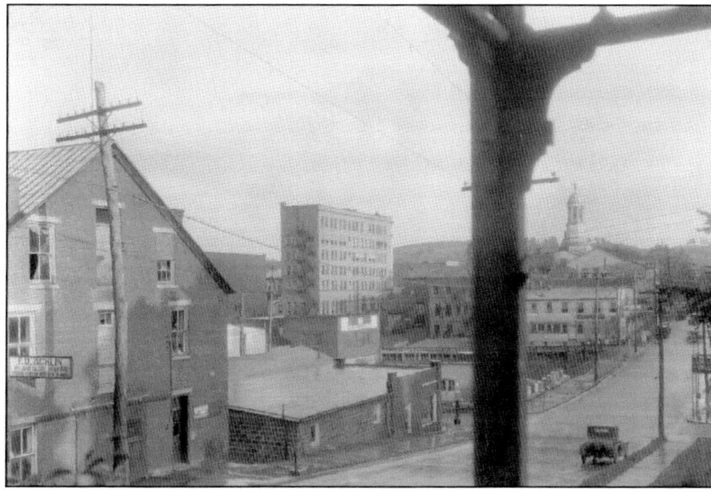

This view is looking south on Washington Street from the site of the Waynesburg College gymnasium, which was under construction. (Photograph by William E.S. Fletcher, courtesy of the Cornerstone Genealogical Society.)

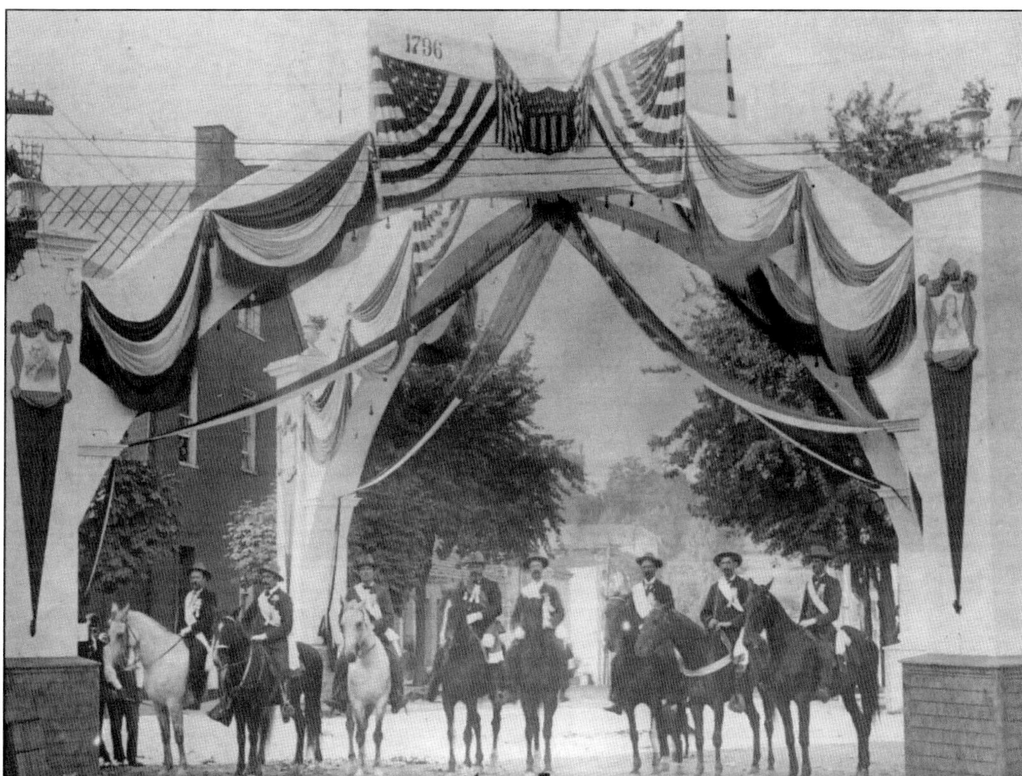

On August 27, 1896, a centennial celebration arch was placed over the intersection of High and Washington Streets. The marshals of the Centennial Parade are, from left to right, Robert Wallace Munnell (1), John Flenniken Pauley Sr. (2), J. B. Rinehart Jr. (3), Dr. J. T. Ullom (4), Thomas Spencer Crago (5), John Martin Wiley (6), Hiram Kent (7), and Eleazer Luse Denny (8). (Courtesy of the Greene County Historical Society.)

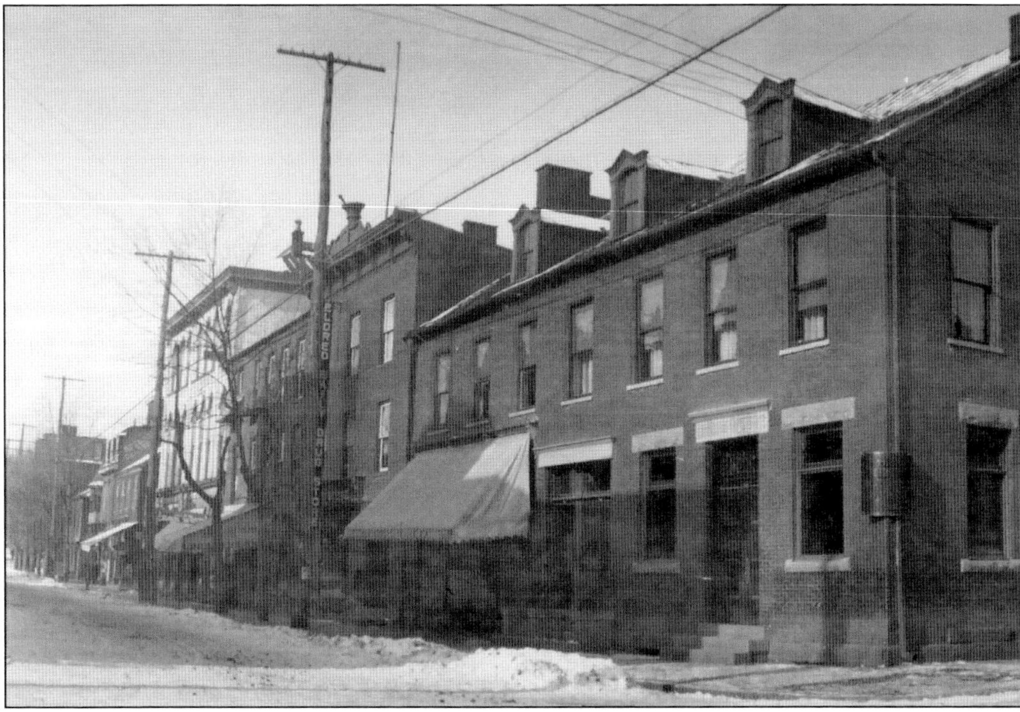

Westward on High Street from Washington Street, the old Citizens National Bank stands on the corner. The large, light-colored building to the left of the image is the opera house, which still stands. (Courtesy of the Greene County Historical Society.)

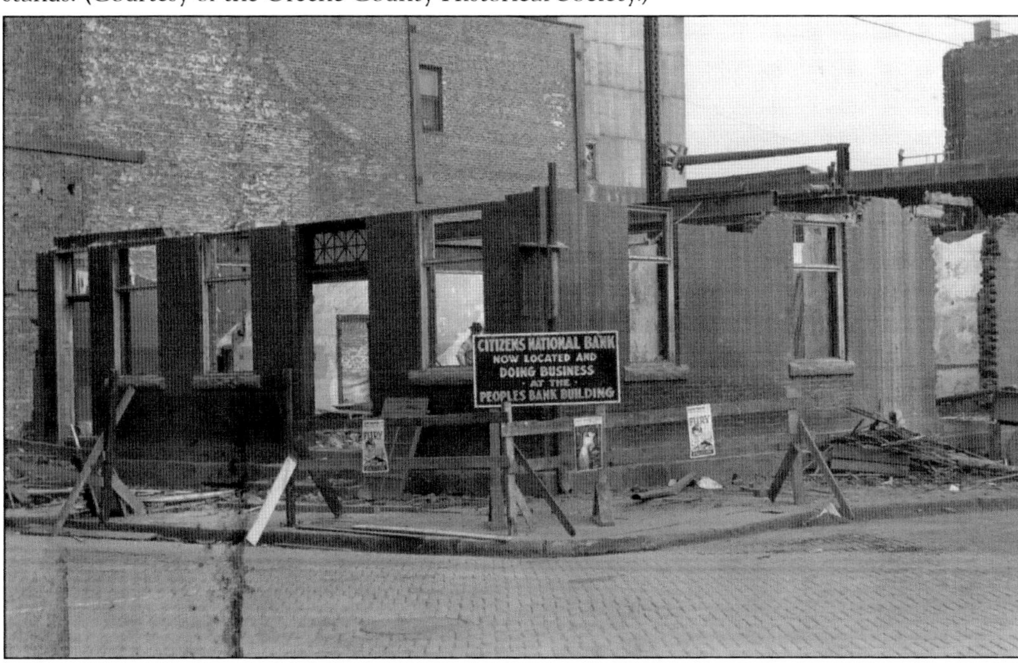

As the old Citizens National Bank building came down on June 23, 1923, clientele were directed to do their business a block east at a temporary location in the Peoples National Bank Building. (Courtesy of the Greene County Historical Society.)

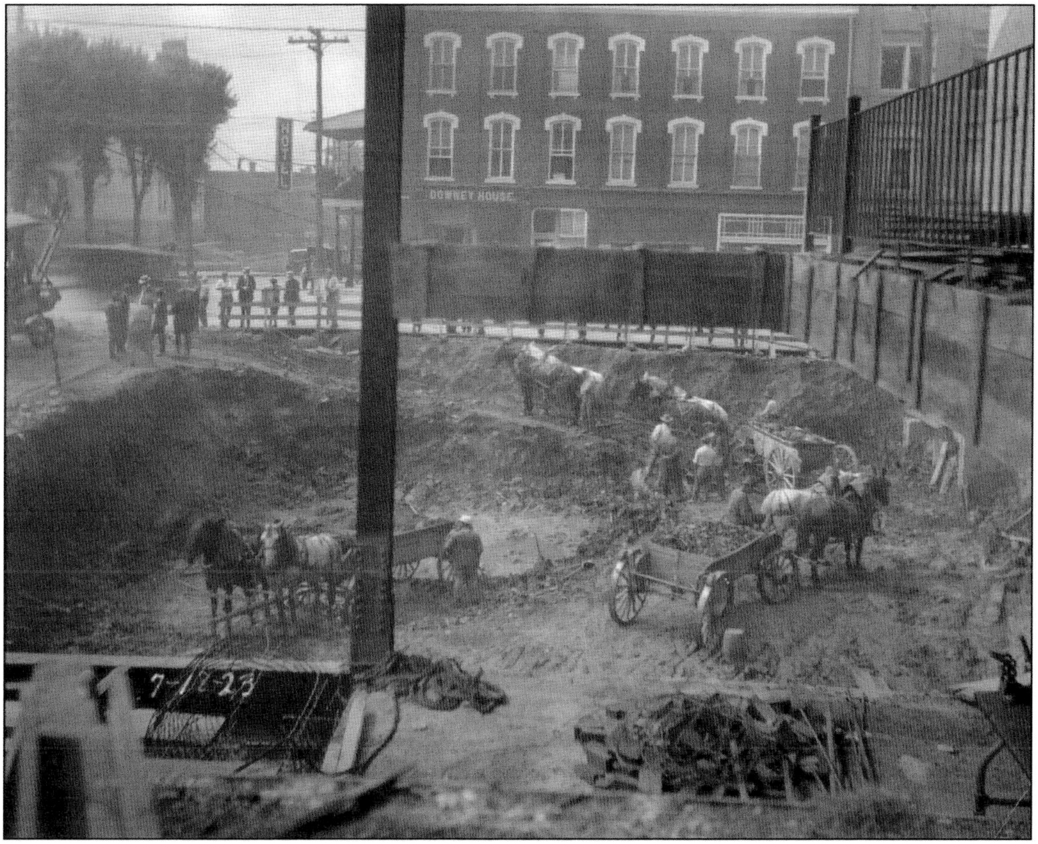

Traditional and modern equipment joined forces on July 18, 1923, as teams of horses partnered with a Keystone Skimmer steam shovel brought down from Beaver Falls, Pennsylvania, during the construction of the new Citizens National Bank on the northwest corner of High and Washington Streets. Above, notice the Downey House standing prominently on the opposite corner; that establishment was doomed to destruction by fire only two years later on December 23, 1925. Below, crowds ignored the "No Loafing Here" signs to watch the action. (Both, courtesy of the Greene County Historical Society.)

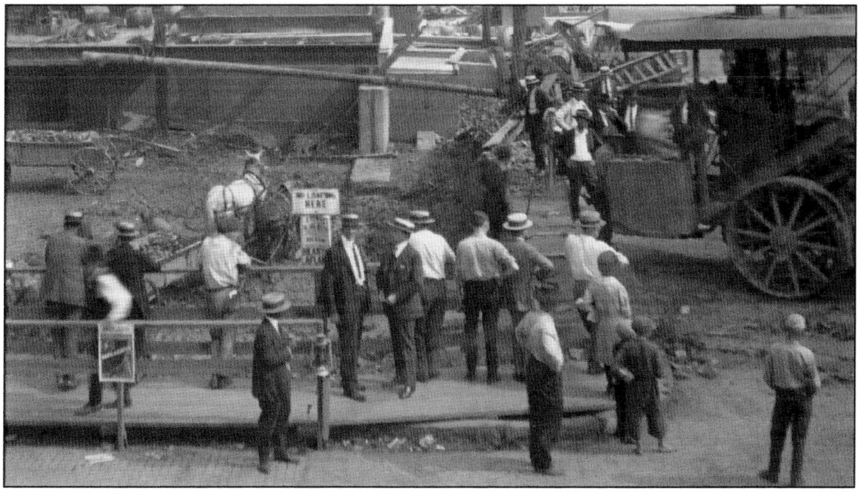

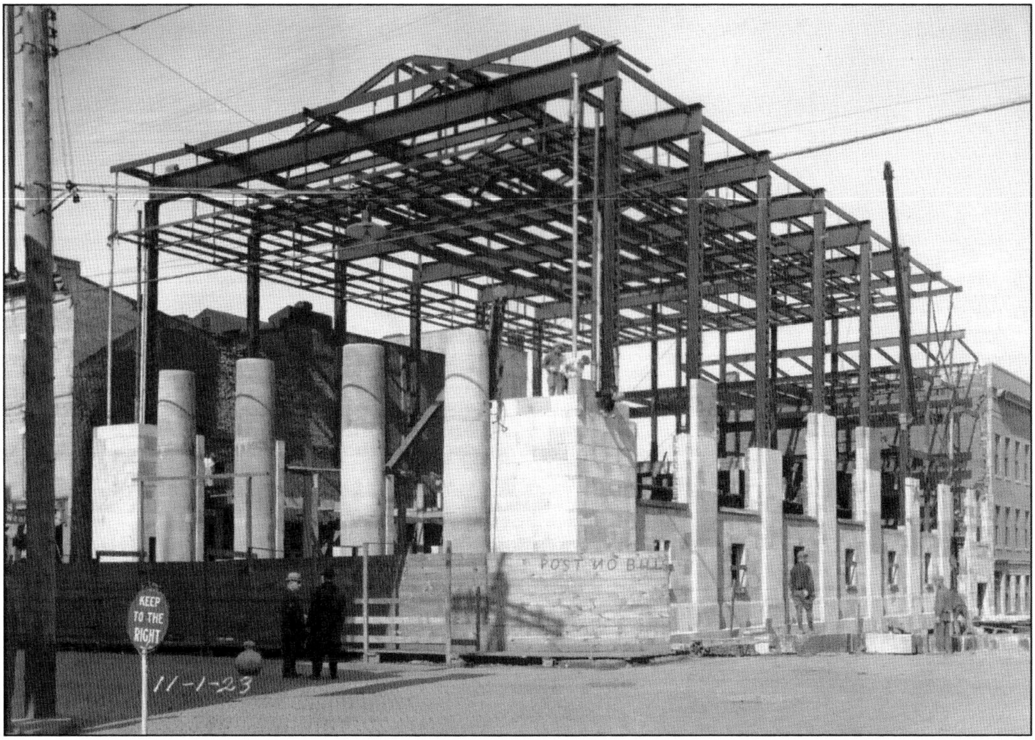

By November 1, 1923, the new Citizens National Bank was rising above the northwest corner of High and Washington Streets. (Courtesy of the Greene County Historical Society.)

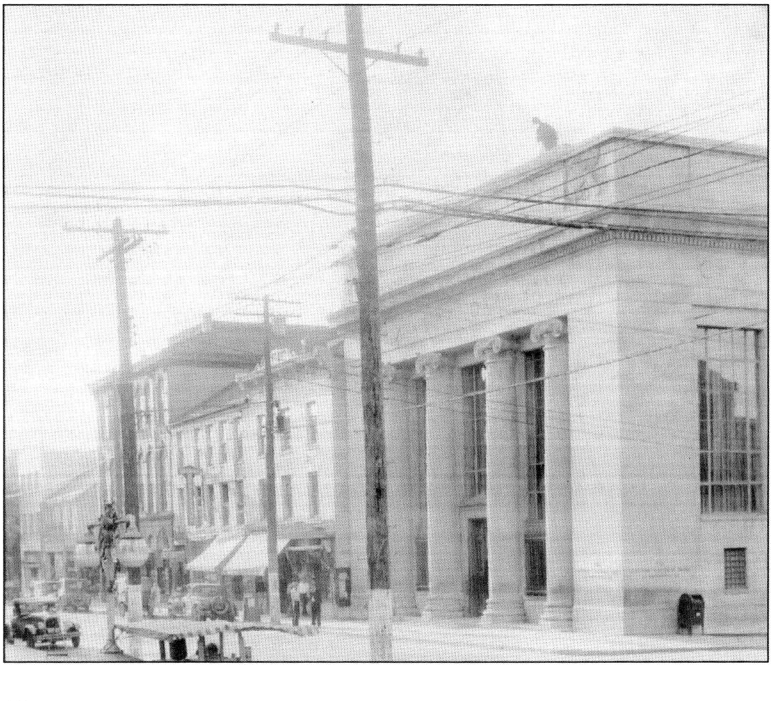

This is a westward view of the new skyline between Washington and Morris Streets. (Photograph by William E.S. Fletcher, courtesy of the Cornerstone Genealogical Society.)

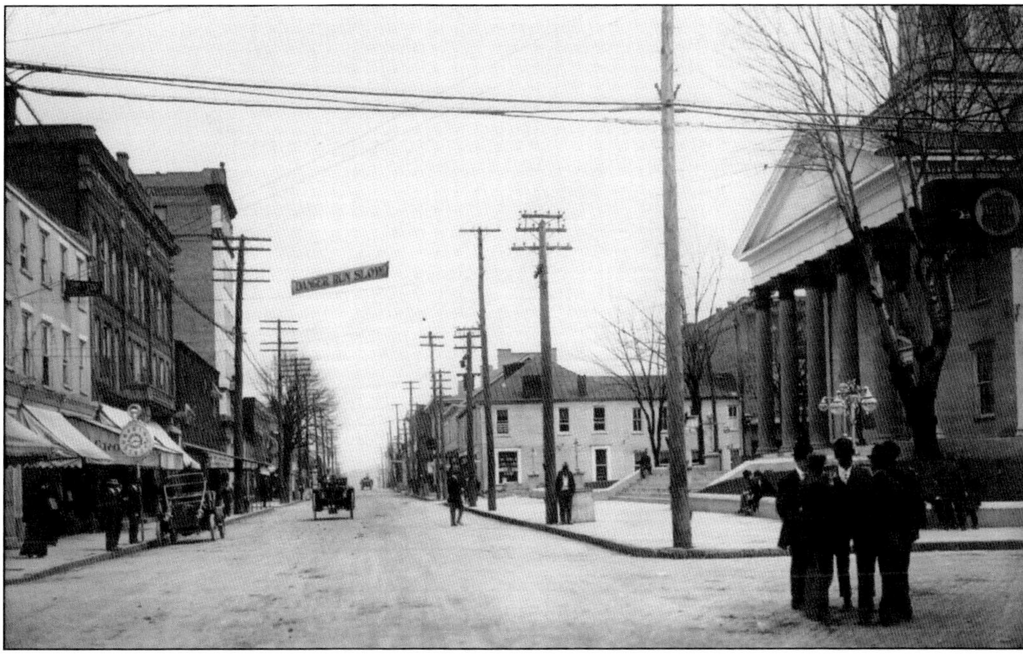

Above, a "Danger Run Slow" sign dangles over a paved High Street, which still provided roadway for both automobiles and horsepower in the early 1900s. Below, a woodcut of downtown Waynesburg, dated 1843, takes High Street back to the era of the previous Greene County Courthouse (in the left foreground), built around 1800 and removed in 1849–1850. It was a brick building that stood on the site of the present courthouse, which was constructed in 1850–1851. To the west (right) of the courthouse, on the corner of High and Washington Streets, is the building best known as the Bull's Head Tavern (also known as the Union Hotel and the Adams Inn). It was built by John Inghram in the town's earliest years. Later proprietors included Elijah Adams and John Strosnider. The iconic hotel structure was removed in the late 1860s for construction of the Downey House. (Above, courtesy of the Waynesburg University Museum; below, courtesy of Candice Buchanan.)

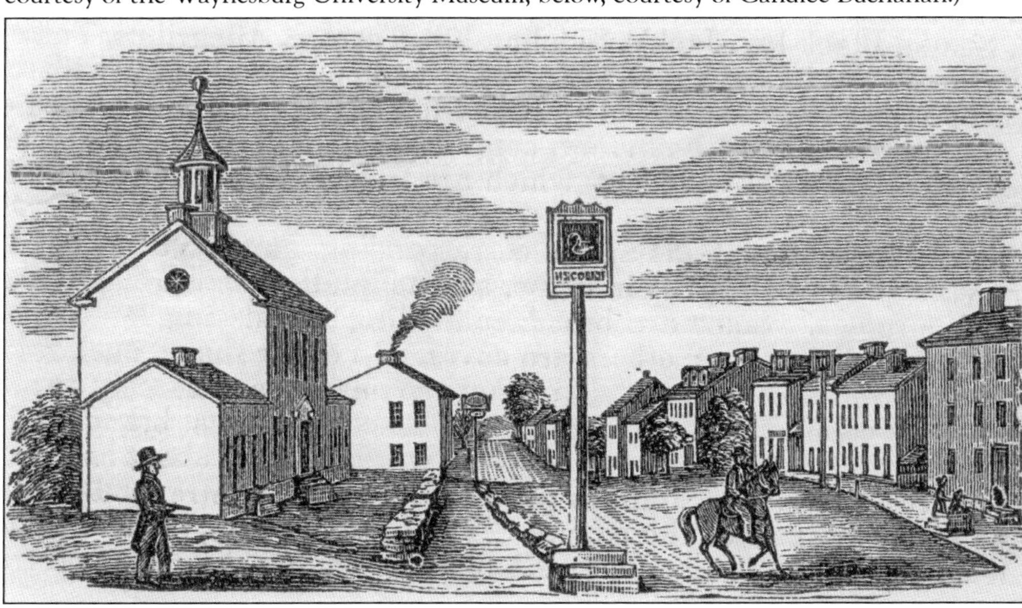

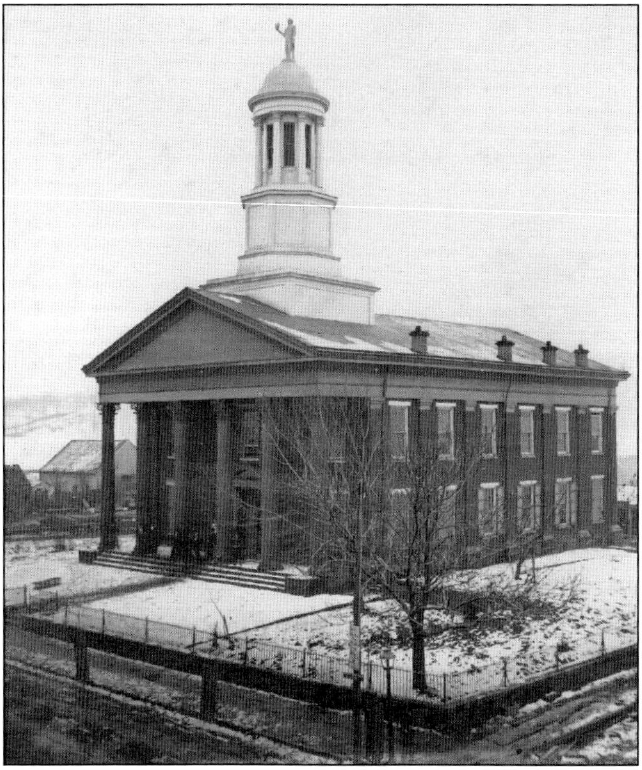

This is an early view of the present Greene County Courthouse, built in 1850–1851. In the background on Church Street is the Sayers & Rinehart marble yard. (Courtesy of Waynesburg Borough.)

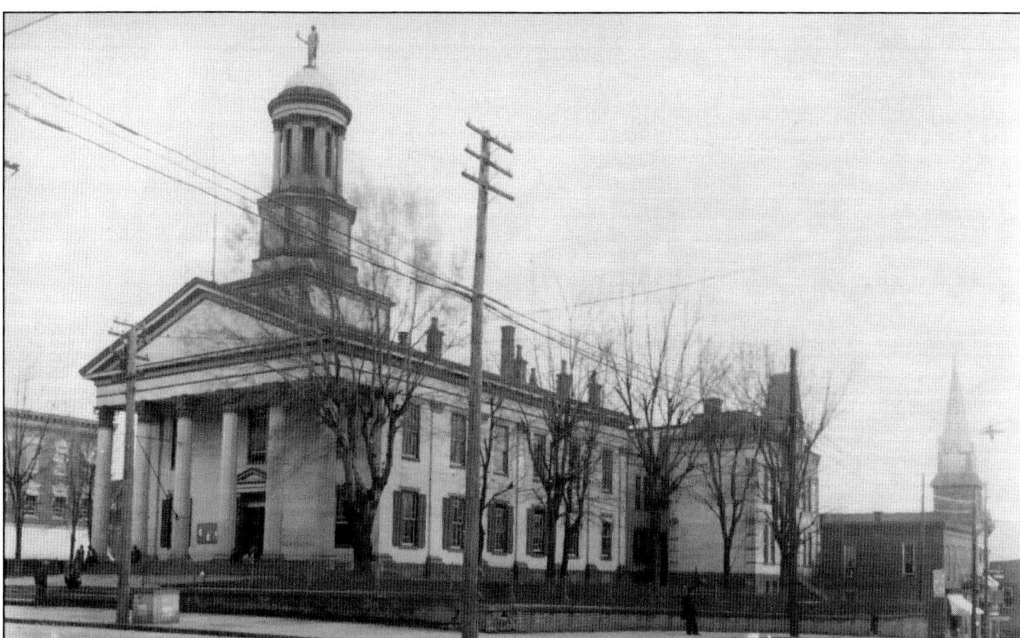

Pictured is the present Greene County Courthouse with the new jail and sheriff's residence, which were added to the south side of the building in 1880–1881. In the background is the L.W. Sayers Building, constructed in 1915 and now Fischer's Antiques. (Courtesy of the Greene County Historical Society.)

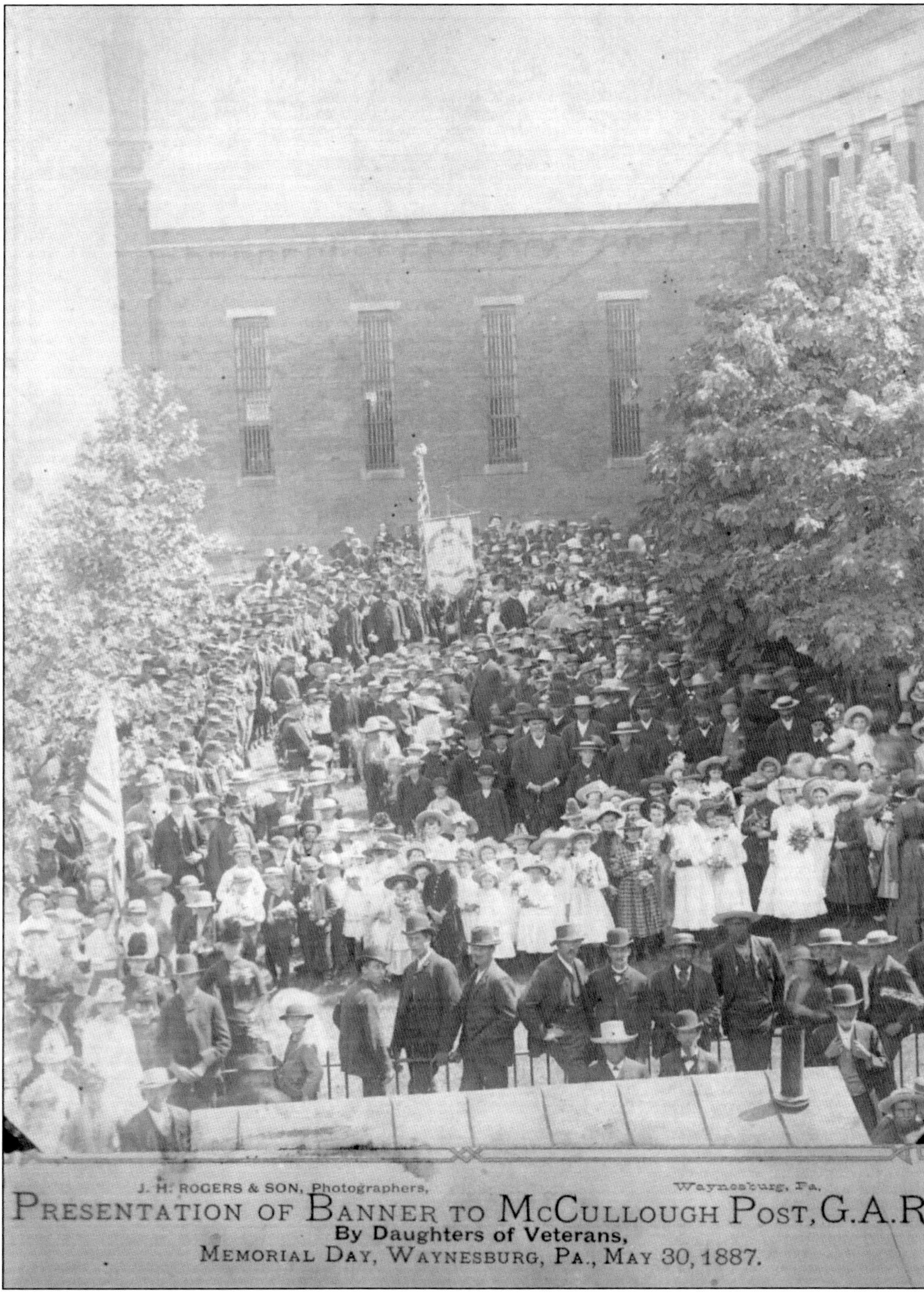

On the east lawn of the present Greene County Courthouse, along Church Street, on Memorial Day, May 30, 1887, this large crowd gathered to deliver a banner from the Daughters of Veterans to the John F. McCullough Post of the Grand Army of the Republic. (Photograph by J.H. Rogers & Son, courtesy of the Greene County Historical Society.)

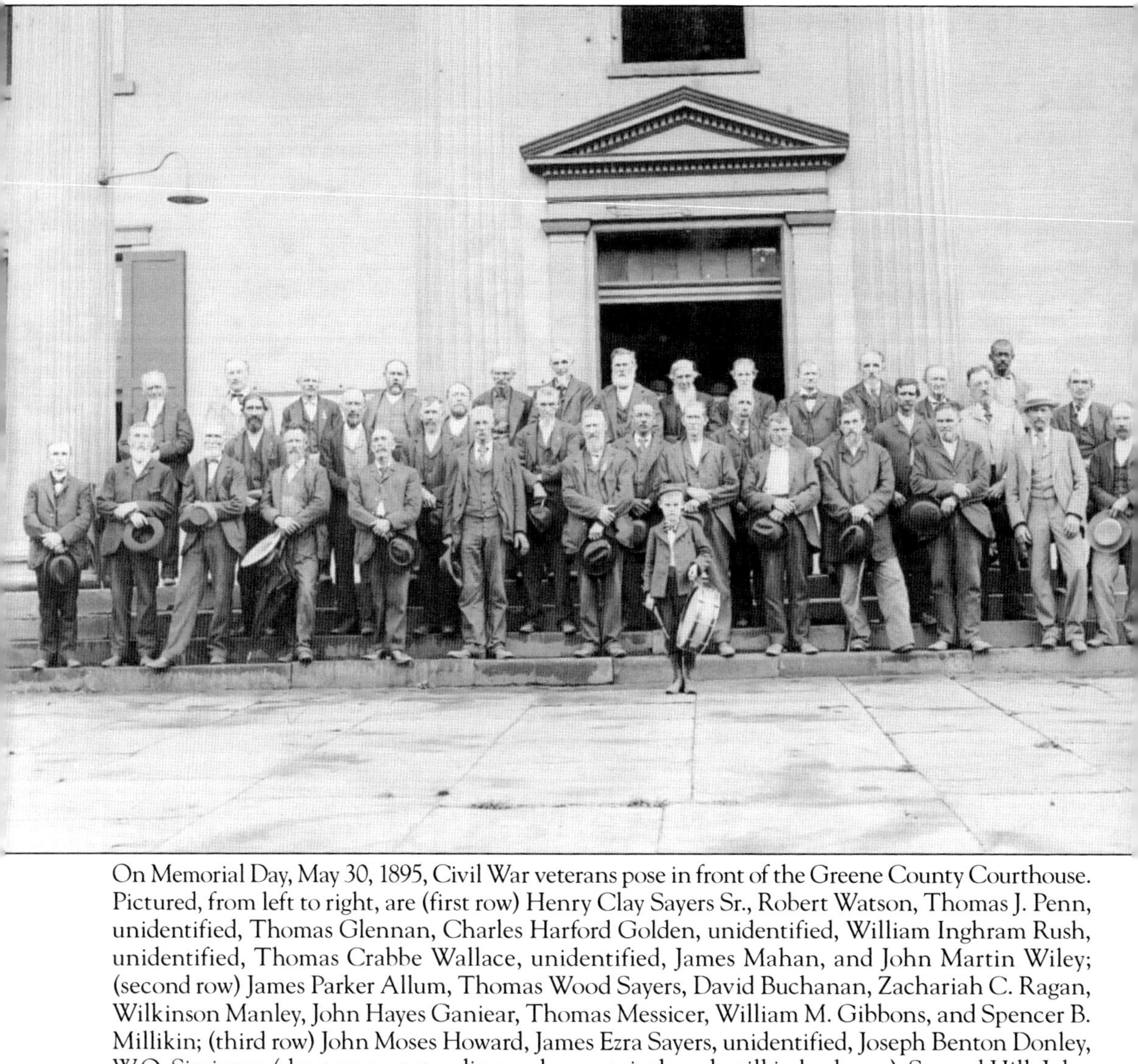

On Memorial Day, May 30, 1895, Civil War veterans pose in front of the Greene County Courthouse. Pictured, from left to right, are (first row) Henry Clay Sayers Sr., Robert Watson, Thomas J. Penn, unidentified, Thomas Glennan, Charles Harford Golden, unidentified, William Inghram Rush, unidentified, Thomas Crabbe Wallace, unidentified, James Mahan, and John Martin Wiley; (second row) James Parker Allum, Thomas Wood Sayers, David Buchanan, Zachariah C. Ragan, Wilkinson Manley, John Hayes Ganiear, Thomas Messicer, William M. Gibbons, and Spencer B. Millikin; (third row) John Moses Howard, James Ezra Sayers, unidentified, Joseph Benton Donley, W.O. Siminton (short man or standing on lower stair though still in back row), Samuel Hill, John Wood, John W. Simpson, Reuben Edgar, Michael Eddy, John Meighen, Edward W. Wood, Nathan Wightman Carter, and unidentified. (Courtesy of the Greene County Historical Society.)

Pictured is a lavish drinking fountain near the Greene County Courthouse on Washington Street that served to water horses from its lower section and people from its upper spouts. (Courtesy of the Greene County Historical Society.)

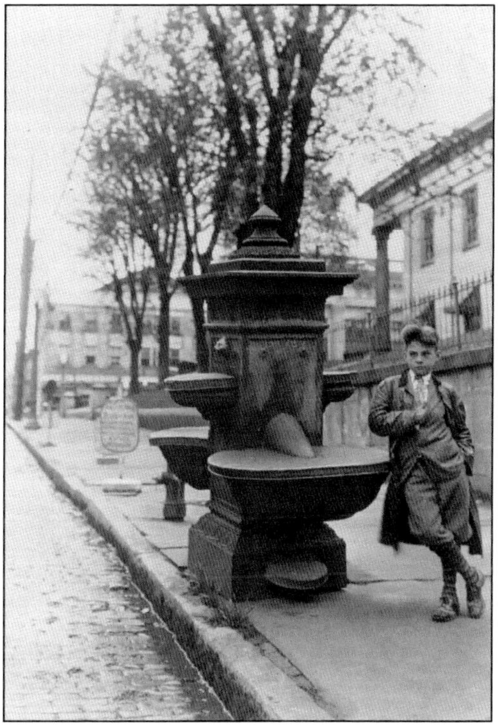

In this southward view of Washington Street, the edge of the Greene County Courthouse can be seen in the left foreground, and the church steeple in the distance is that of the old Methodist Episcopal church. The first structure south of the alley on the right is the blacksmith shop of Joseph Wiley Jr. Today, that site is the location of Baily Insurance. (Courtesy of the Greene County Historical Society.)

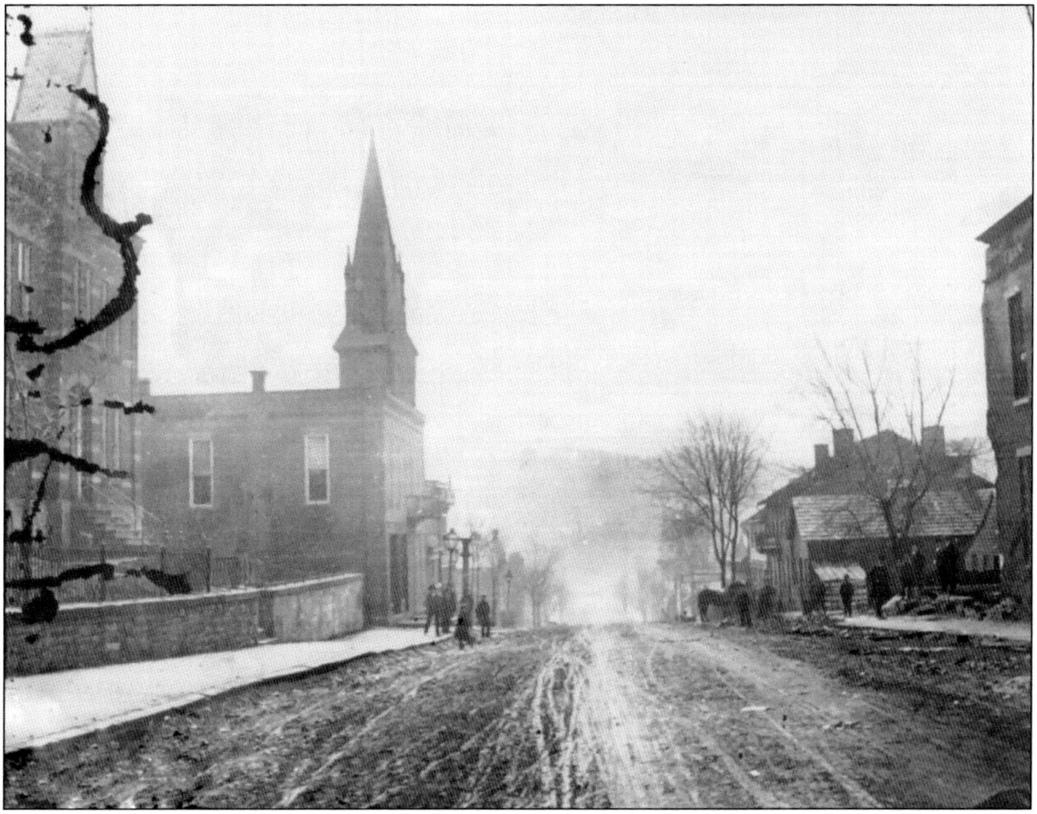

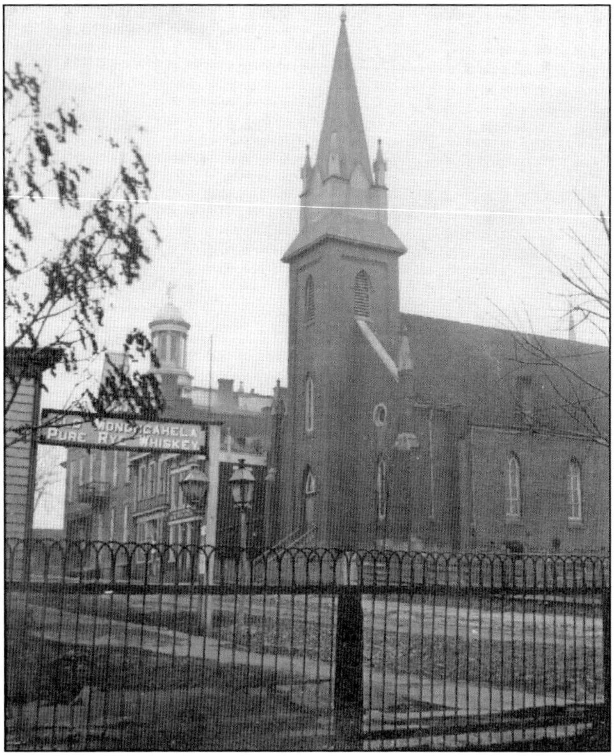

The old Methodist Episcopal church is seen beside the Greene County Courthouse on Washington Street. Notice the sign across the street for Old Monongahela Pure Rye Whiskey. This was a whiskey distilled in the region whose early producers were certainly part of the Whiskey Rebellion. (Courtesy of Waynesburg Borough.)

In 1860, hotels dotted High Street. Travelers who came to Waynesburg to attend court or transact business often traveled long and far on harsh roads by horse and buggy. Besides the popular Bull's Head Tavern on the corner, on this block alone were also the Worley House, just a few doors down, and the Hamilton House, which later became the Messenger Building. (Courtesy of the Greene County Historical Society.)

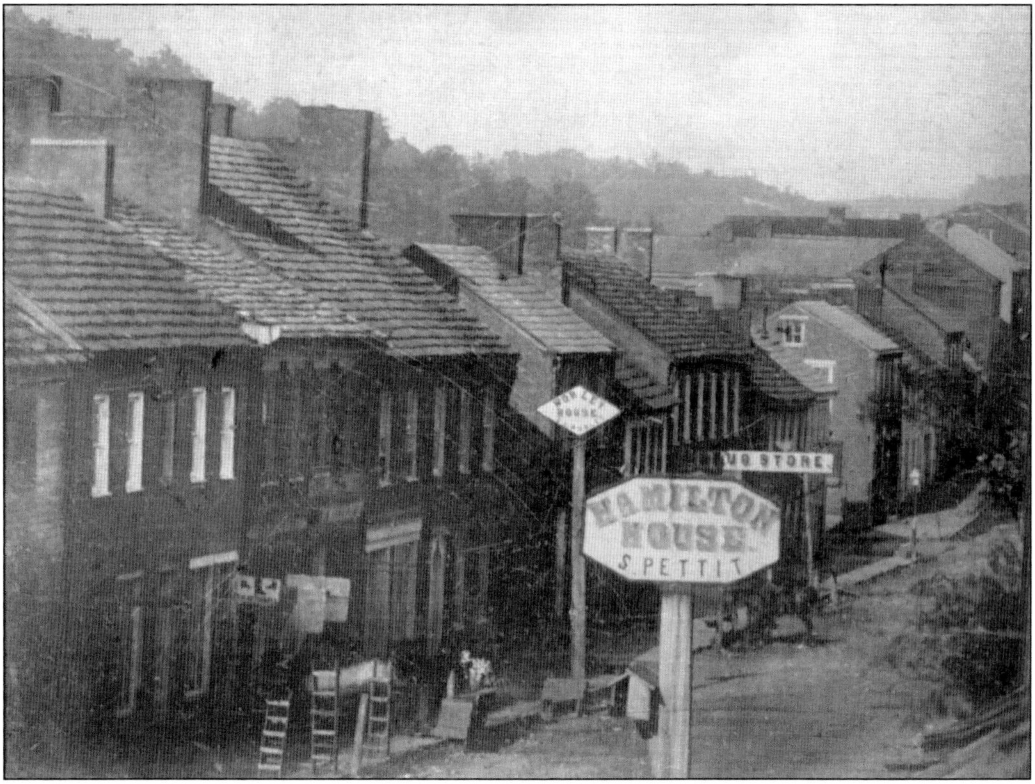

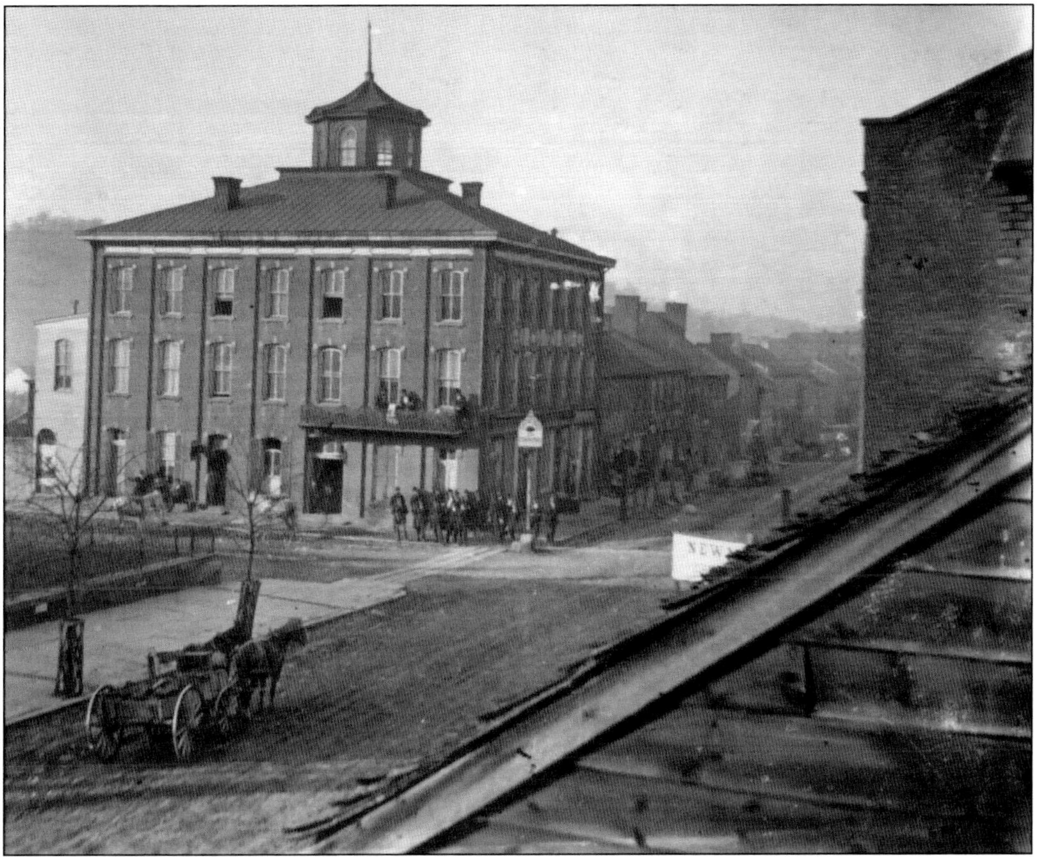

The Downey House, Waynesburg's premier hotel in its day, built in 1869, added a new sense of style to High Street. The addition to the hotel seen at right had not yet been built when the above image was taken. The addition was constructed between 1877 and 1890. (Both, courtesy of the Greene County Historical Society.)

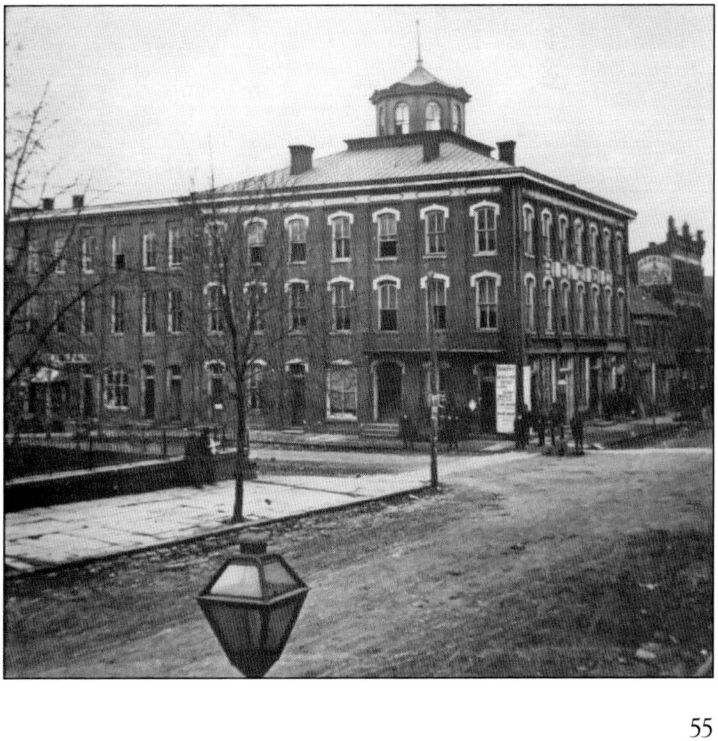

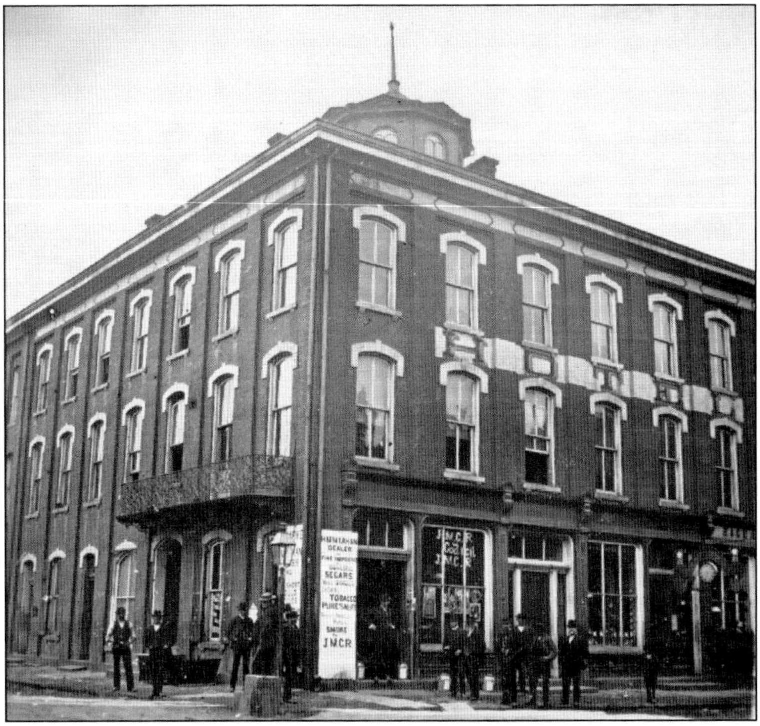

The Downey House was a hub of activity. More than just a hotel, it housed local businesses including restaurants, shops, and services. (Left, courtesy of the Greene County Historical Society; below, courtesy of Waynesburg Borough.)

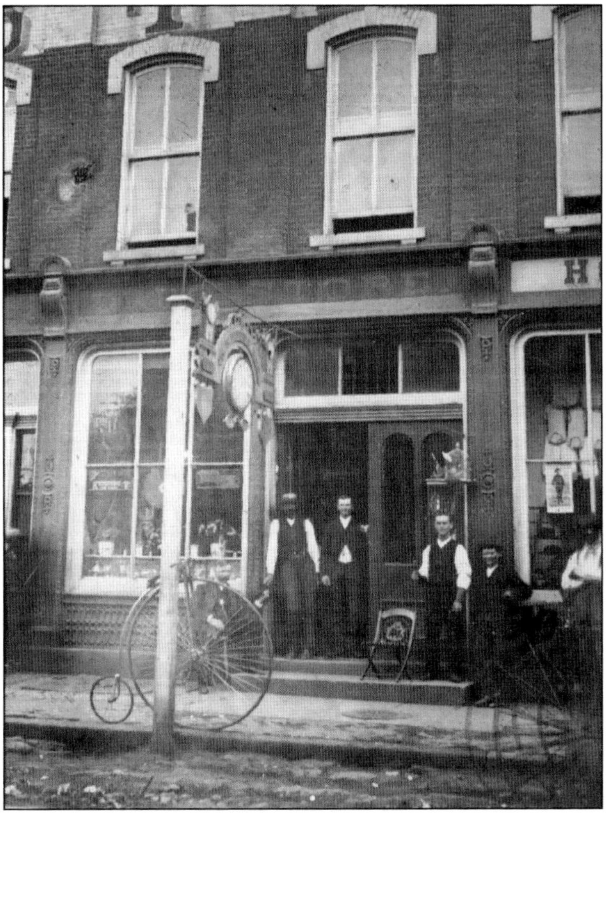

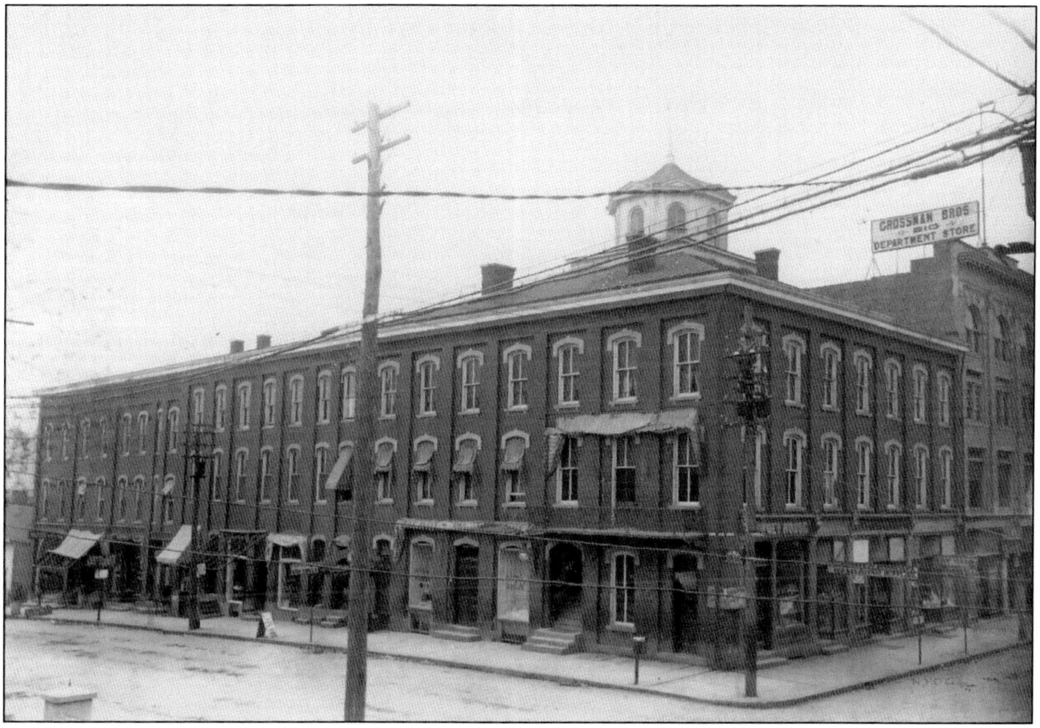

Between 1869 and 1925, as buildings rose and fell around them, the Greene County Courthouse, Downey House, and the Messenger Building (out of view across High Street) represented the heart of downtown Waynesburg. (Above, photograph by W.T. Hays, courtesy of Waynesburg Borough; below, courtesy of the Greene County Historical Society.)

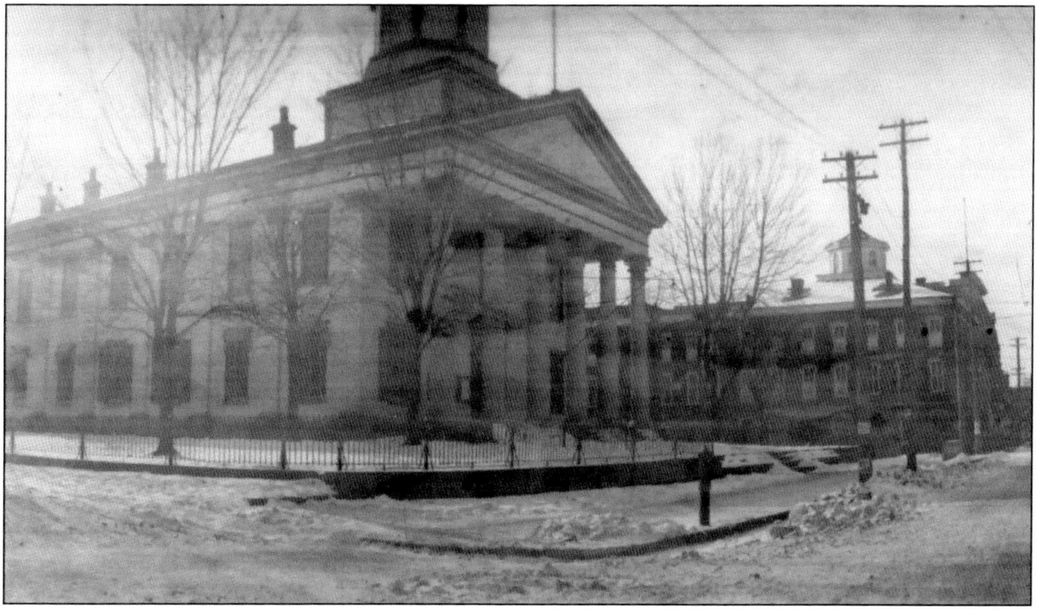

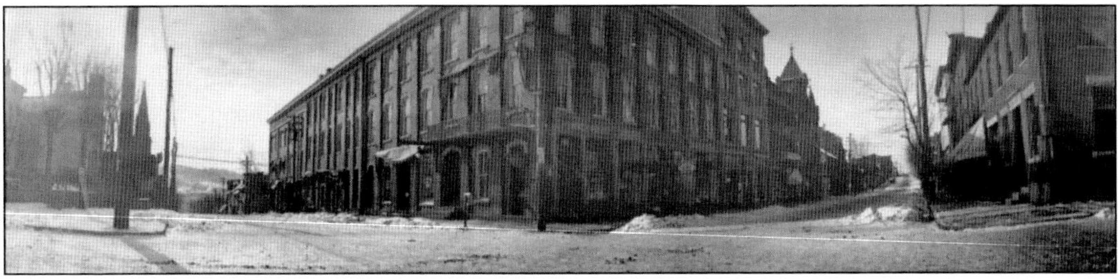

Notice the fallen snow covering the streets and the gray, wintry sky providing the framing for this wide-angle photograph of the Downey House corner. The actual date of this photograph is unknown, but it was on a wintry morning like this when a tragic fire destroyed this structure on December 23, 1925. Five young men fighting the fire lost their lives when a brick wall from the neighboring Grossman Building (right of the Downey House), also consumed in the blaze, came crashing down upon them. A small memorial plaque on the front of the Fort Jackson Building, which currently occupies this location, lists the names of those who perished—Harvey Call Jr., William Andrew Finch, J. Thurman Long, Joseph Rifenberg, and Victor Hoy Silveus. (Courtesy of the Greene County Historical Society.)

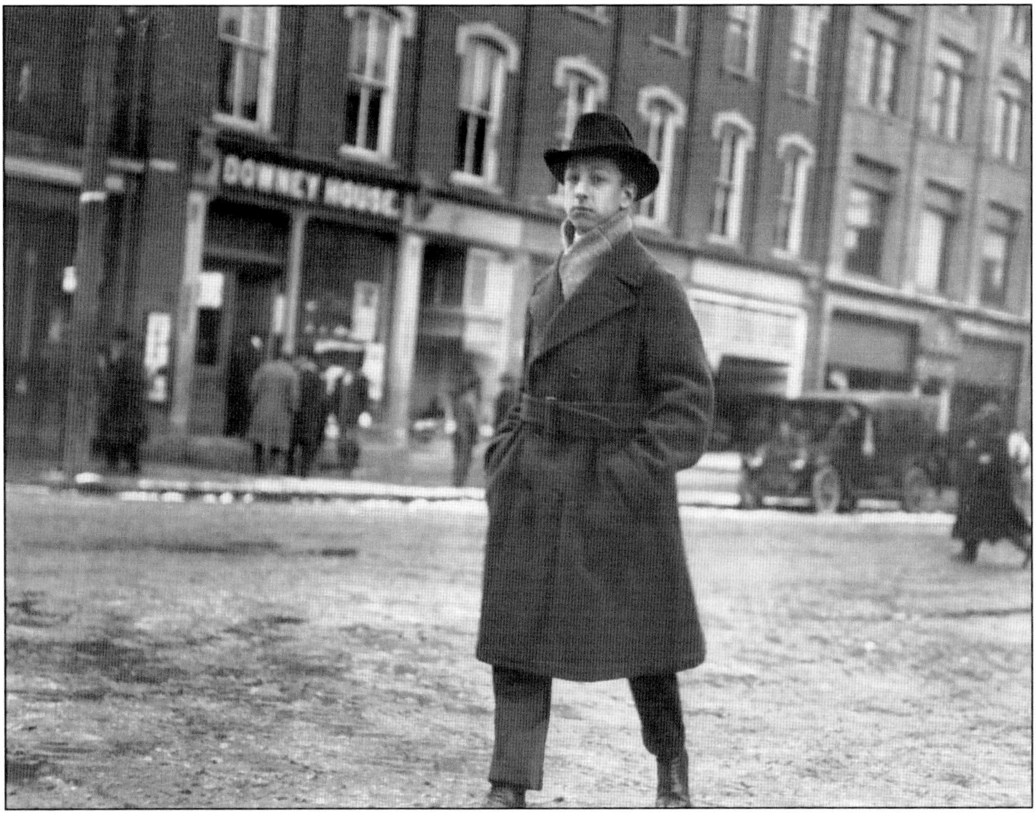

An unidentified young man crosses Washington Street, from the northwest corner with High Street, in front of the Downey House. (Courtesy of Waynesburg Borough.)

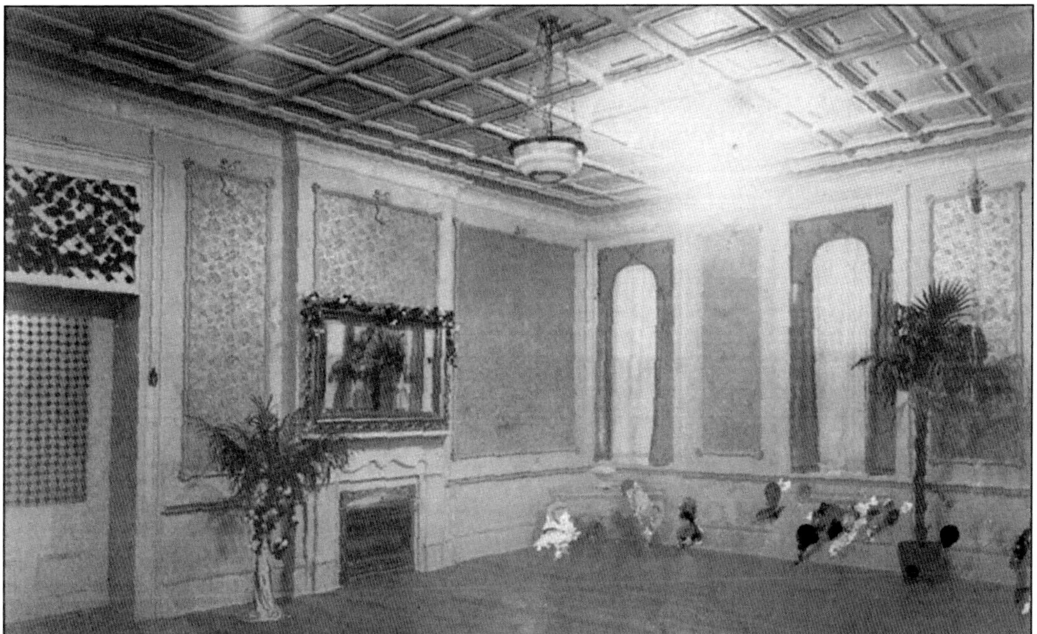

Images of interior rooms at the Downey House show areas that served as spaces for weddings, meals, and meetings. (Both, courtesy of Richard Walton Caperton and Joanne Christina Walton.)

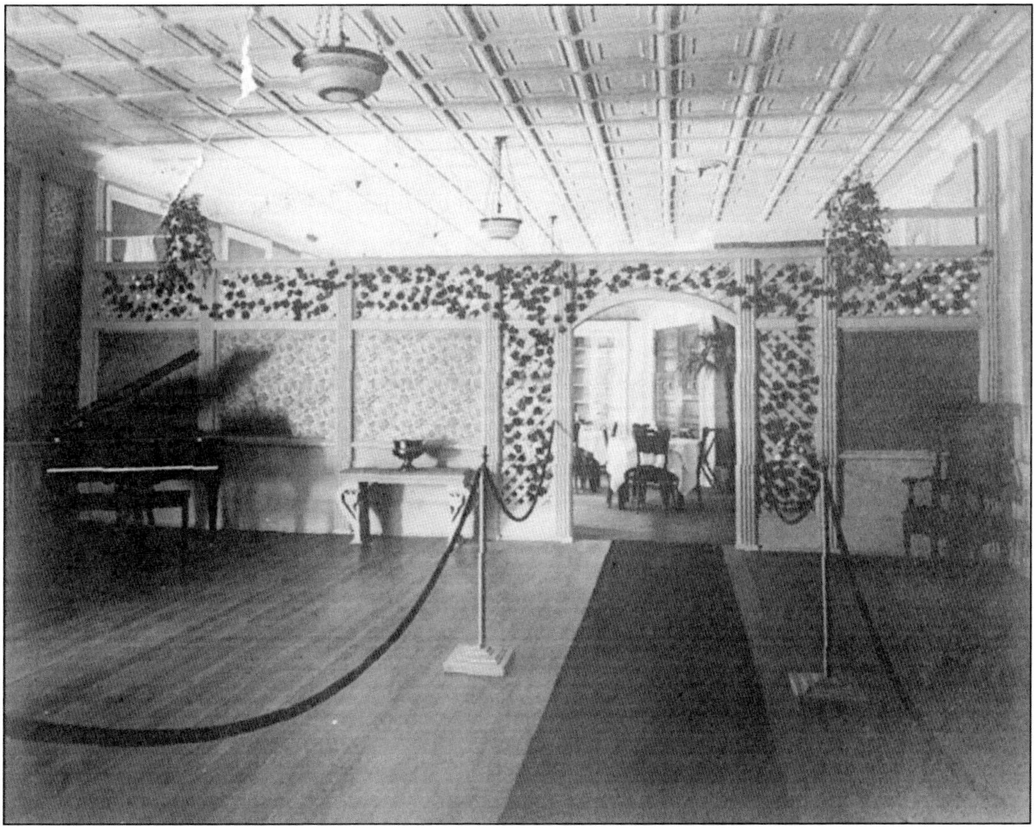

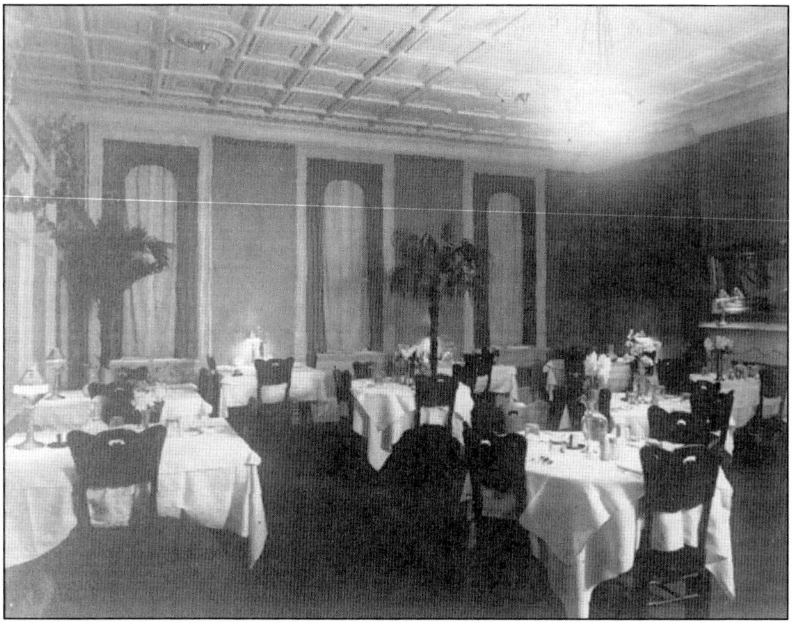

Another image of an interior room shows a formal dining room at the Downey House. (Courtesy of Richard Walton Caperton and Joanne Christina Walton.)

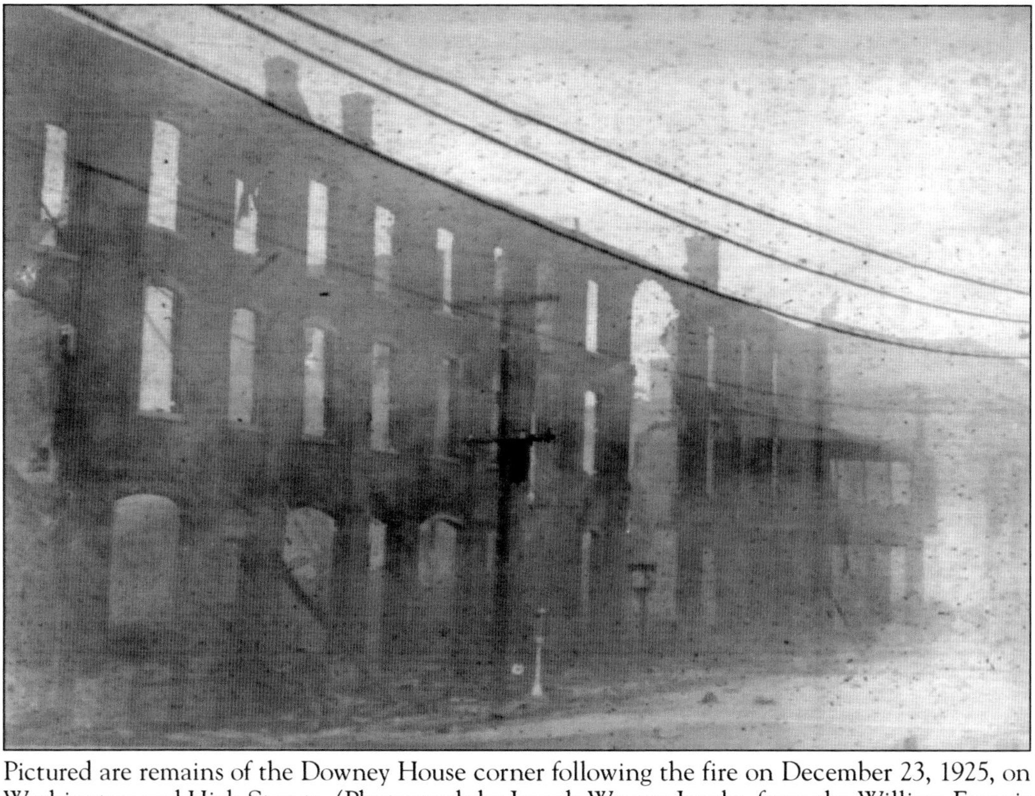

Pictured are remains of the Downey House corner following the fire on December 23, 1925, on Washington and High Streets. (Photograph by Joseph Warren Jacobs, from the William Francis Jacobs Collection, courtesy of David Kent Jacobs.)

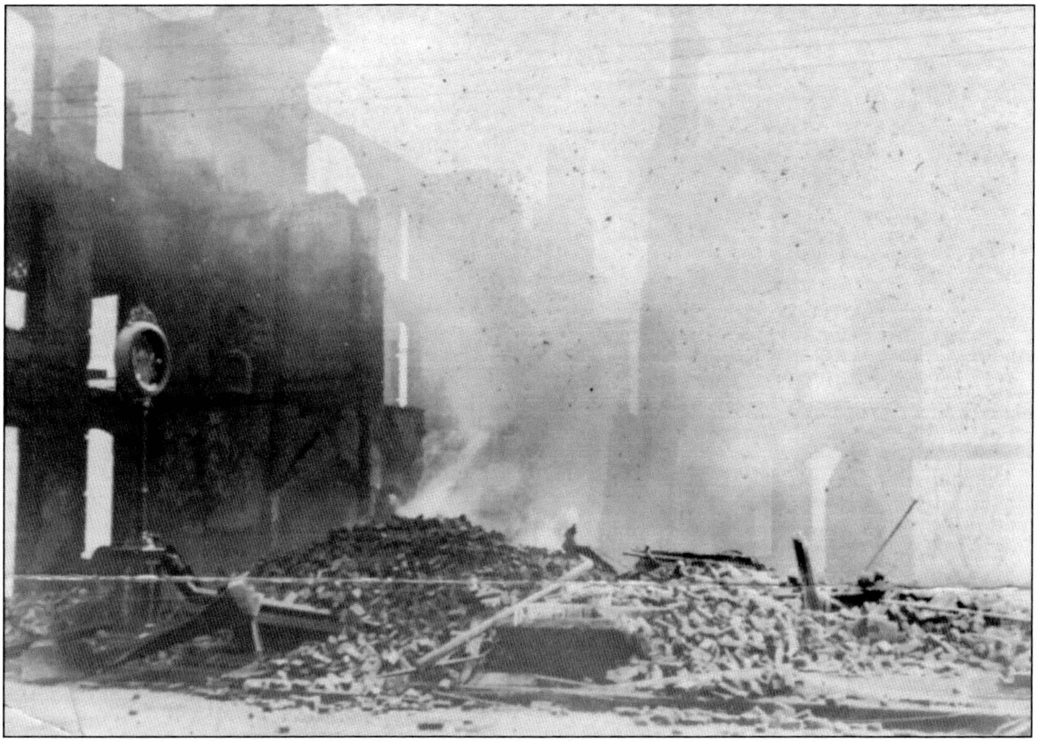

More smoldering remains of the Downey House corner on Washington and High Streets following the fire on December 23, 1925, are seen here. Notice the clock still standing after the whole of the ordeal was done, just as it had been positioned on the sidewalk in front of the hotel before the fire started. (Both, photograph by Joseph Warren Jacobs, from the William Francis Jacobs Collection, courtesy of David Kent Jacobs.)

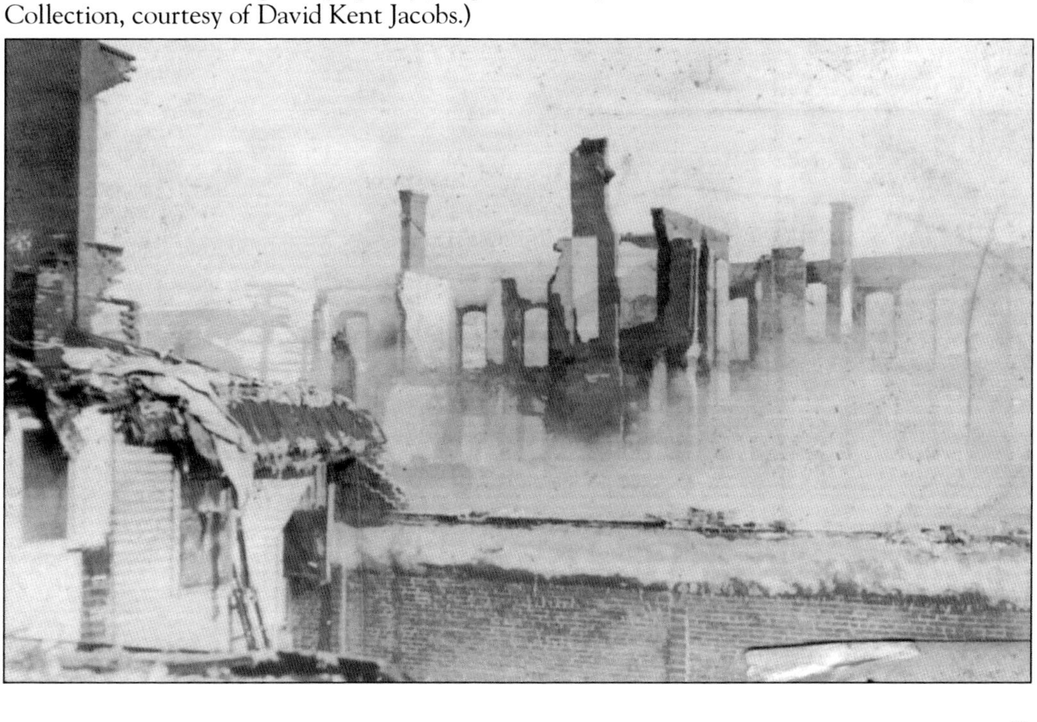

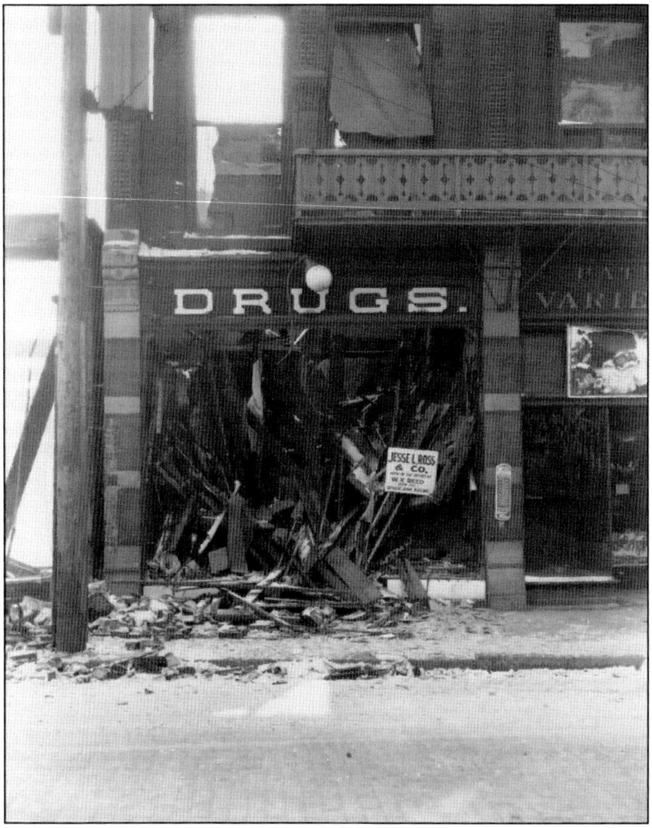

Inside the Ross Drug Store during its prime, to the front left in suspenders is store owner Jesse Lazear Ross; behind him to the right wearing glasses and a bow tie is Newt Penn. The Ross Drug Store was housed in the Silveus Building, neighboring the Grossman Building, the latter of which was destroyed on December 23, 1925, in the Downey House fire. When the remains of the Grossman Building were being torn down, its west wall collapsed onto the Silveus Building, damaging it so severely that it had to be torn down and rebuilt. (Left, courtesy of the Greene County Historical Society; below, courtesy of Mary Luna [Furman] Berryman.)

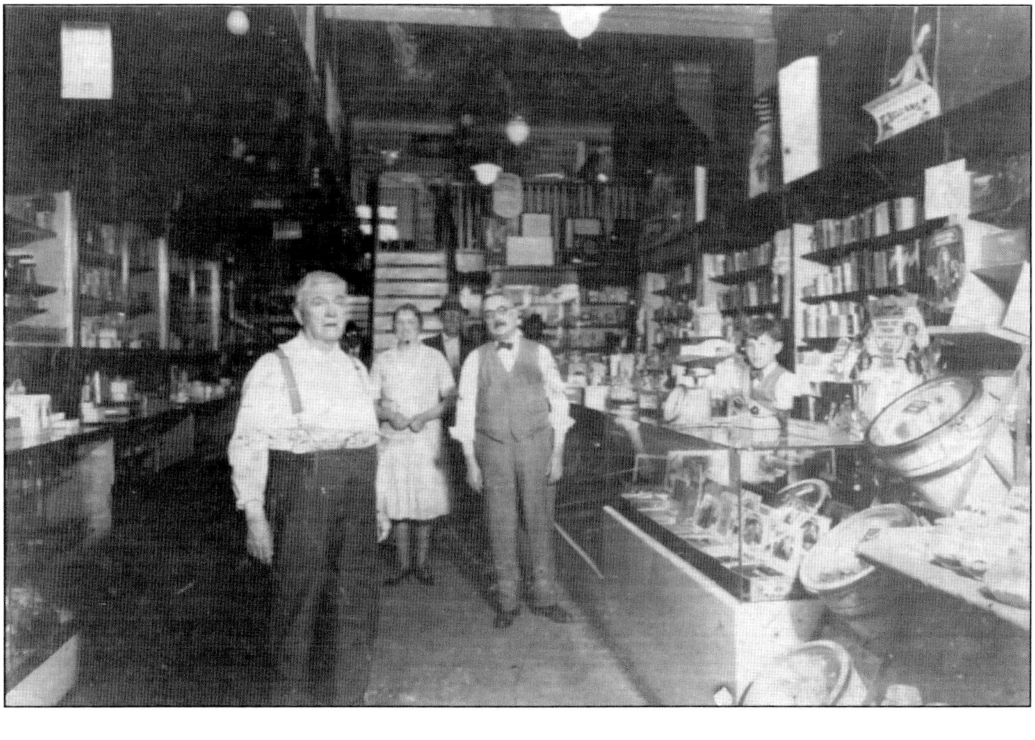

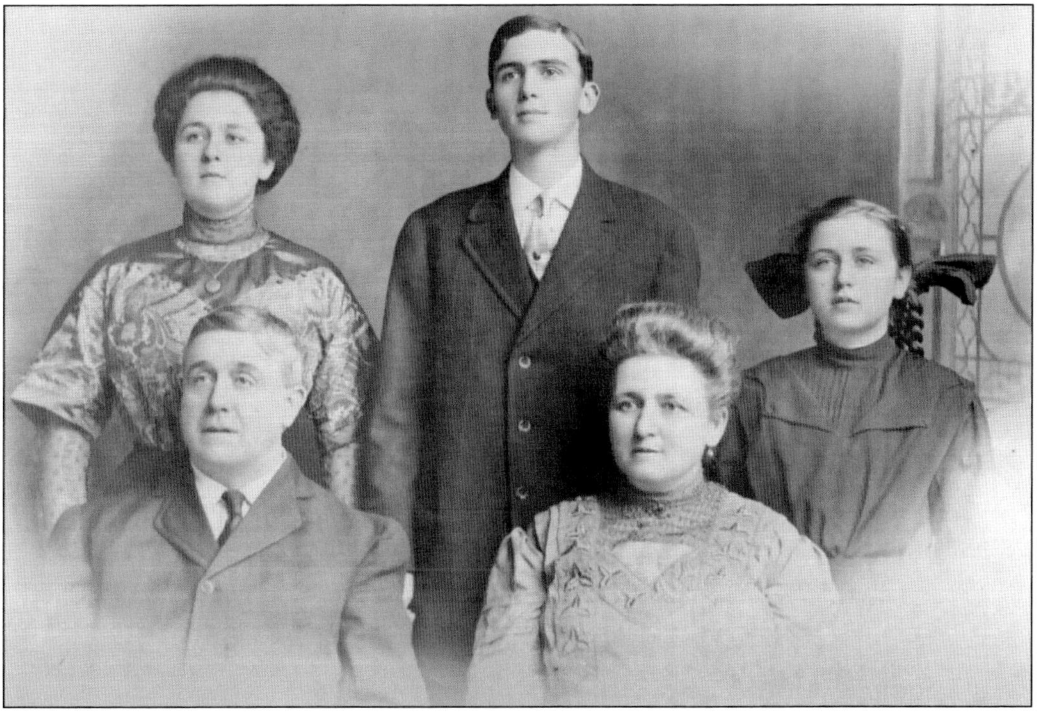

The Jesse Lazear Ross and Mary Catherine (Donahoo) Ross family are seen here; from left to right are (first row) Jesse Lazear Ross and Mary Catherine (Donahoo) Ross; (second row) Jane M. (Ross) Reed, John H. Ross, and Mary Helen (Ross) Furman. (Photograph by Mercer, courtesy of Mary Luna [Furman] Berryman.)

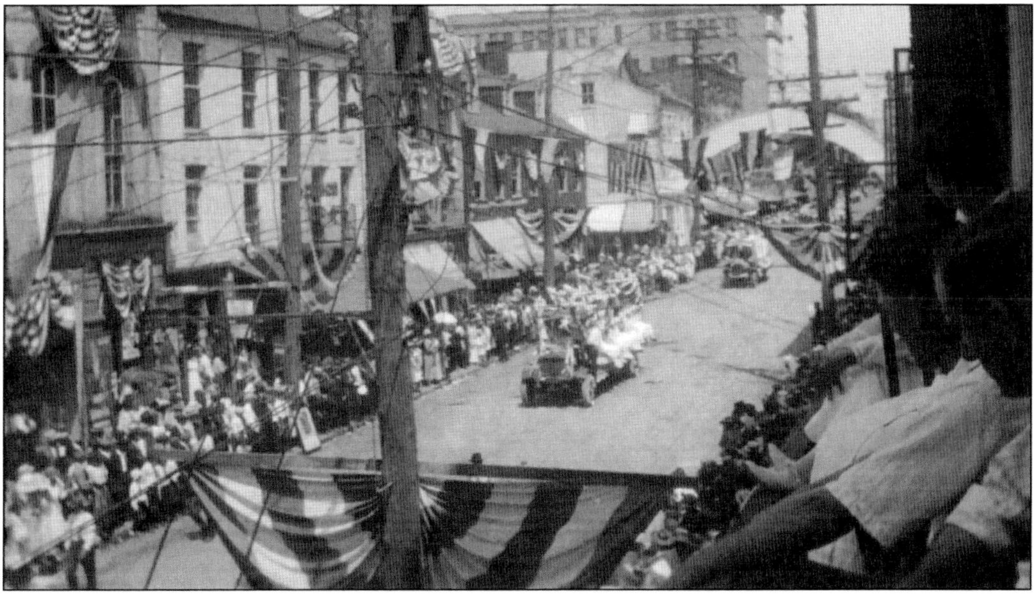

On July 4, 1919, a victory arch over High Street and a patriotic parade were just a portion of the celebration to welcome back the soldiers from World War I. For the families of the 54 young men that Greene County lost in the war, this must have been a bittersweet day. (Courtesy of the Greene County Historical Society.)

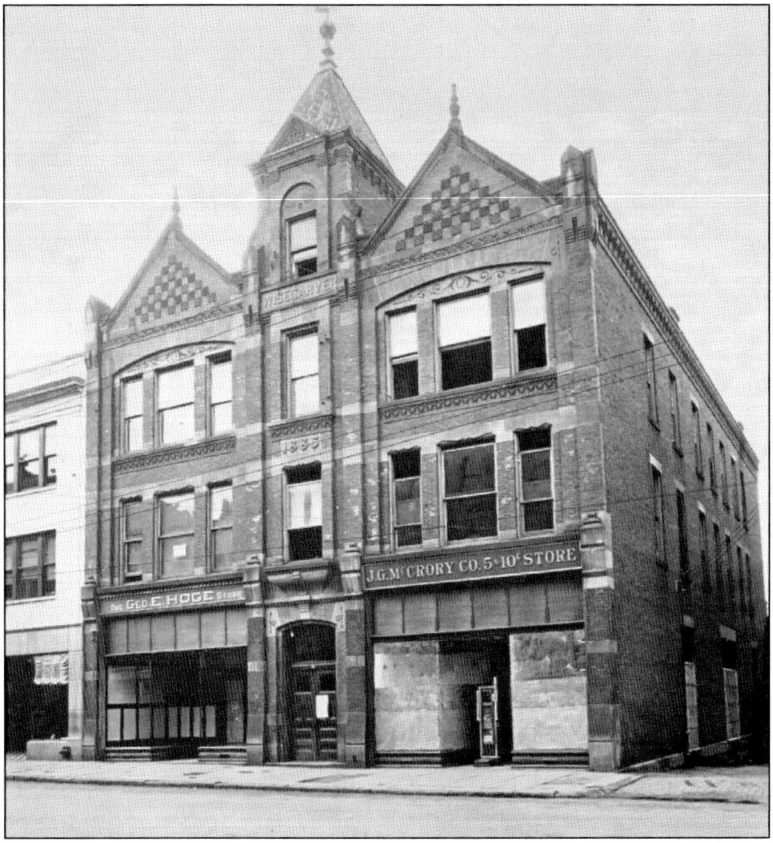

The McCrory's five-and-dime store was one of many businesses housed in the Wisecarver Building, since its establishment in 1885, on the southeast corner of High Street and Fruit Alley. Ultimately, the business took over the location, removed the top two floors, and added the Art Deco cornice, much of which remains today. The building is currently the location of InMotion Dance and Fitness Center. (Both, courtesy of the Greene County Historical Society.)

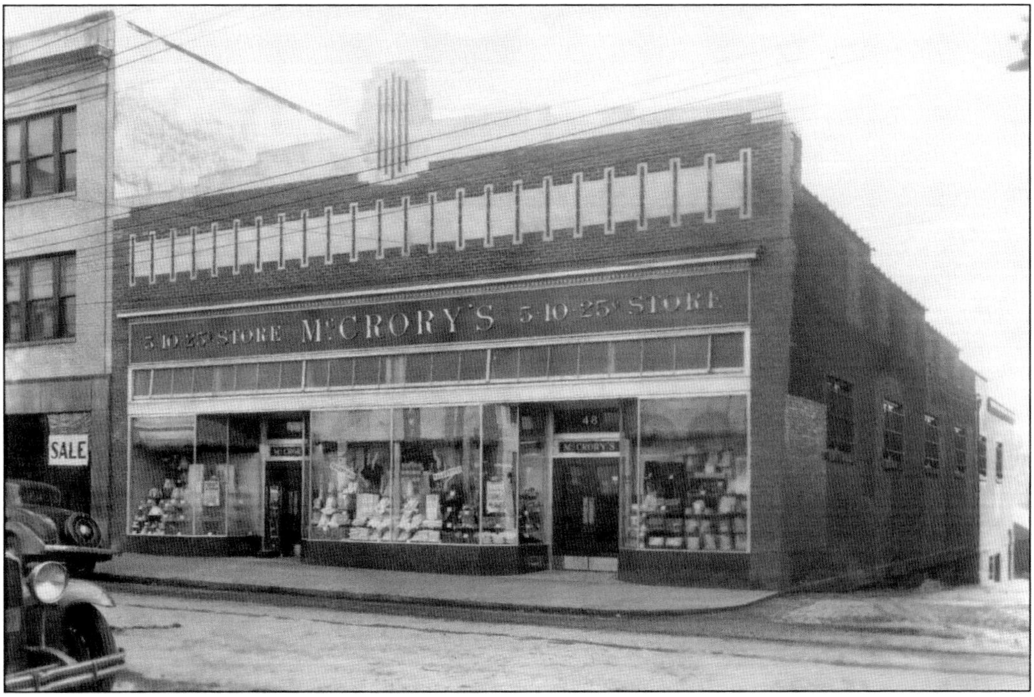

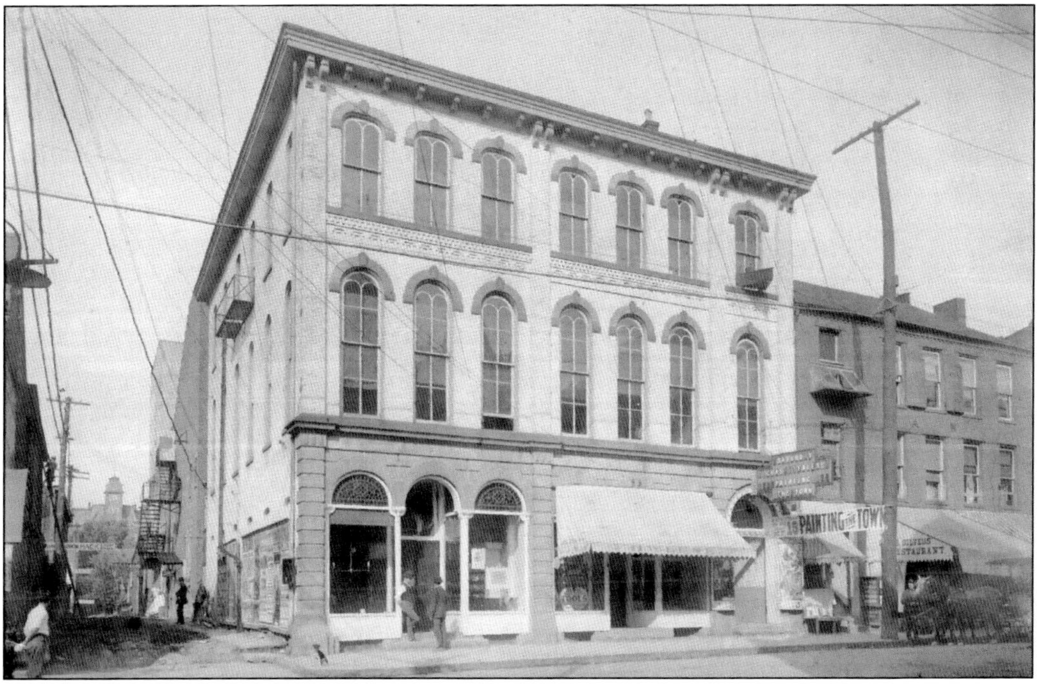

Built in 1870–1871, the Independent Order of Odd Fellows building was converted from the Waynesburg Town Hall to the opera house in 1889. It is currently the home of the Fashion Shop. The building to its right was constructed in 1853 and demolished in 2012. (Photograph by Adamson, courtesy of Waynesburg Borough.)

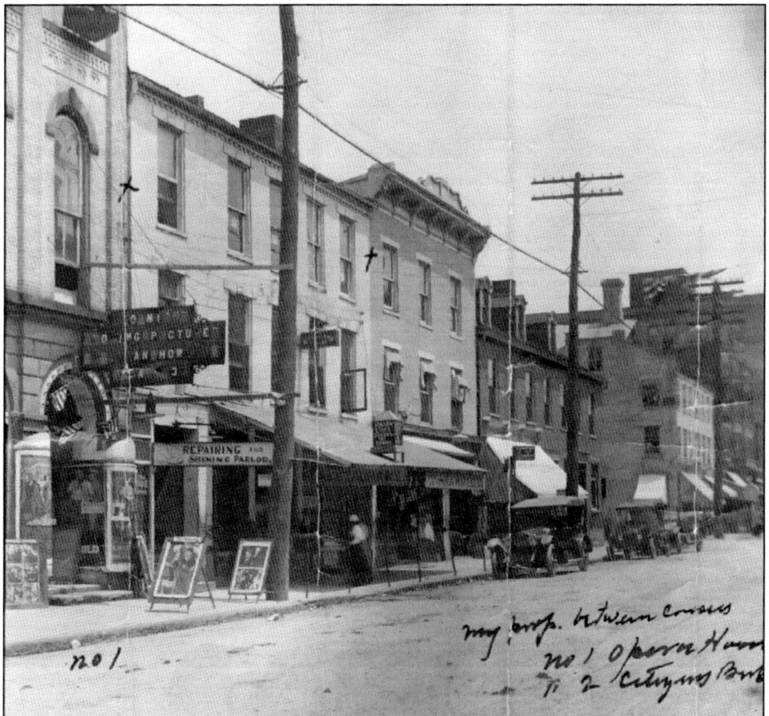

In a view looking east down the north side of High Street, the opera house is easy to spot, with moving pictures posters on display. Next door, the Union Café advertises "cigars and candy." Harrison & Cohen shared the Citizens National Bank building on the corner; and across Washington Street, the Messenger Building and Jacobs & Headley Building can be seen with awnings deployed. (Courtesy of the Greene County Historical Society.)

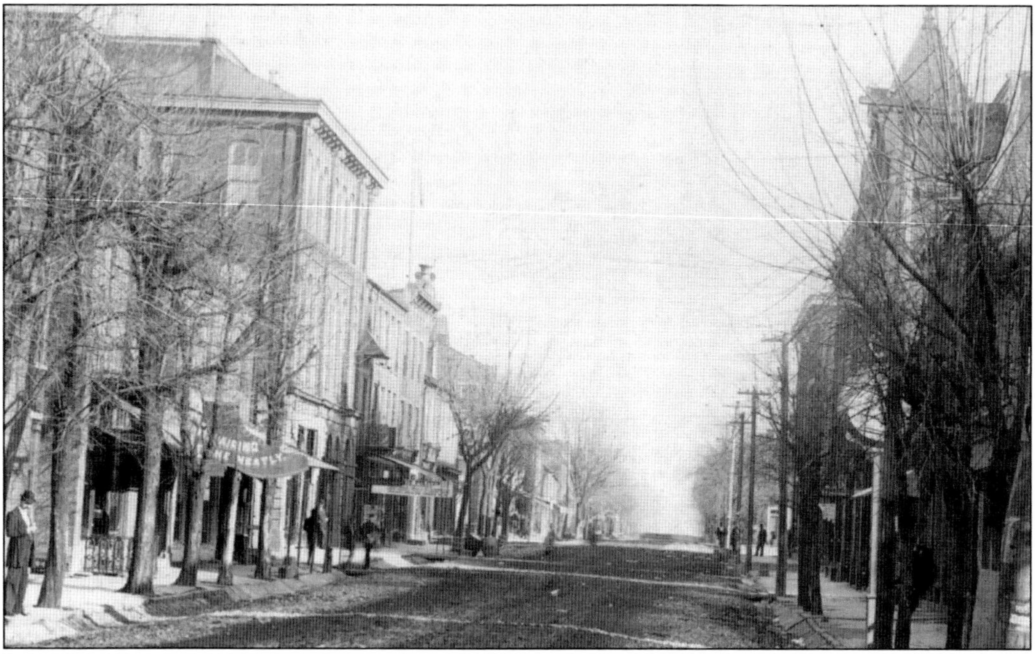

Photographed from a little further west on High Street, this view also looks east down the north side of High Street before the brick pavers had been installed. (Courtesy of the Greene County Historical Society.)

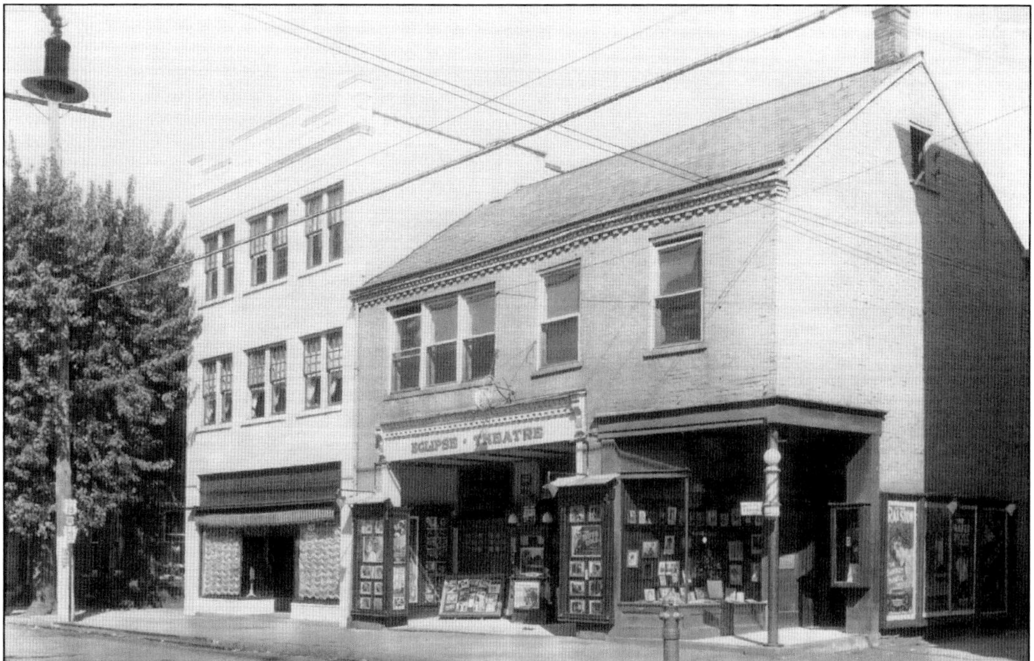

The R.H. Goldberg Building (built 1925) and the Eclipse Theater (which became Wayne Theater in 1935) were located on the northwest corner of High Street and Fruit Alley. (Courtesy of the Greene County Historical Society.)

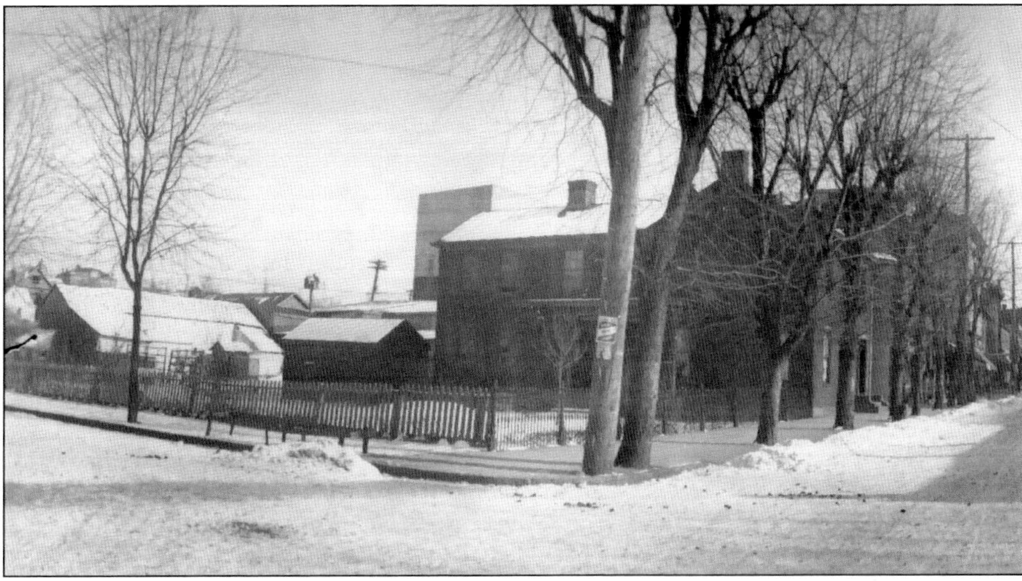

This is the home of Judge James Inghram and his wife, Mary (Black) Inghram, on the northeast corner of High and Morris Streets. It was formerly the home of her parents, Charles A. and Maria (Allison) Black. Today, this property is the location of PNC Bank. (Courtesy of the Greene County Historical Society.)

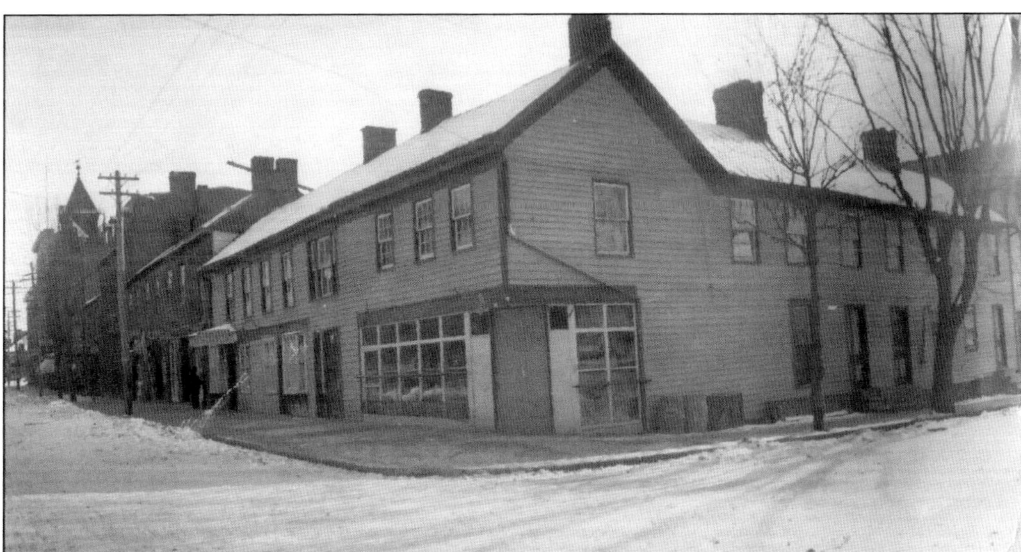

The Johnson House, located on the southeast corner of High and Morris Streets, was destroyed by fire in 1924. The John F. Reagan Building, which still stands, was built on this site in 1935. (Courtesy of the Greene County Historical Society.)

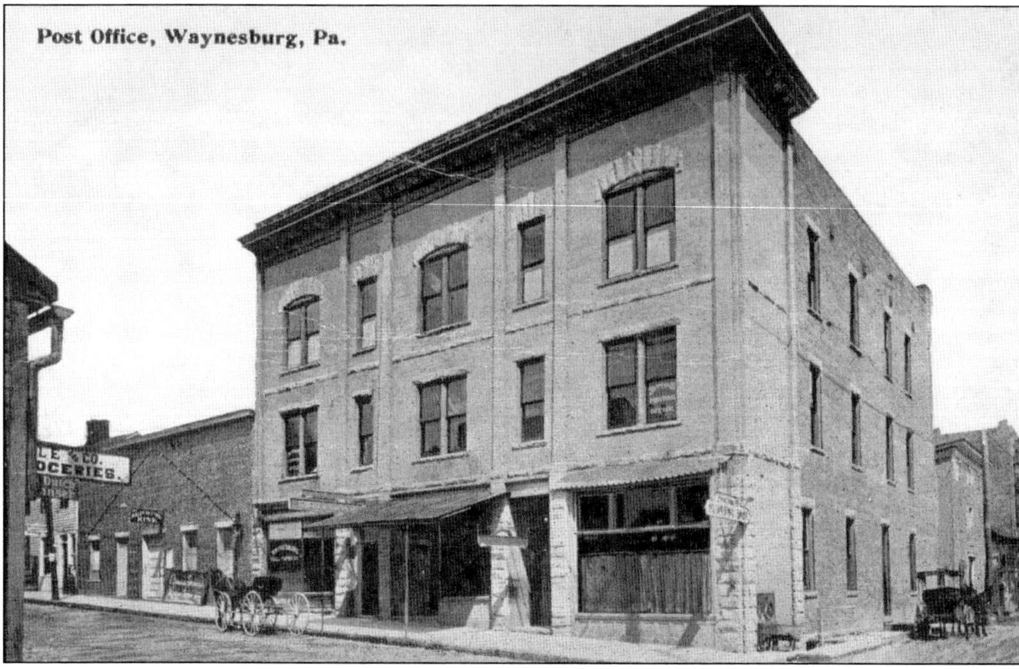

In November 1904, the first floor of the Ross Building on Morris Street, became home to the Waynesburg Post Office, where it stayed until moving to the J.M. Burns Building on High Street in December 1922. In December 1904, the Ross Building's third floor was adopted as armory headquarters for Company K. It is currently home to Hot Rods restaurant. (From the Walter "Blackie" Markiewich Postcard Collection, courtesy of Brice and Linda Rush.)

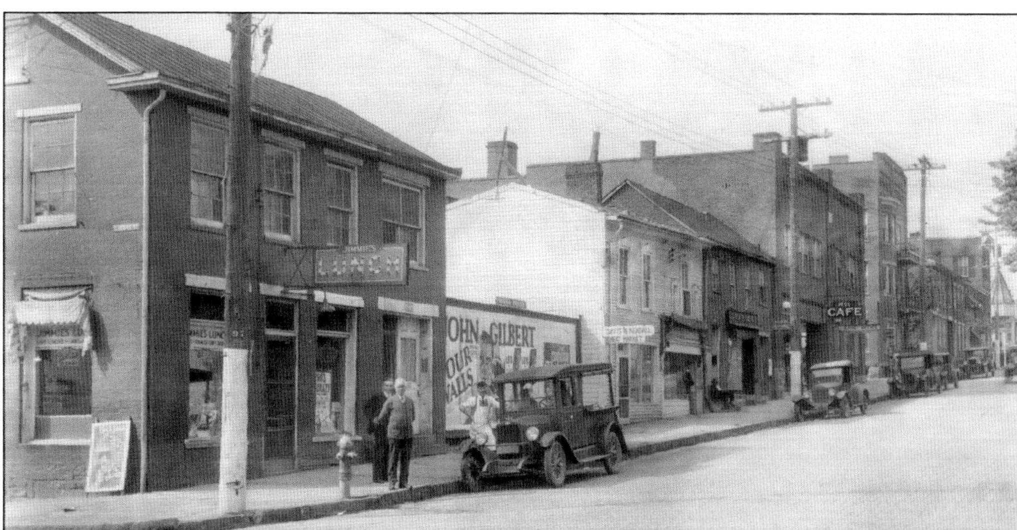

Jimmie's Lunch, situated on the southwest corner of High and Morris Streets, was a favorite hangout best known for hot dogs "run through the garden." Westward are the Davis & Kendall Meat Market, the Hess Cafe, and the Waynesburg Post Office. The opera house billboard advertises the silent dramatic film *Four Walls* starring John Gilbert, which was released in 1928. (Courtesy of the Greene County Historical Society.)

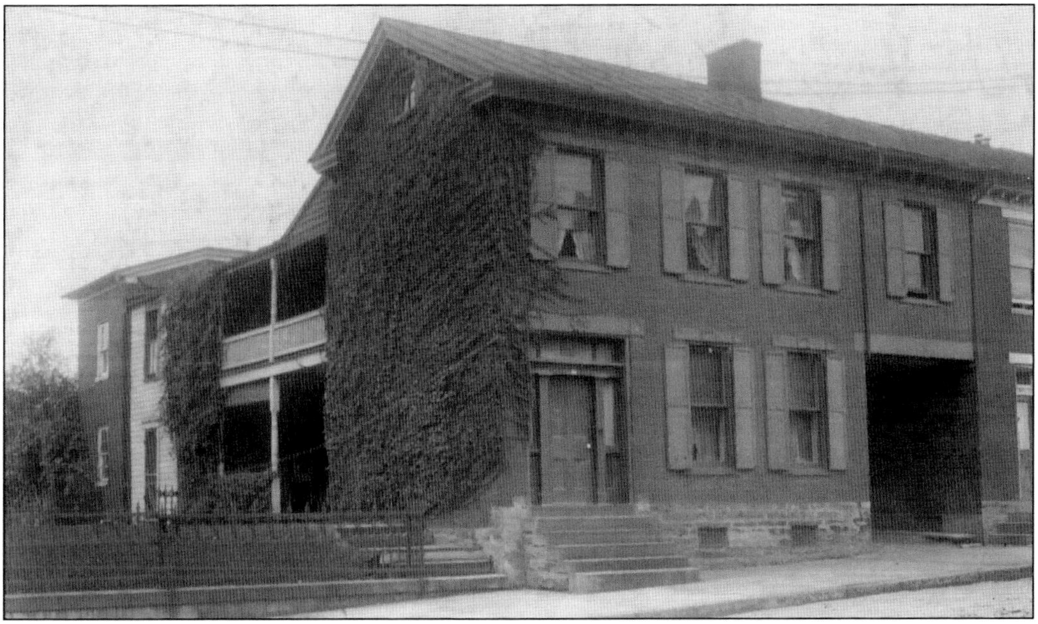

Encompassing three generations, the Waynesburg home of Civil War–era judge James Lindsey and his wife, Sarah (Inghram) Lindsey, was passed to their daughter Anna Laura Lindsey, who married Robert Wallace Munnell. Their only surviving child, Mary Inghram (Munnell) Rinehart, owned the house in turn. Judge Lindsey died unexpectedly from illness in 1864 after riding horseback from hearings in Washington County. (Courtesy of the Greene County Historical Society.)

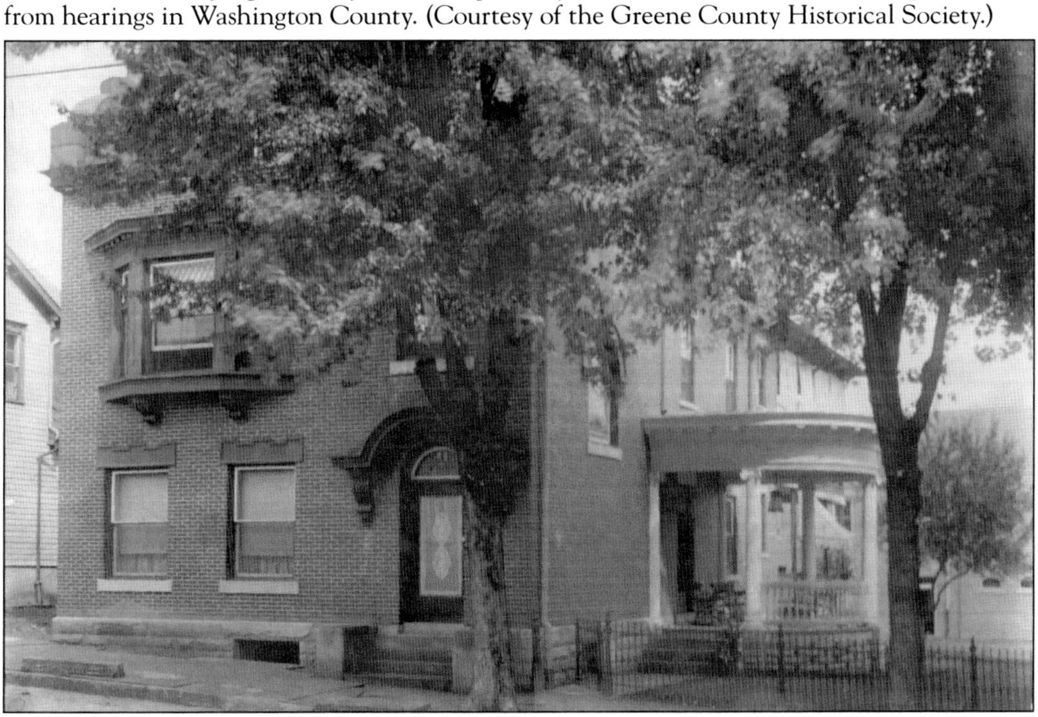

The Eleazer Luse and Louise (Inghram) Denny family home still stands on High Street. Eleazer was a successful businessman who sold supplies by the railcar to meet the needs of the area's oil and gas boom in the early 1900s. (Courtesy of the Greene County Historical Society.)

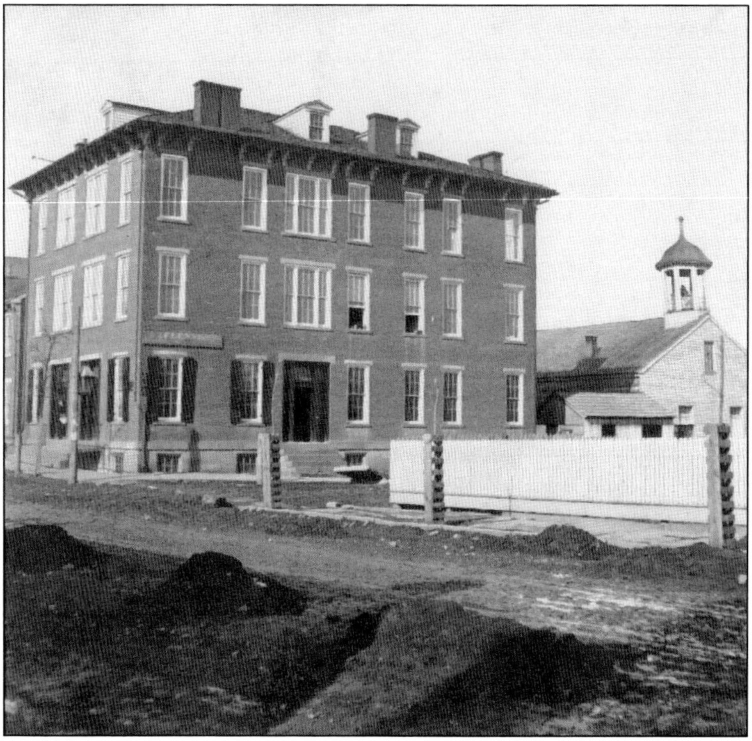

The Walton Hotel on the northwest corner of High and Morris Streets, was one of the finest hotels in the tristate area. After the Civil War, it was expanded from a small tavern to a full-sized hotel with ballroom. The photograph below shows the mansard roof added in 1881. Behind the hotel, the Presbyterian church's first building was constructed in 1849. This entire area is now Waynesburg Borough parking lots. (Left, courtesy of Waynesburg Borough; below, courtesy of the Greene County Historical Society.)

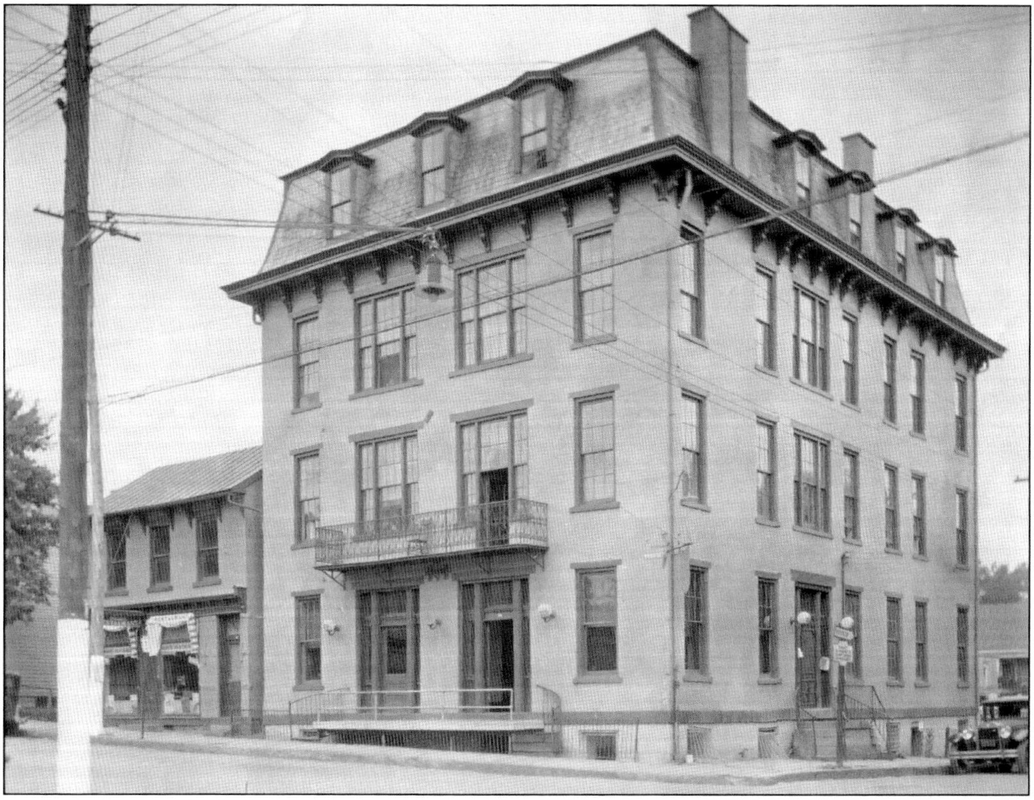

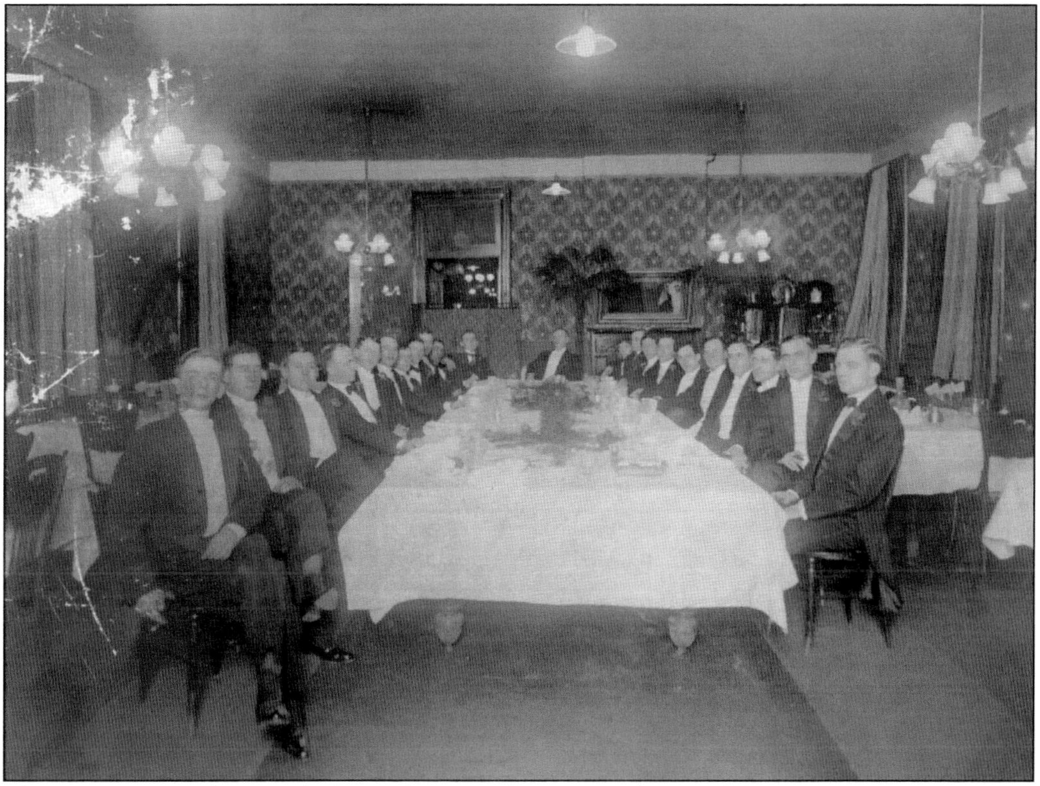

This picture was taken inside the Walton Hotel, a venue often used for community events. Pres. Ulysses S. Grant met with local Civil War veterans at the hotel when he visited Waynesburg. (Courtesy of Richard Walton Caperton and Joanne Christina Walton.)

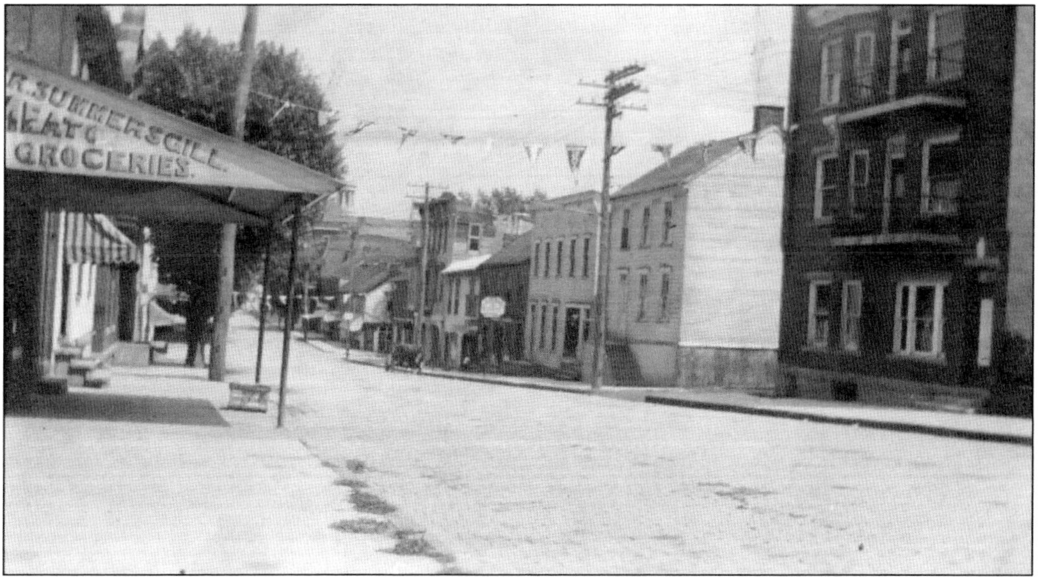

The view in this image looks east on High Street from near the current location of the Family Dollar store. The three-story apartment building shown at the far right of this picture still exists today. (Courtesy of Scott and Teresa [Crouse] Roberts.)

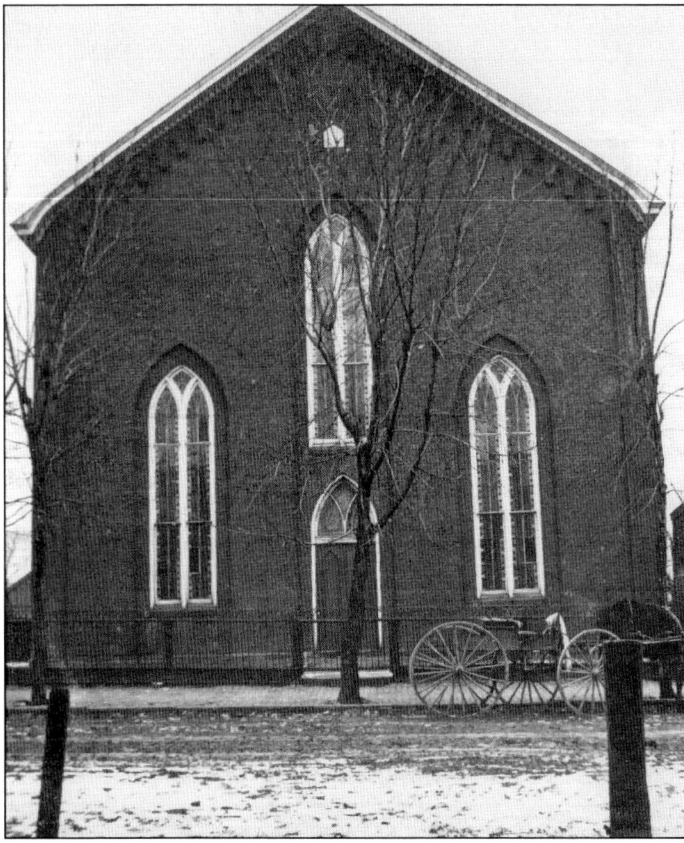

The Cumberland Presbyterian Church on High Street was built in 1868, when it replaced the original "Church on the Hill" that had been near Wayne Street in the Monument Park area. In 1906, when the Cumberland Presbyterian and Presbyterian congregations of Waynesburg merged to form the First Presbyterian Church, they began to hold services in the Presbyterian building on Church Street, using the Cumberland Presbyterian building on High Street for Sunday school and social functions only. The High Street building was torn down in 1941. (Left, courtesy of Waynesburg Borough; below, photograph by William E.S. Fletcher, courtesy of the Cornerstone Genealogical Society.)

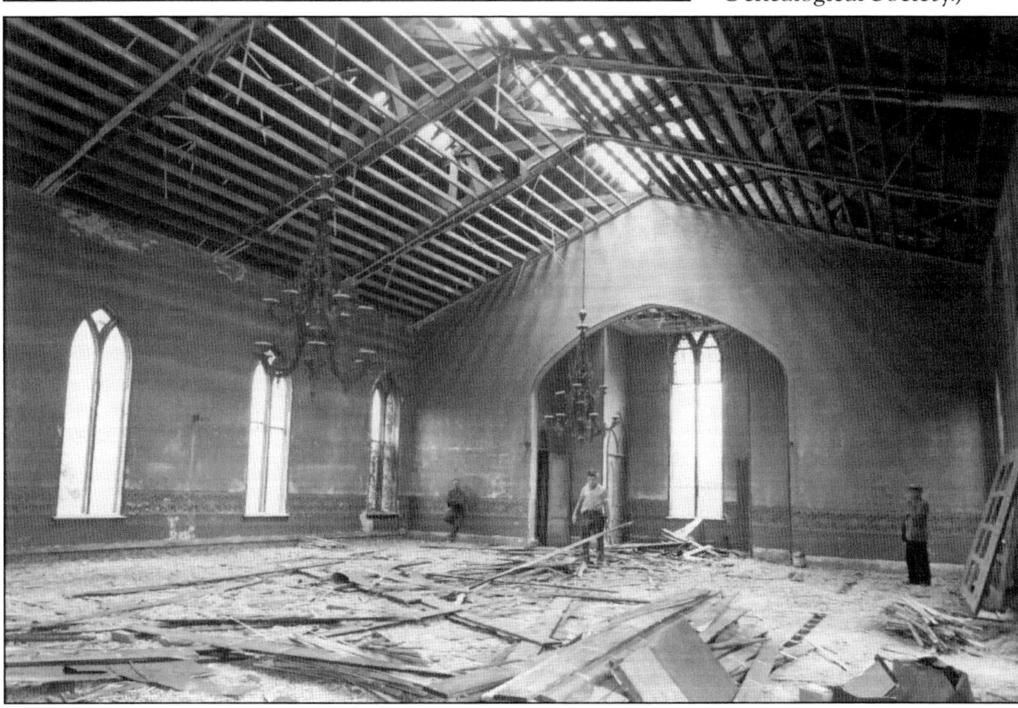

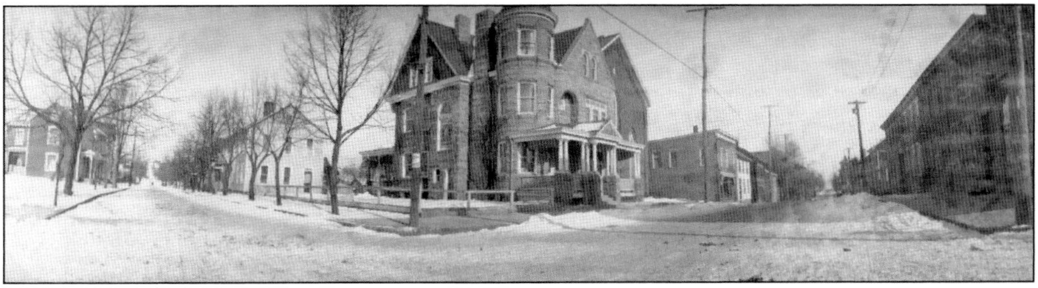

In this image with a view looking northeast toward the intersection of High and Richhill Streets, Dr. J.T. Ullom's house is at the center. The building currently houses the Hook Law Offices. The Cumberland Presbyterian Church is to its right. (Courtesy of the Greene County Historical Society.)

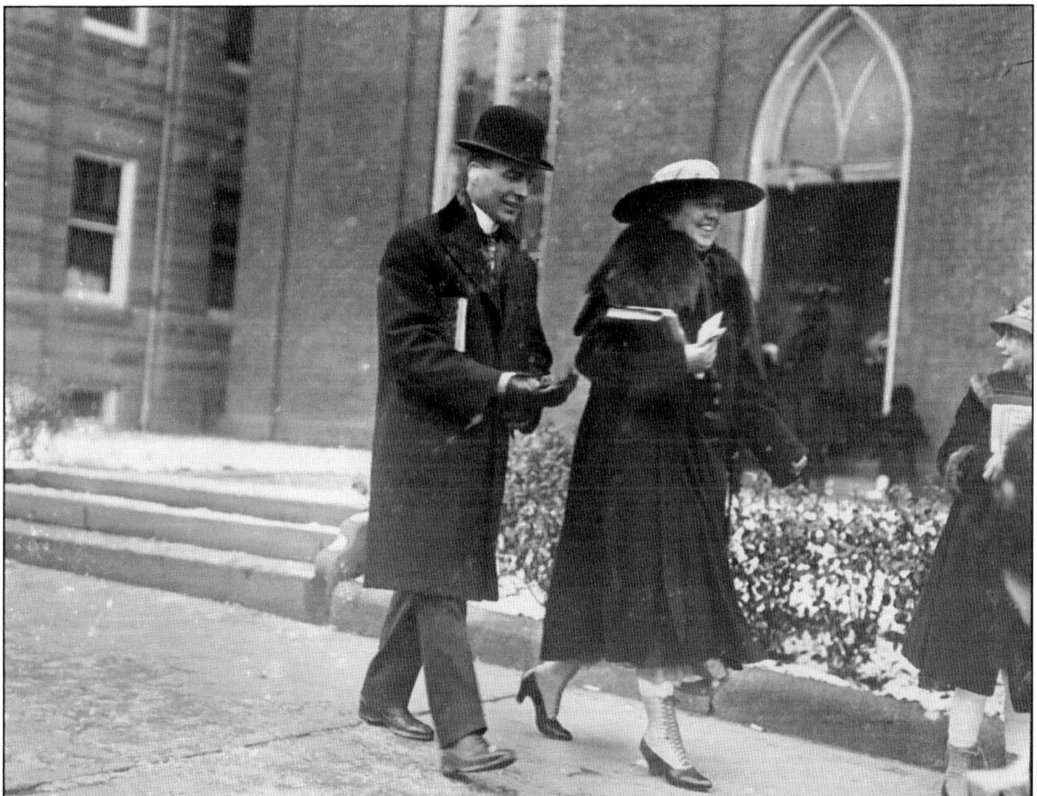

This candid shot taken outside the former Cumberland Presbyterian Church on High Street was likely snapped after a joyful gathering of the First Presbyterian Church congregation, which was using the building for social events by this time. (Courtesy of Waynesburg Borough.)

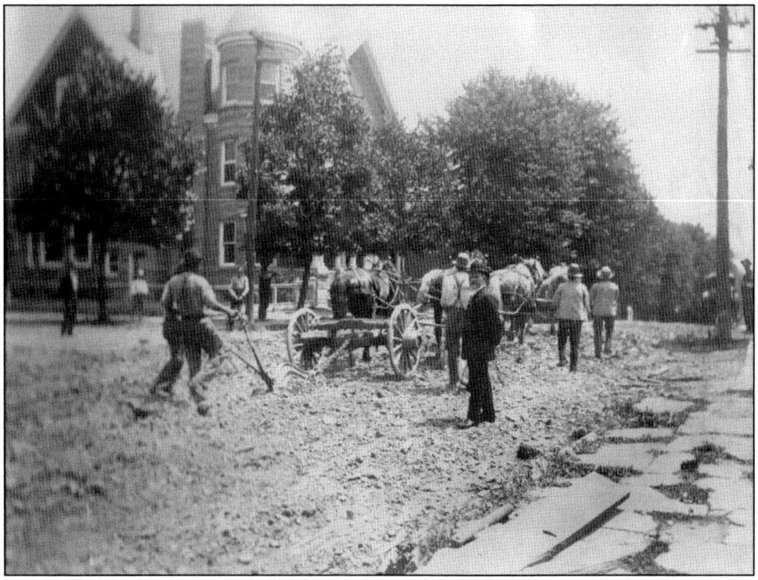

Road-paving preparation on High Street at the corner of Richhill Street takes place in this scene. (From the George David Jenkins Collection, courtesy of the Greene County Historical Society.)

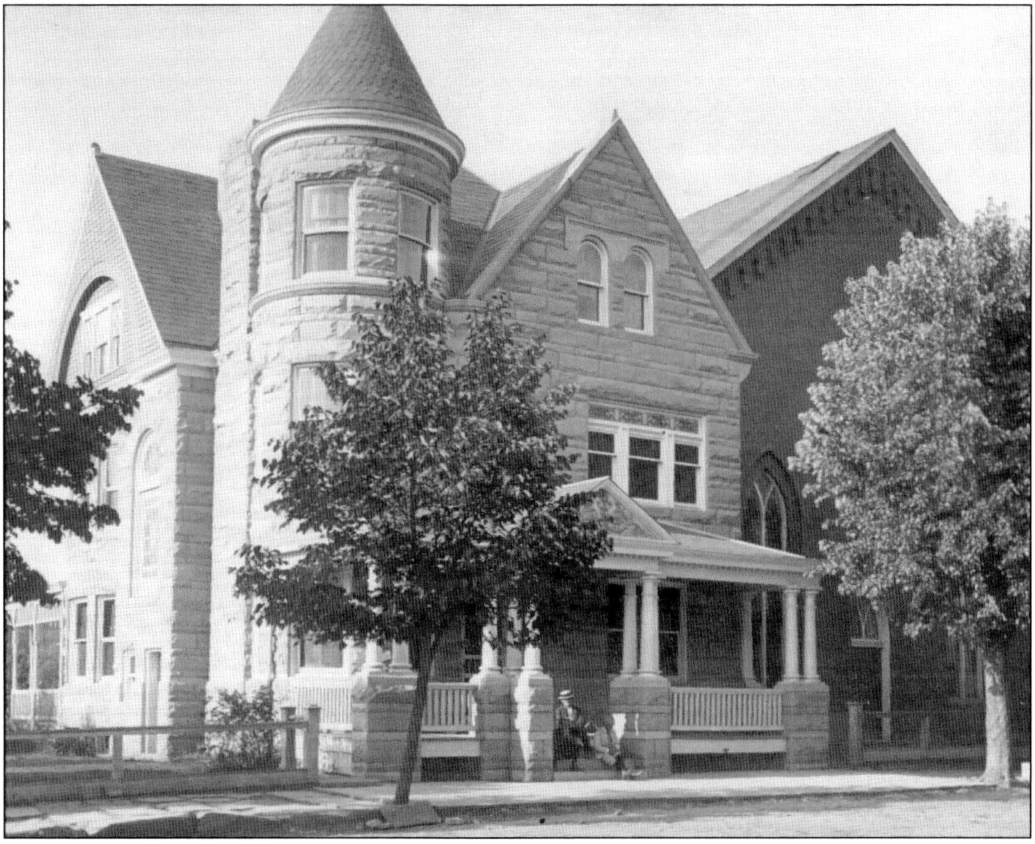

The Dr. J.T. Ullom family home was located on the corner of High and Richhill Streets. It featured two doors on the front porch: One led to the residence and the other to the doctor's office. To the right of the house is the Cumberland Presbyterian Church. (Courtesy of the Greene County Historical Society.)

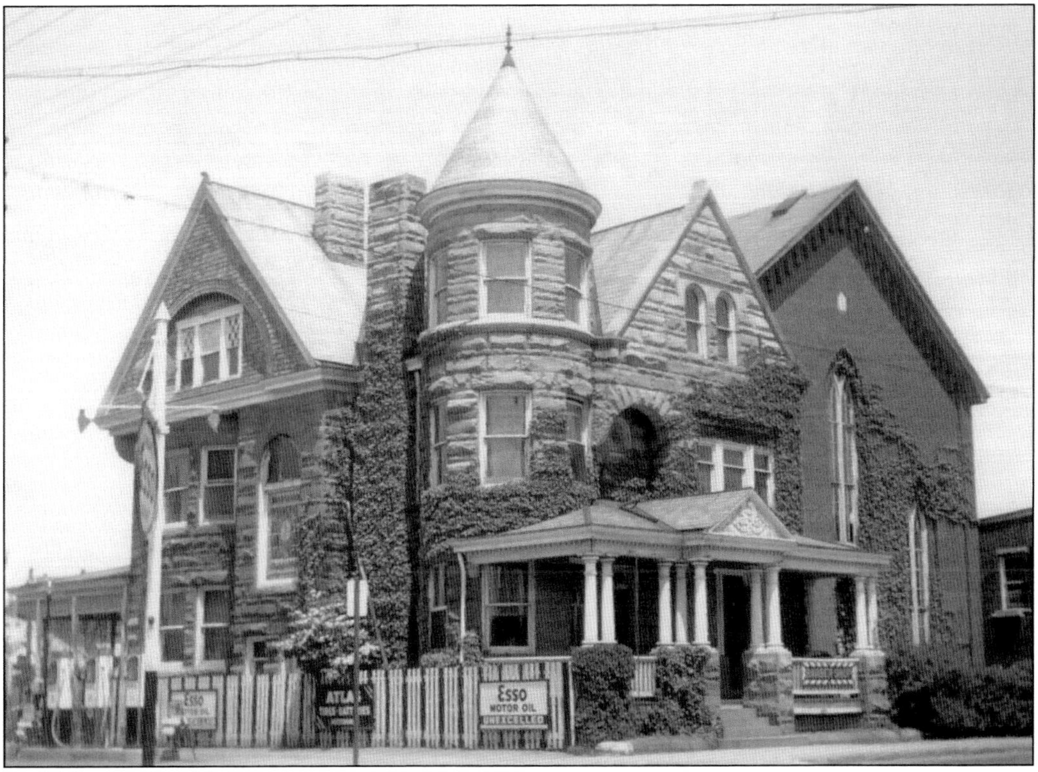

The Ullom family home is seen here at a time when an active gasoline station operated from the corner lot of High and Richhill Streets. (Courtesy of the Greene County Historical Society.)

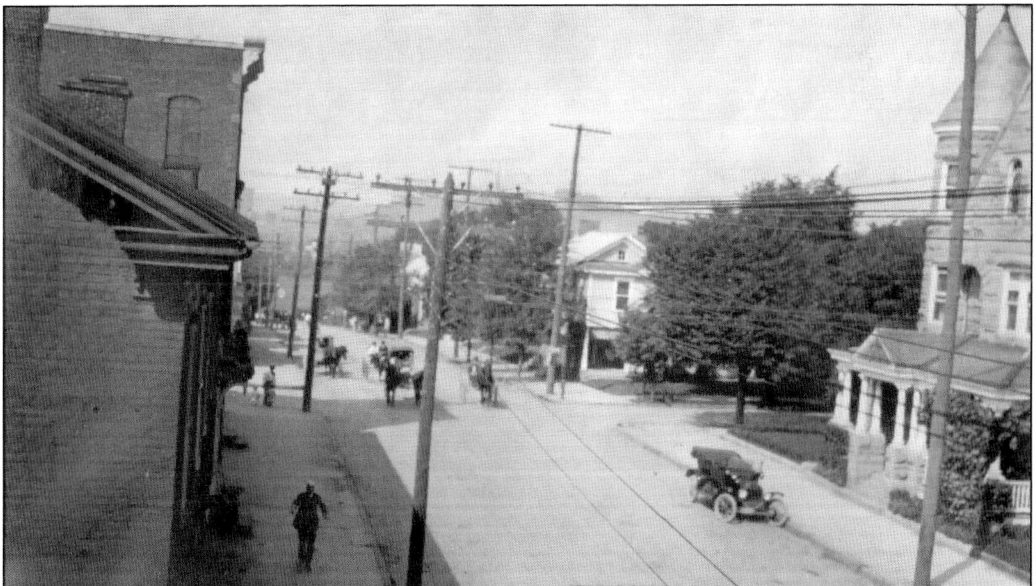

In this view looking west down High Street in 1915, the center of the picture would eventually be the current location of the Food Depot grocery store. (From the George David Jenkins Collection, courtesy of the Greene County Historical Society.)

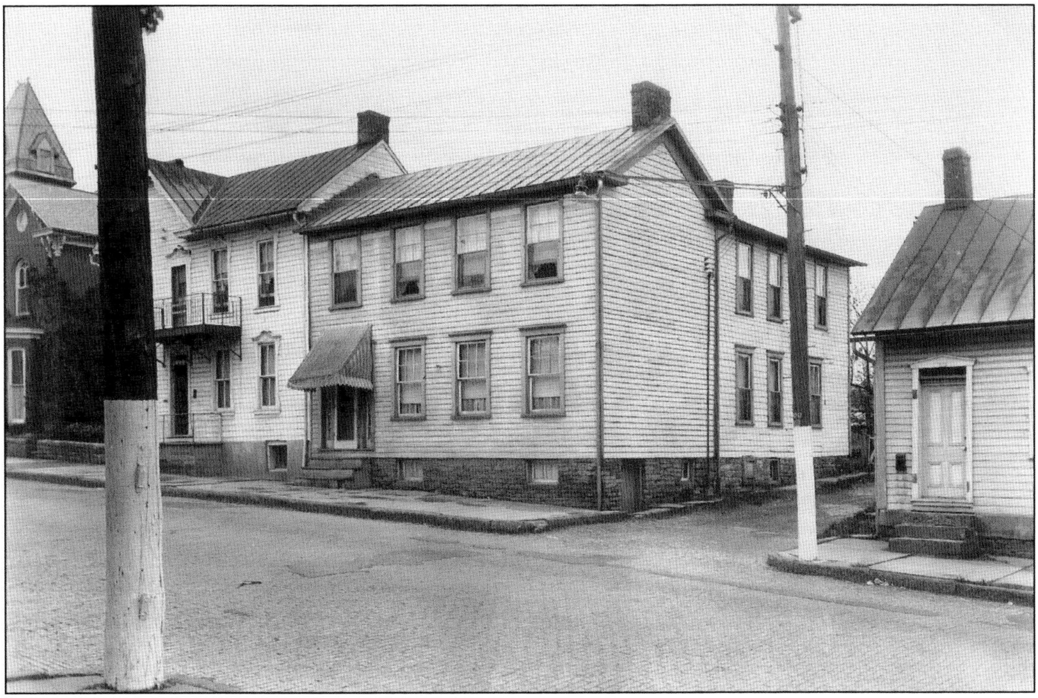

The houses in this view facing northwest are on High Street and stand near the intersection with Richhill Street. This area is located across High Street from where the Food Depot grocery store stands today and is currently the location of the Kalsey Insurance Agency. (Courtesy of the Greene County Historical Society.)

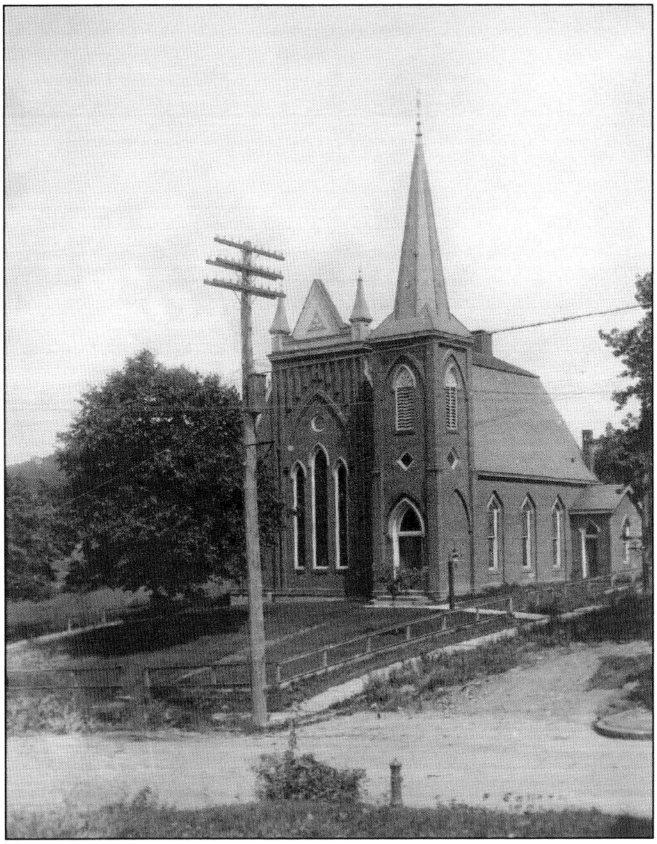

The First Baptist Church, located on the corner of High and West Streets, is pictured in 1903. This brick building was dedicated in 1884, replacing one destroyed by a tornado. In 1916, an educational addition was built at the rear of the church. The sanctuary shown here was replaced in 1962. (Courtesy of the First Baptist Church.)

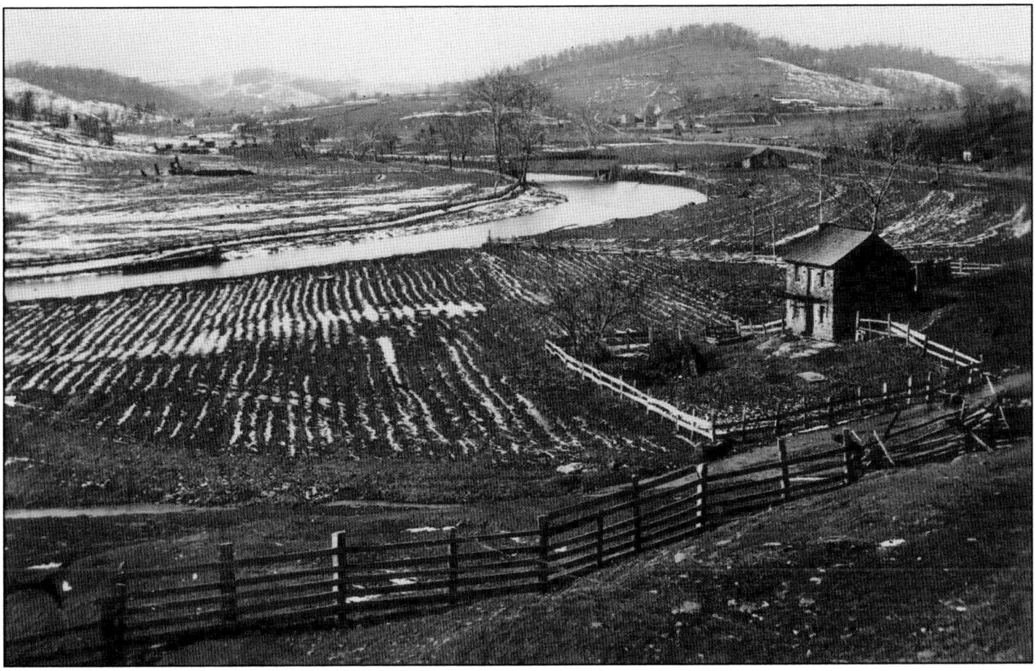

The Capt. James Seals homestead in West Waynesburg is pictured. The stone house was built in 1792. (Both, courtesy of the Greene County Historical Society.)

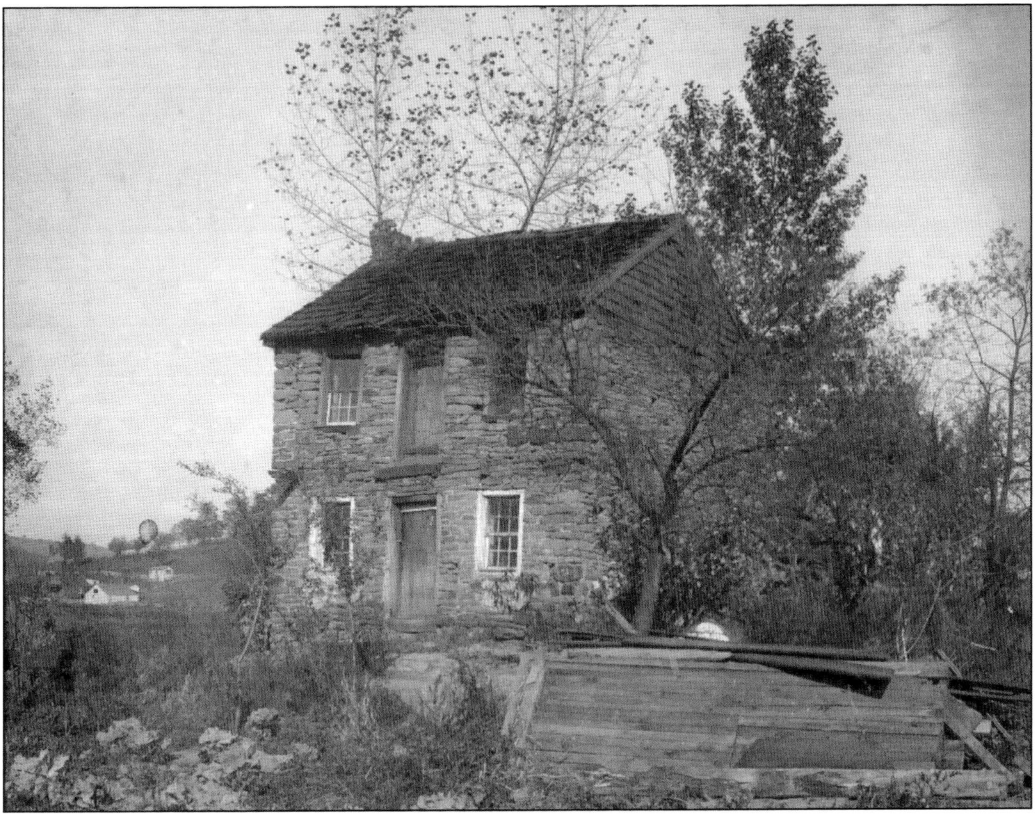

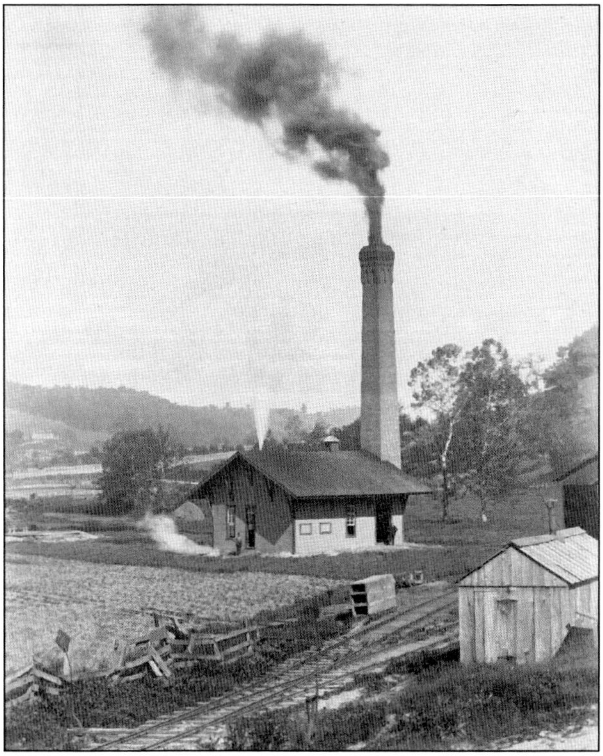

The water pumping station in West Waynesburg sits in proximity to the current small dam crossing Ten Mile Creek at the far western portion of town. (Courtesy of the Greene County Historical Society.)

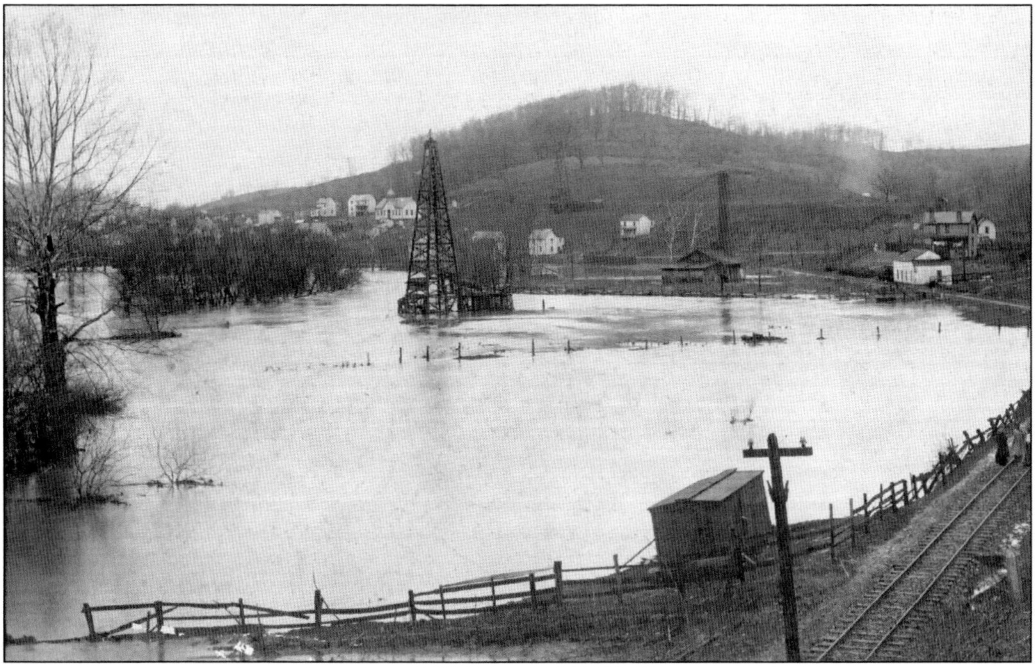

An oil derrick can be seen in the middle of the high water of Ten Mile Creek in West Waynesburg, while other derricks are visible in the background. Notice the people walking along the Waynesburg & Washington Railroad tracks at the far right. (Courtesy of the Waynesburg University Museum.)

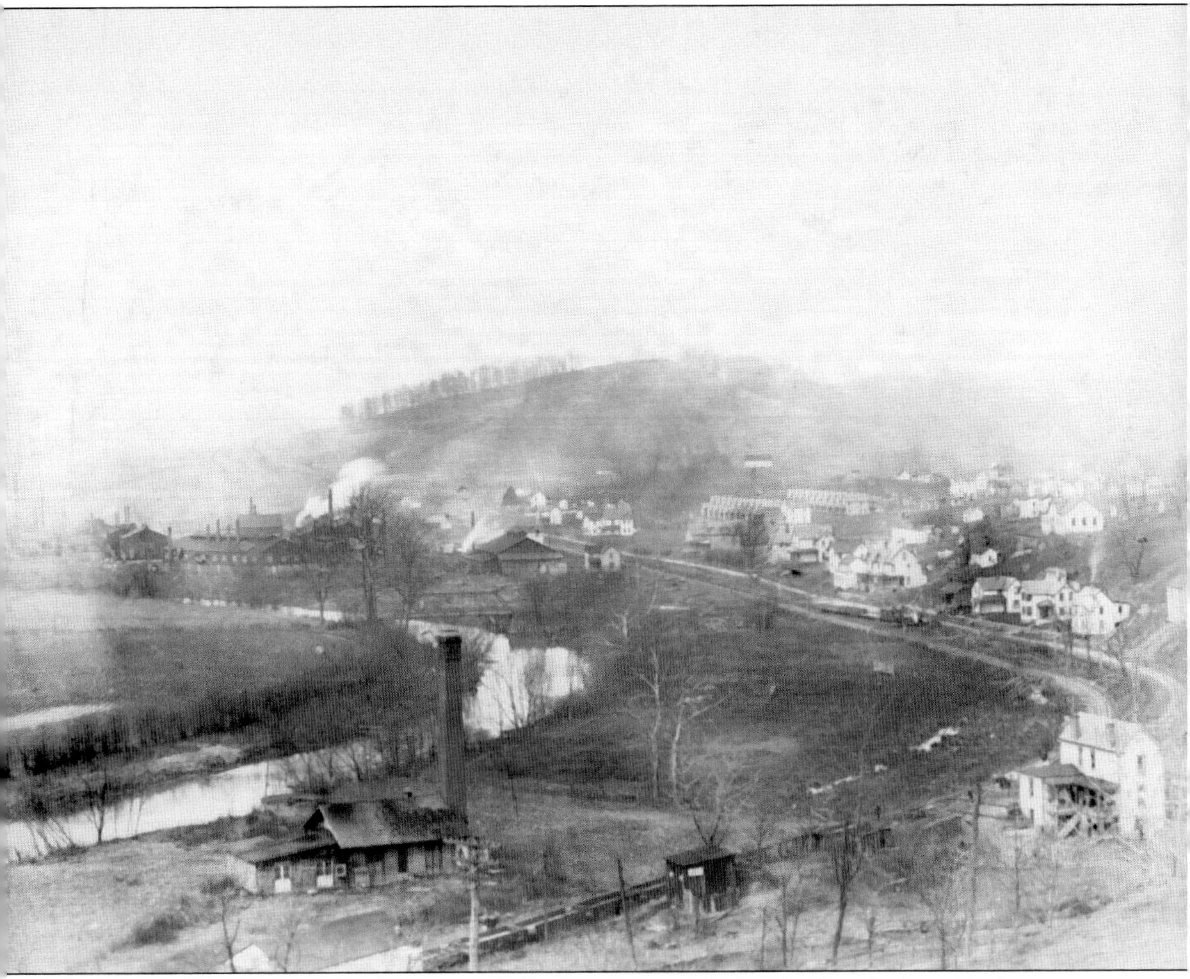

West Waynesburg is often referred to as "Bucktown," owing to James Andrew Jackson Buchanan, a prominent landowner during Waynesburg's growth in the late 1800s and early 1900s. The son of Congressman Andrew Buchanan, James was a forward thinker who enabled rights-of-way for the Waynesburg & Washington Railroad and sold land to businesses such as the Tin Mill, which built its workers' houses on James's former farm. (Courtesy of Waynesburg Borough.)

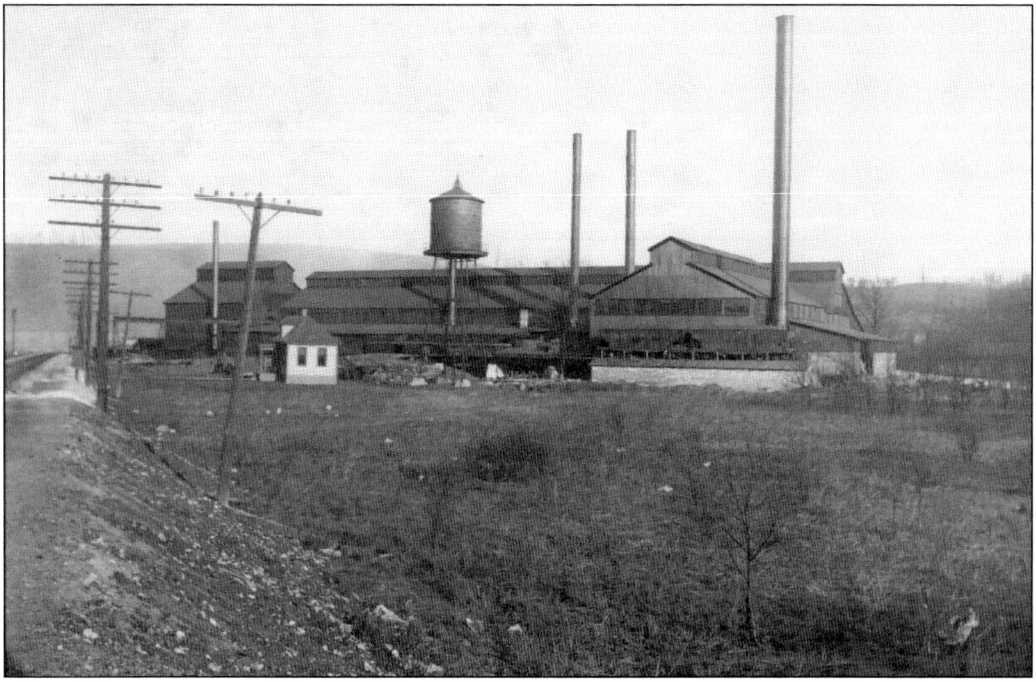

The Tin Mill in West Waynesburg was one of the many local industries that fell victim to the financial collapse of the community upon the failure of the Farmers & Drovers Bank in 1906. (Courtesy of the Greene County Historical Society.)

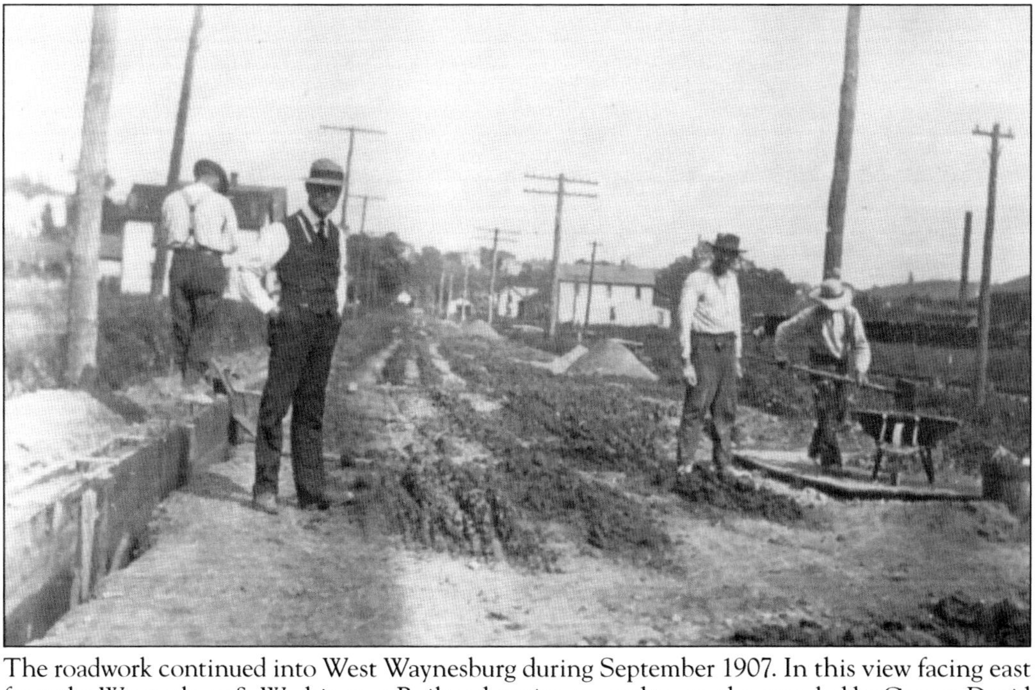

The roadwork continued into West Waynesburg during September 1907. In this view facing east from the Waynesburg & Washington Railroad station toward town, the crew led by George David Jenkins (second from left) keeps on with the improvements to modernize the roadways. (From the George David Jenkins Collection, courtesy of the Greene County Historical Society.)

Three

North Side Neighbors

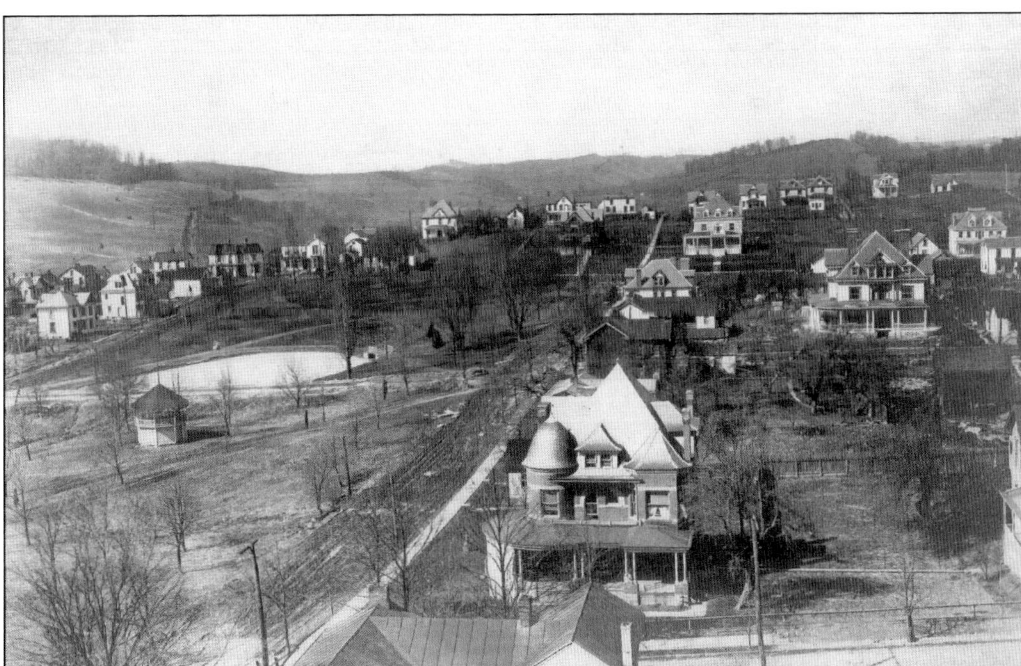

This view looks west from Miller Hall on the Waynesburg College campus. The Ritchie Park gazebo can be seen to the left, as can the former location of the pond in West Park, where its iron bridge still stands today. (Courtesy of the Waynesburg University Museum.)

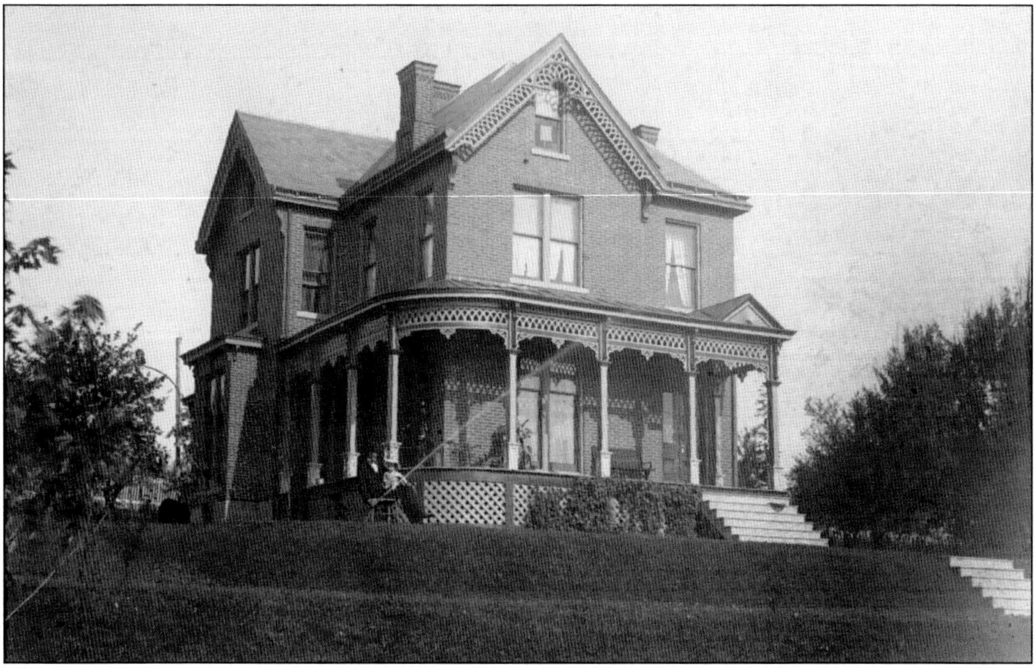

The Timothy Johns and Avadaney "Vada" (Spragg) Wisecarver family home once stood to the left of the Bowlby family home, which later became the Eva K. Bowlby Public Library, on West Street. In the photograph above, Timothy Johns Wisecarver sprays a water hose in front of an early version of the house prior to its expansion, as can be seen in the image below. Notice the rail in front of the house for tying up a horse, as well as the steps set for helping to enter a horse-drawn carriage. (Above, courtesy of the Greene County Historical Society; below, from the Walter "Blackie" Markiewich Postcard Collection, courtesy of Brice and Linda Rush.)

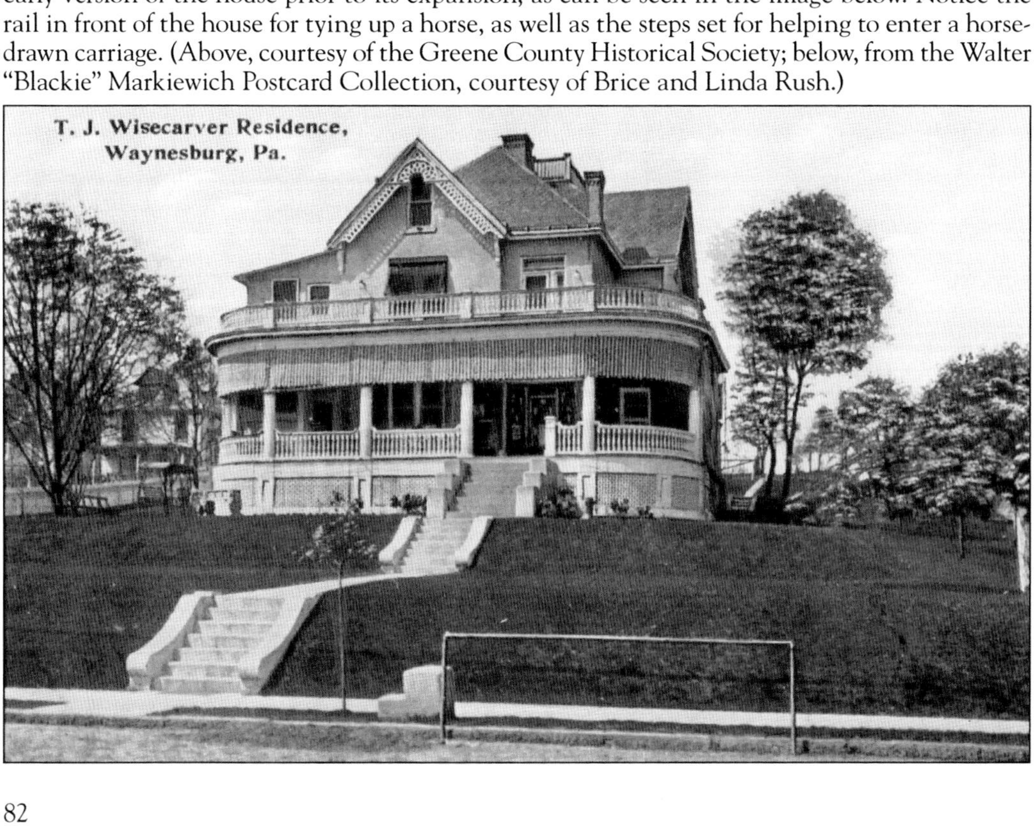

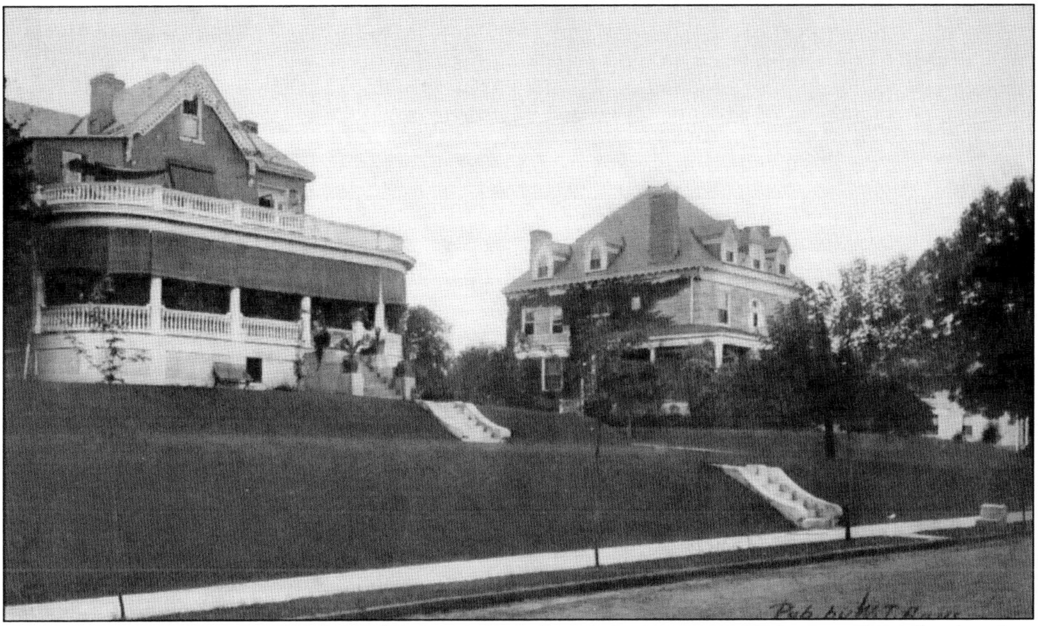

The homes of socialite neighbors the Timothy Johns Wisecarver and Carhart Bowlby families on West Street are good examples of the *Waynesburg Prosperous & Beautiful* theme of the era. West Street was so named because it was the furthermost street on the western boundary to be established in the original plot of Waynesburg in 1796. (Photograph by W.T. Hays, from the Walter "Blackie" Markiewich Postcard Collection, courtesy of Brice and Linda Rush.)

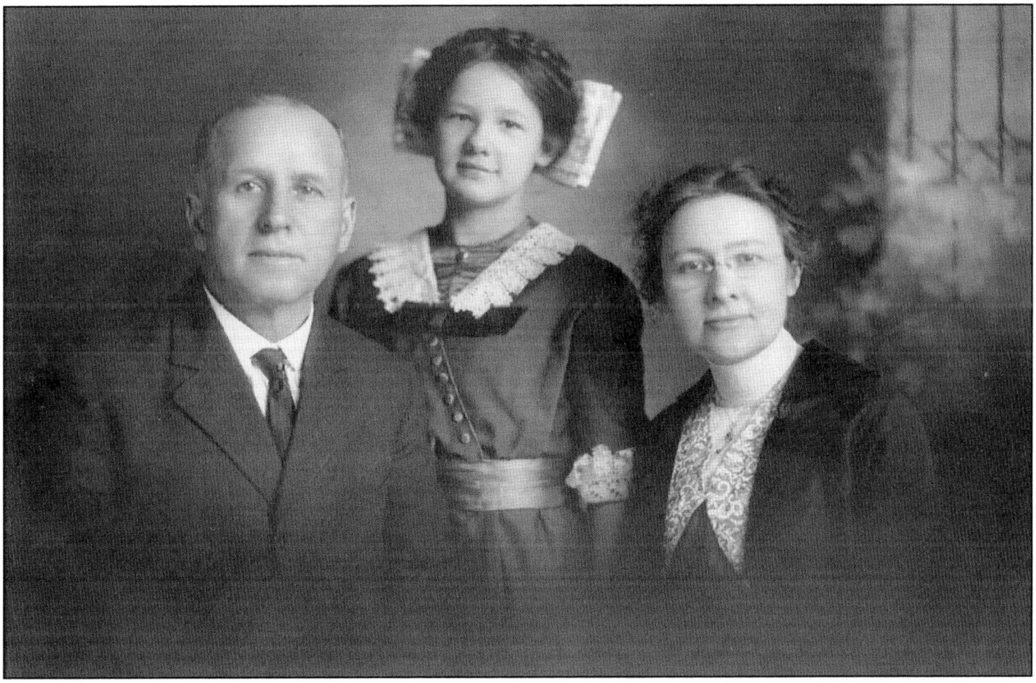

Pictured are Carhart Bowlby and his wife, Eva (Kendall) Bowlby, with their daughter, Dorothy Bowlby (later Connor). Their home now serves the community as the Eva K. Bowlby Public Library. (From the Catherine Miranda [Staggers] Bowlby Collection, courtesy of the Bowlby family.)

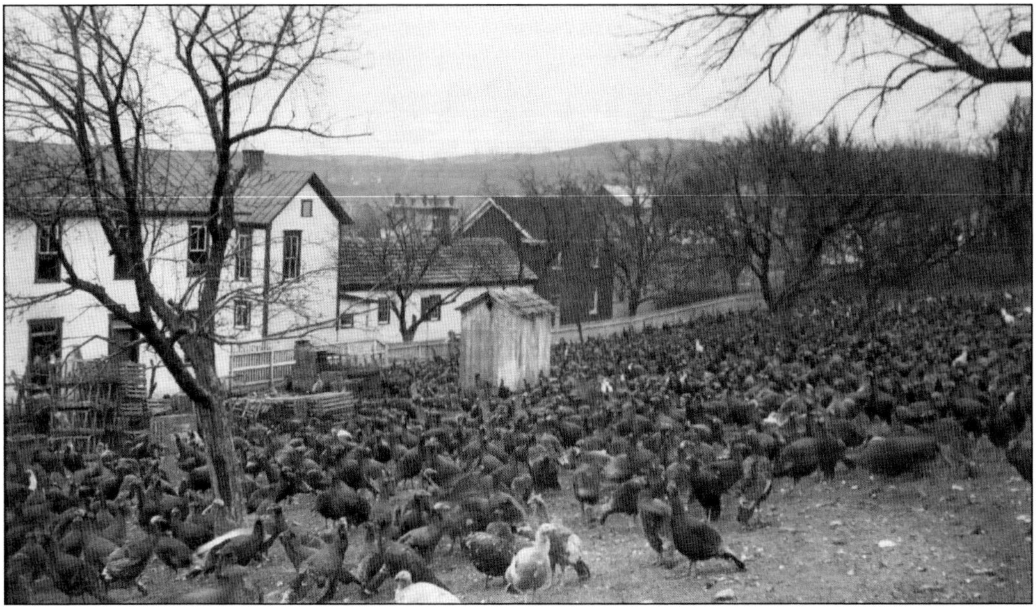

The Illig Turkey Farm existed above where Bowlby Street is today. In the photograph below, taken on butchering day, the only man identified is Frank Conklin, who is noted as the "man standing in doorway with hatchet." A 65-acre portion of the Illig farm was purchased in 1899 to develop 118 residential lots that stretched west of West Street. The 14 new blocks extended from College Street north to Sixth Avenue. Bowlby Street, Huffman Street, and Ross Street were named in honor of the Illig Addition's principal developers. (Both, courtesy of the Greene County Historical Society.)

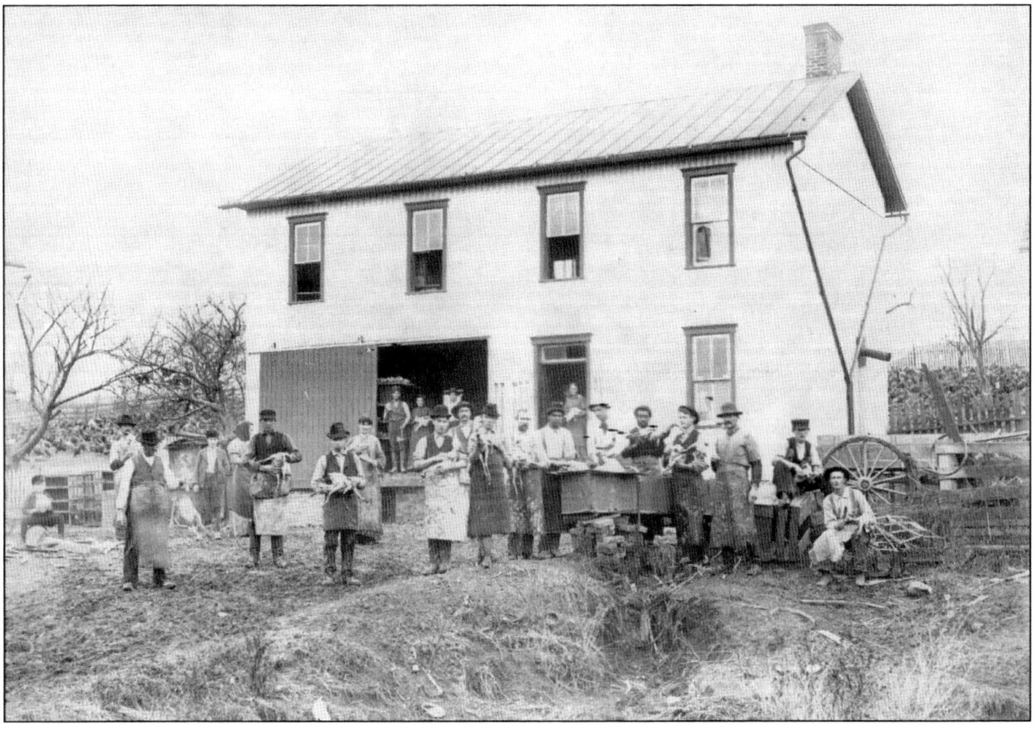

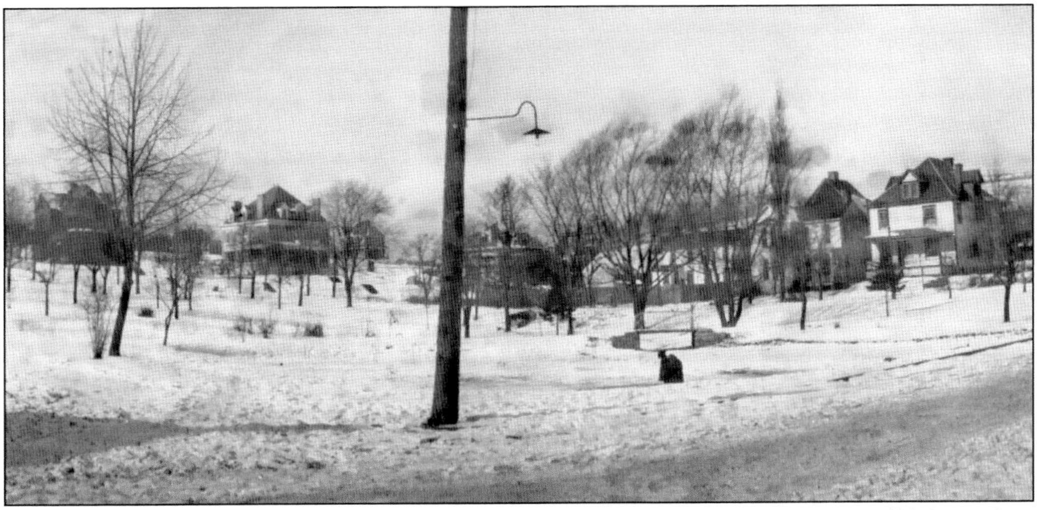

This view looks northwest from the corner of Wayne and Richhill Streets. A small lake and an iron bridge to cross it were added to West Park in 1894. The 12-by-11-foot bridge can be seen over the frozen lake where ice-skaters enjoyed winter amusement. In the background, on West Street, are the Wisecarver and Bowlby houses. (Courtesy of the Greene County Historical Society.)

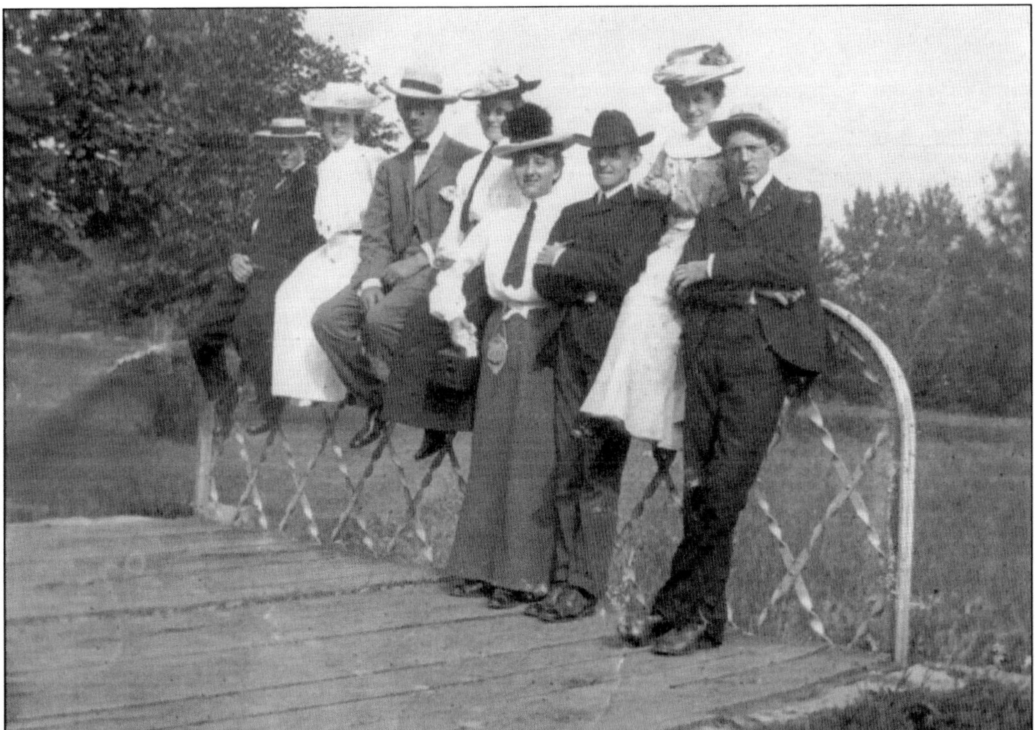

George David Jenkins (perched on the rail, third from left) and friends pose on the iron bridge in West Park in the early 1900s. Jenkins served as the borough engineer during much of the town's early development, such as the installation of sewer lines, bricked streets, and paved sidewalks. (From the George David Jenkins Collection, courtesy of the Greene County Historical Society.)

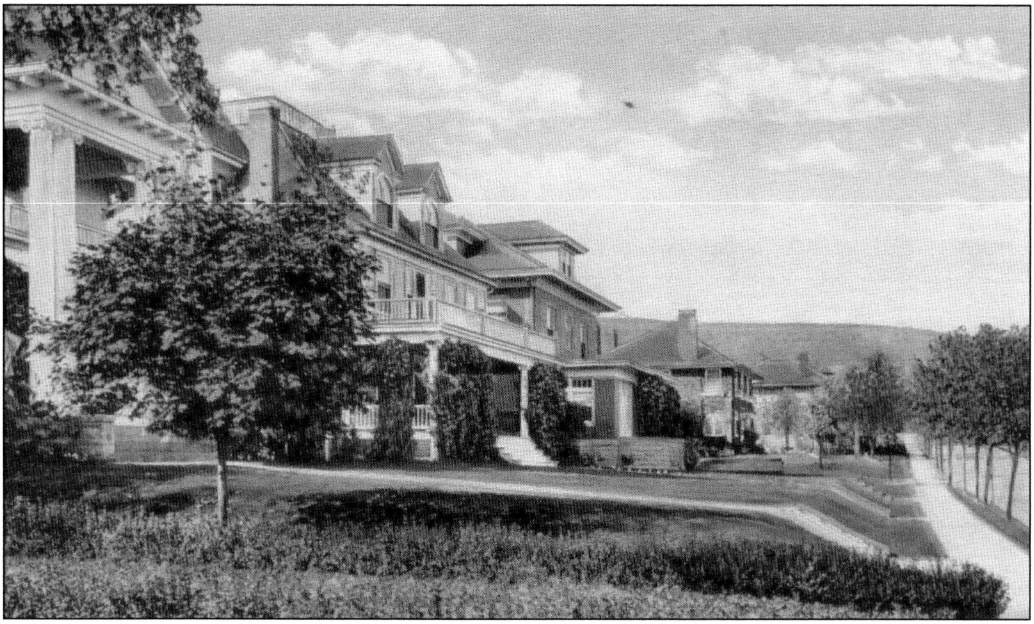

This postcard rendition of West Street is unique because this view stands intact today. (From the Walter "Blackie" Markiewich Postcard Collection, courtesy of Brice and Linda Rush.)

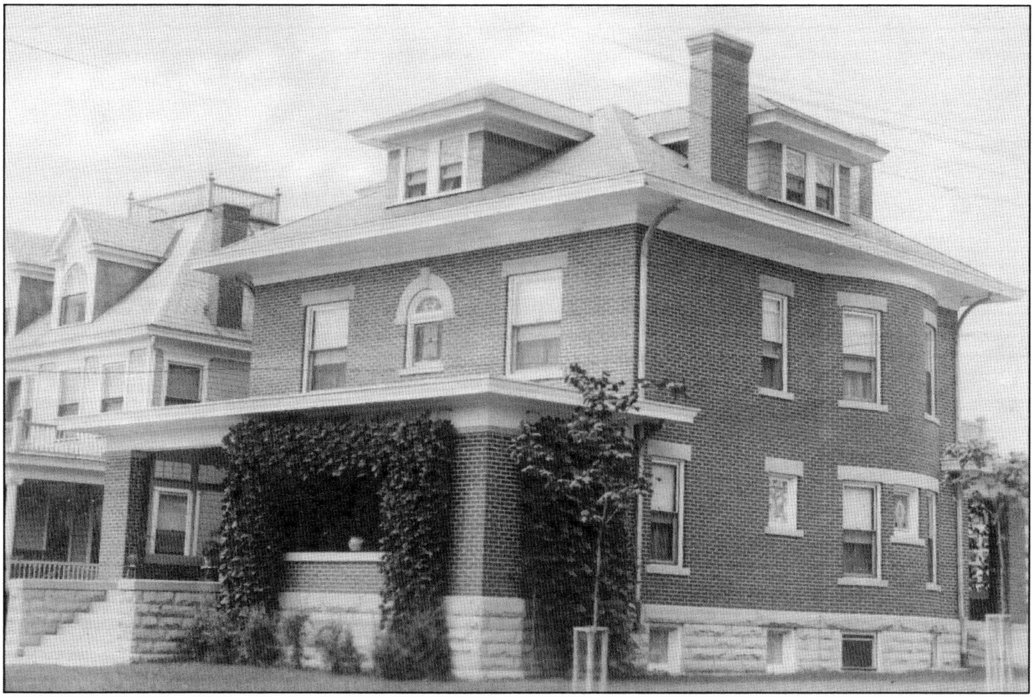

On the corner of West Street and First Avenue, this home built in 1911 by William Davis and Nancy (Scott) Cotterrel still stands. (Courtesy of Richard and Beverly Krill.)

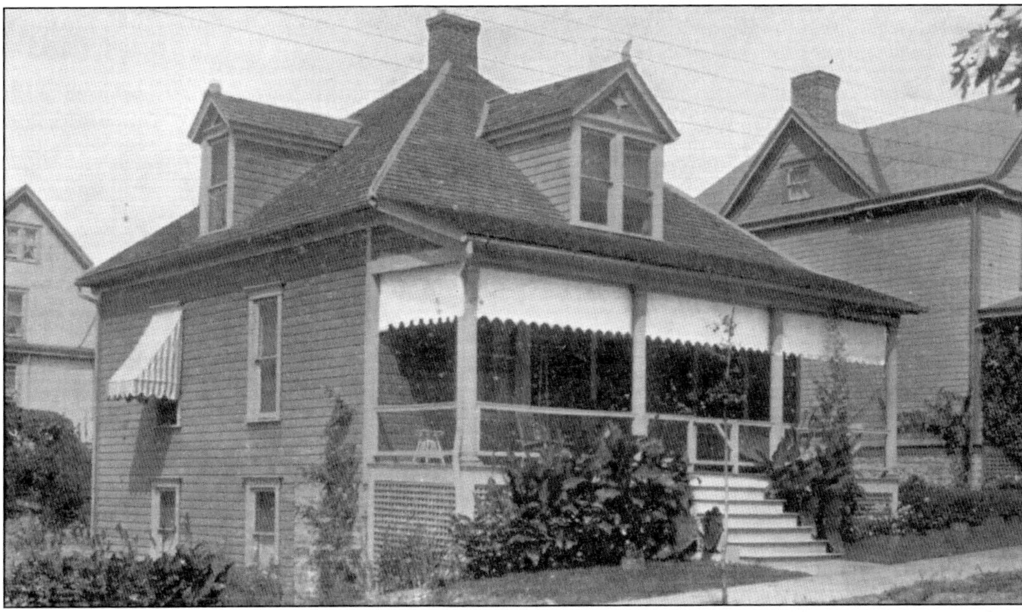

This is the home of J. Harry Babbitt on West Street near Third Avenue. Babbitt was a Waynesburg photographer whose name appears embossed on many of the antique images in local collections. (Photograph by W.T. Hays, from the Walter "Blackie" Markiewich Postcard Collection, courtesy of Brice and Linda Rush.)

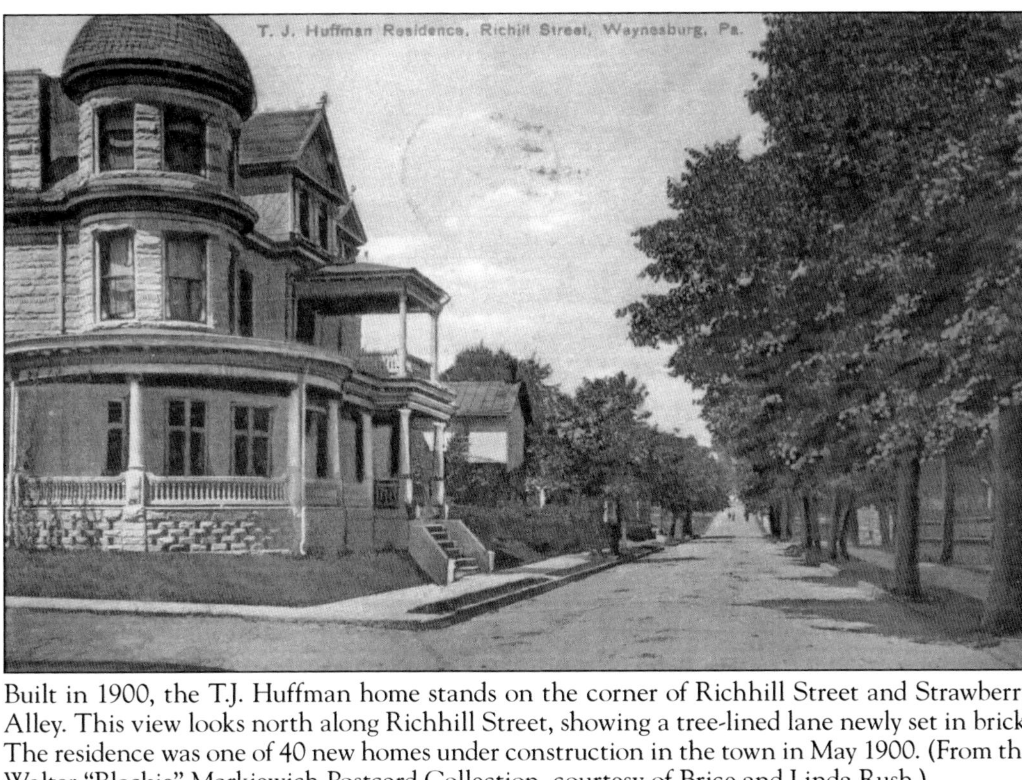

Built in 1900, the T.J. Huffman home stands on the corner of Richhill Street and Strawberry Alley. This view looks north along Richhill Street, showing a tree-lined lane newly set in brick. The residence was one of 40 new homes under construction in the town in May 1900. (From the Walter "Blackie" Markiewich Postcard Collection, courtesy of Brice and Linda Rush.)

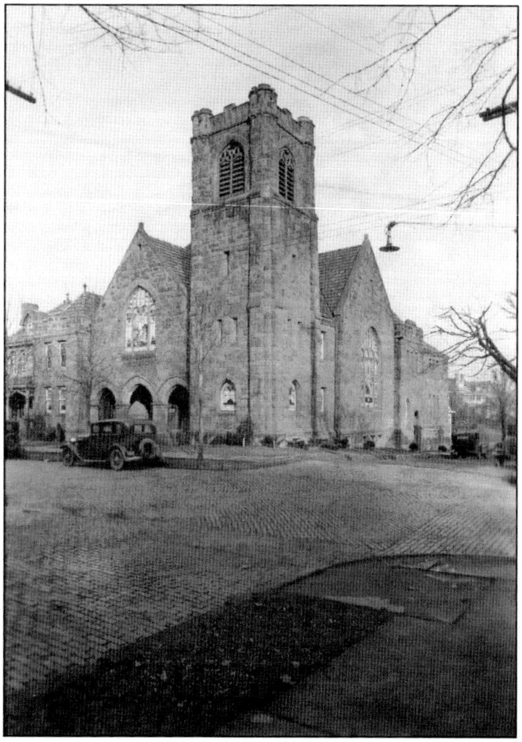

Brownstone from Hummelstown, Pennsylvania, was used for the exterior of the Methodist Episcopal church, later the First United Methodist Church, on the corner of Franklin and Richhill Streets, dedicated September 29, 1907. In 1908, Andrew Carnegie donated one half of the cost of the original Hinner pipe organ. This church construction was completed in spite of the failure of the Farmers & Drovers Bank. (Courtesy of the Greene County Historical Society.)

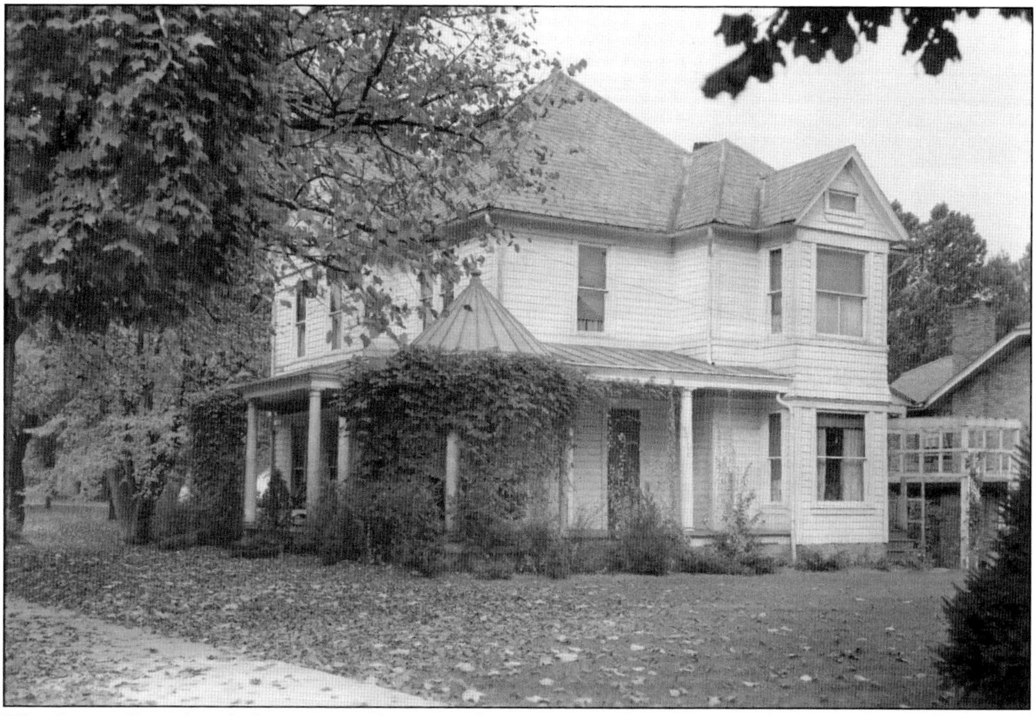

The former Day family home, seen here on the southeast corner of Wayne and Richhill Streets, was replaced with the current brick house on the property of the First United Methodist Church. (Courtesy of the Greene County Historical Society.)

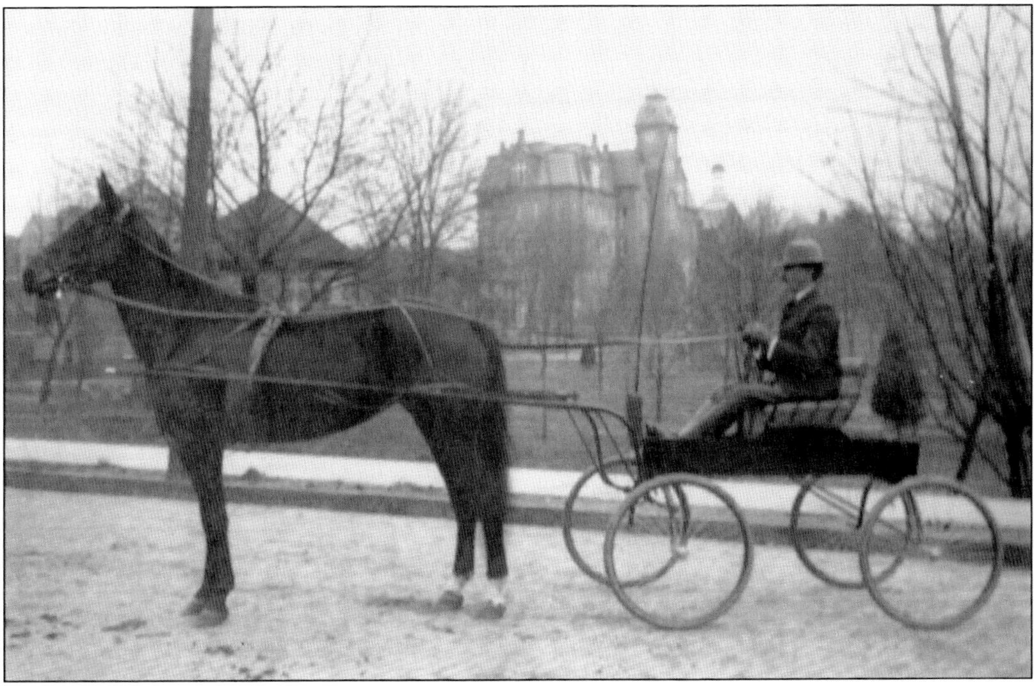

Eleazer Luse Denny rides north on Richhill Street. Behind him is the gazebo in Ritchie Park, as well as Miller and Hanna Halls on the Waynesburg College campus. (Photograph by J. Harry Babbitt, from the Josephine Denny Collection, courtesy of Farley Toothman.)

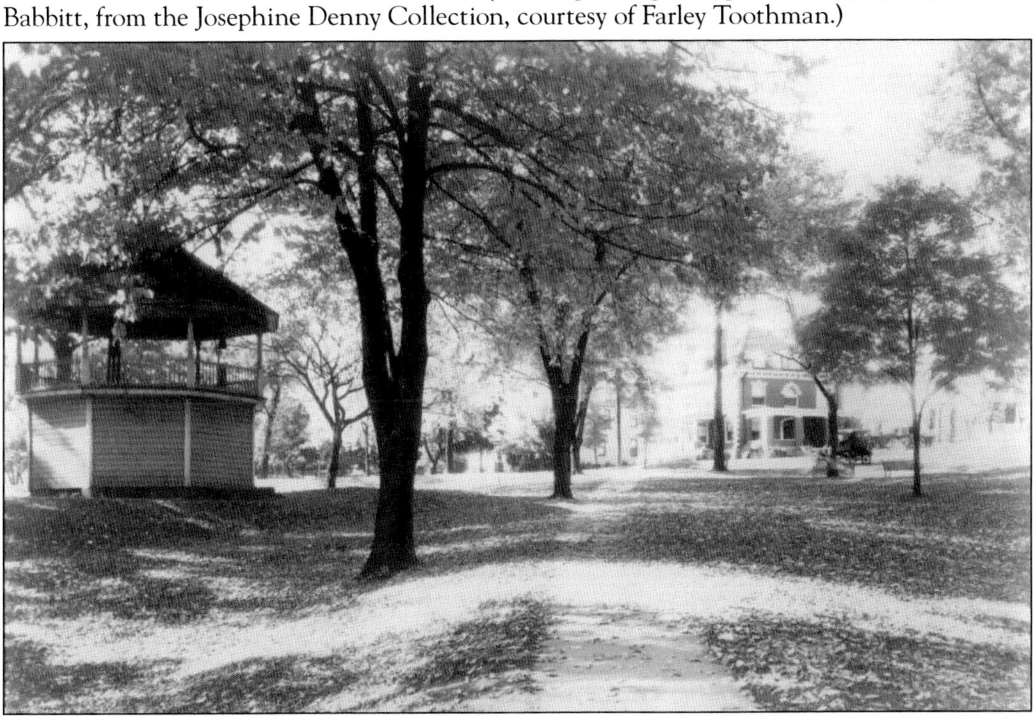

The view in this image looks northwest from Ritchie Park. The original gazebo was constructed at this location in 1901. It was a popular venue for local concerts; the first was held on August 11, 1901. (Photograph by William E.S. Fletcher, courtesy of the Cornerstone Genealogical Society.)

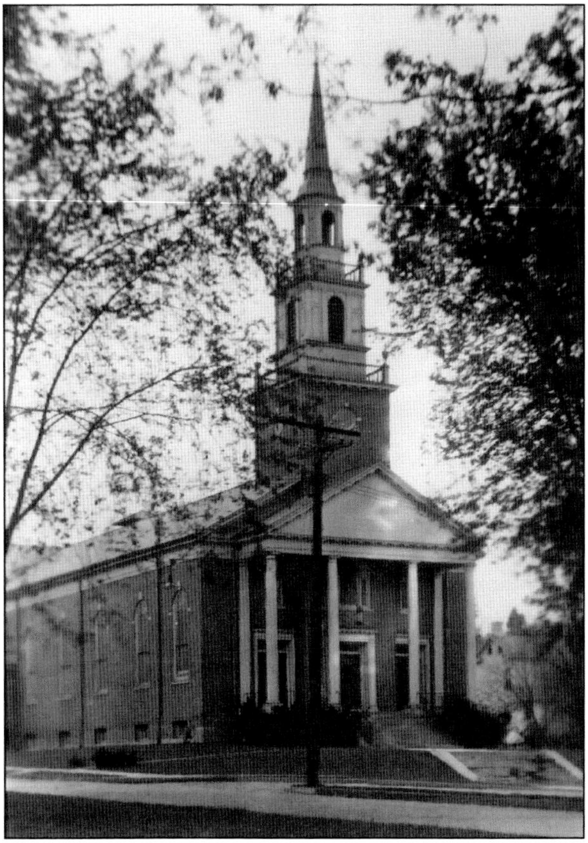

The First Presbyterian Church, located on the corner of College and Richhill Streets, was dedicated on October 31, 1926. The building was designed by architects Smith and Walker of Boston and built by Edward A. Wehr of Pittsburgh. (Courtesy of the Greene County Historical Society.)

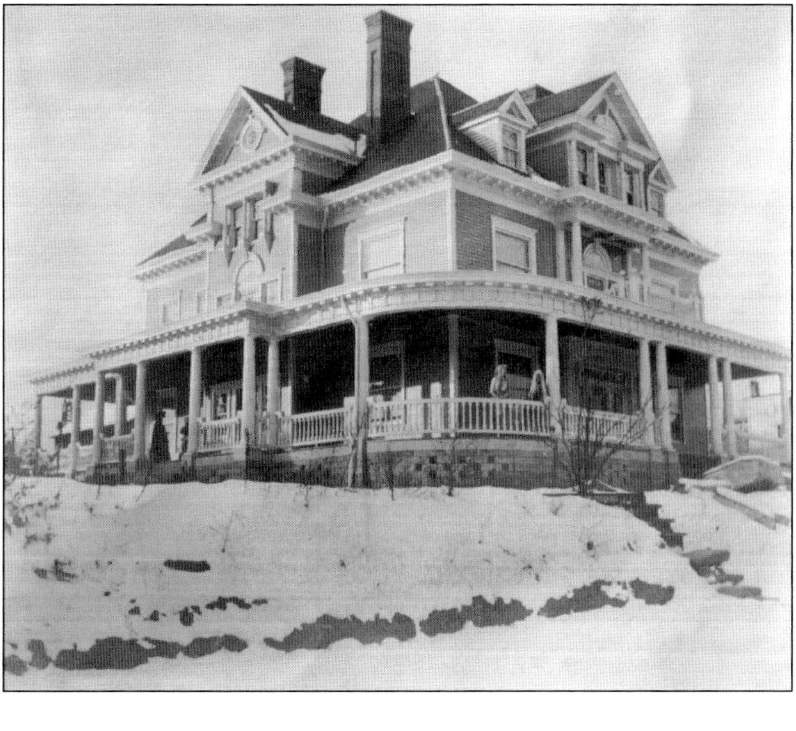

The James L. Iams residence on Richhill Street, across from the First Presbyterian Church, later served as the community senior center. Today, the site is a parking lot for church members. (From the George David Jenkins Collection, courtesy of the Greene County Historical Society.)

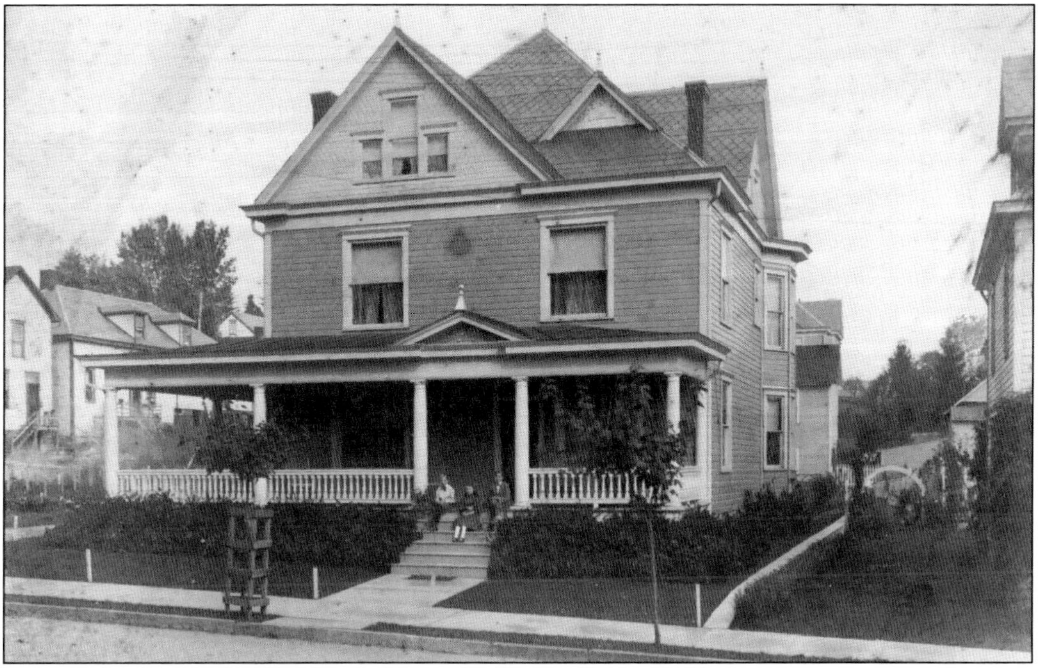

This is a family home of Thomas Morford and Annie (Webster) Throckmorton on Richhill Street. Their children are seated on the porch in the photograph above; they are, from left to right, Alfred, Nancy, and William. Before William left to serve his country with Company K during World War I, the Throckmorton family posed in their yard for the photograph below; from left to right are (first row) Thomas and Annie; (second row) Alfred, William, and Nancy. William was injured in battle on July 29, 1918, and died in France on September 18, 1918. Within a year, his brother Alfred succumbed to the flu epidemic and was buried on July 29, 1919, a year to the day of his brother's injury. The home was later used by Waynesburg College as a fraternity house and ultimately torn down. (Above, courtesy of the Waynesburg University Museum; below, from the Nancy Laureanne [Throckmorton] Meighen Collection, courtesy of the Cornerstone Genealogical Society.)

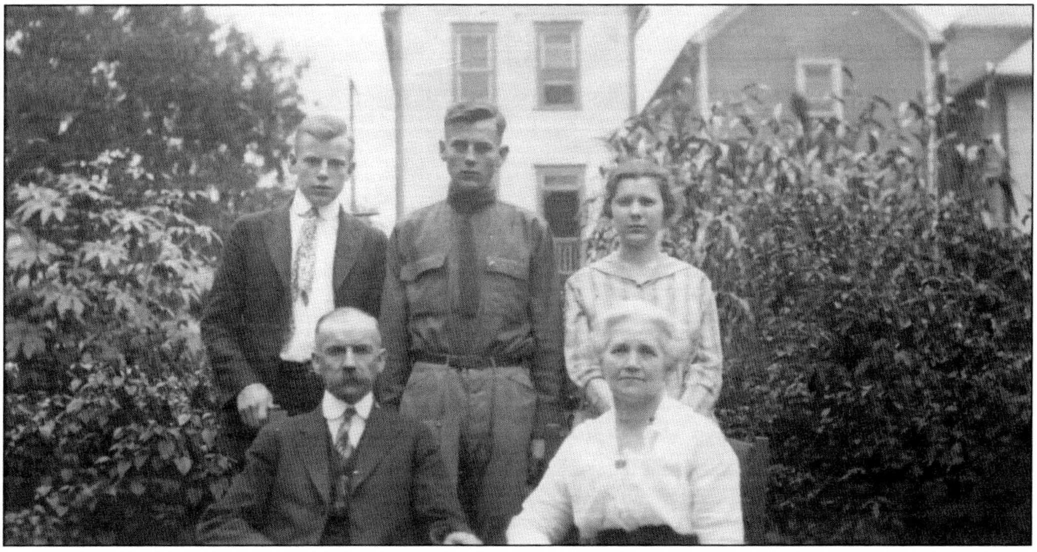

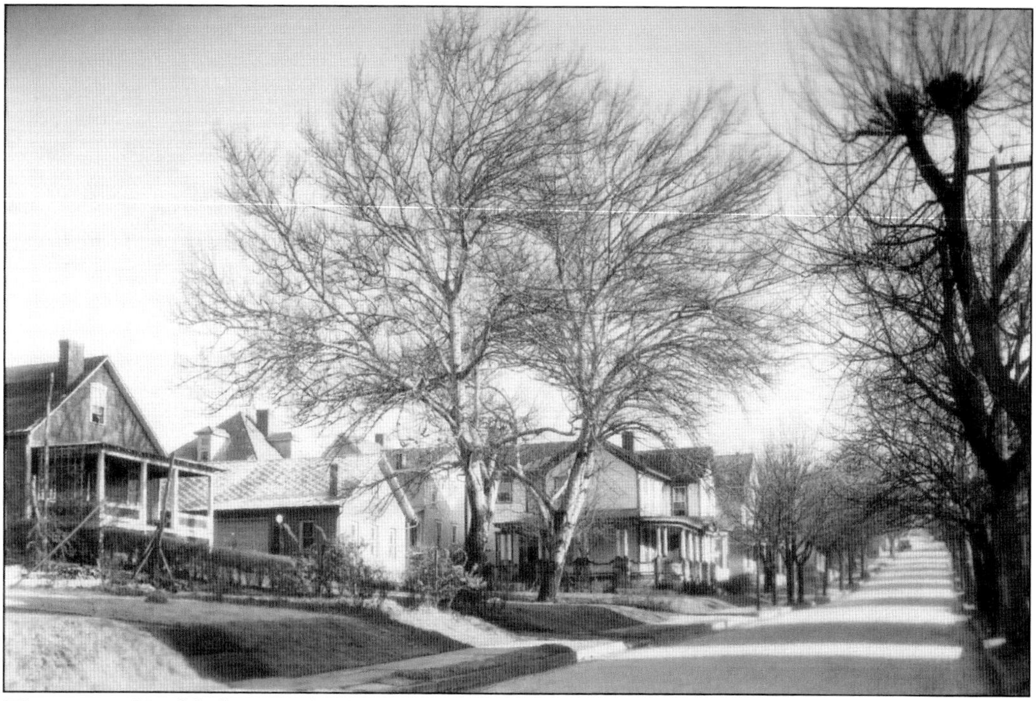

This view of Richhill Street looks north from Second Avenue and appears very much the same today. (Courtesy of the Greene County Historical Society.)

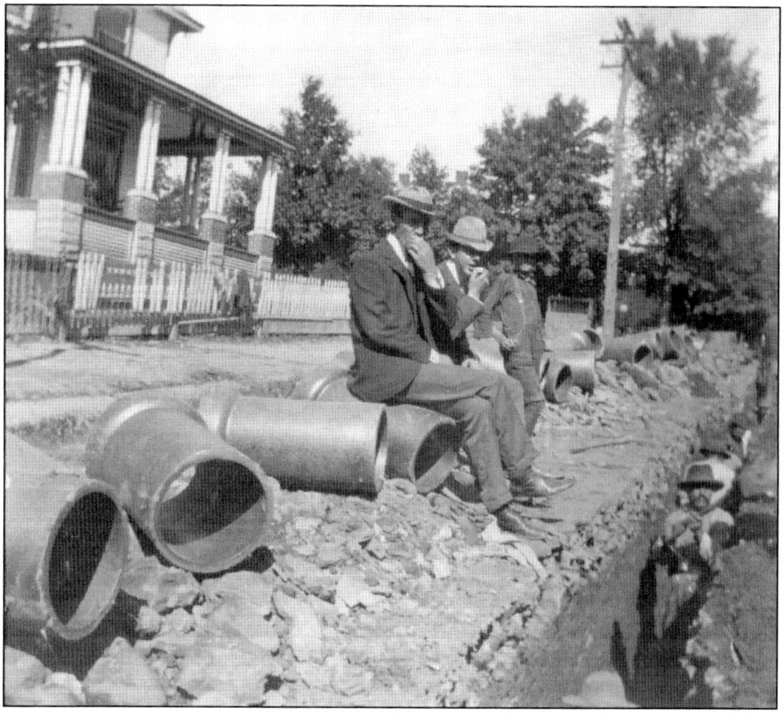

A sewer line is being laid along Richhill Street in this early-1900s image. Much of the town's infrastructure was done via Italian immigrant workers specifically hired by the community for this purpose. They are seen in the depths of the ditch in this photograph. (From the George David Jenkins Collection, courtesy of the Greene County Historical Society.)

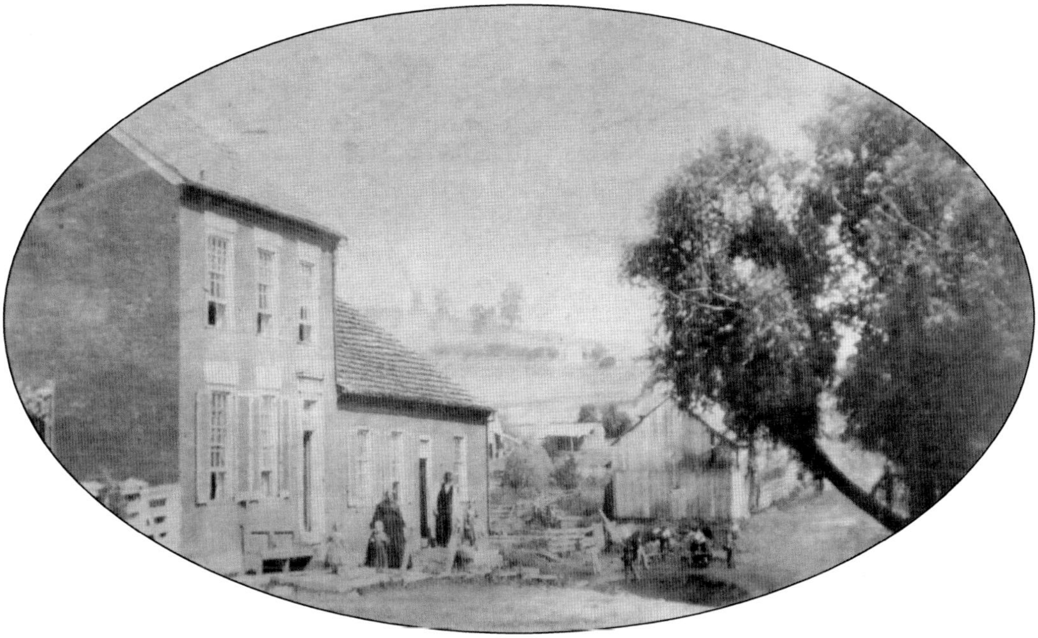

On March 10, 1800, Robert Adams purchased lot 48 of the original plan of Waynesburg. On this corner of Franklin and Morris Streets, Robert and Rebecca (Blackmore) Adams, pictured below, built their home and tanyard, pictured above in the summer of 1864. They raised a large family of children who intermarried with such Waynesburg families as the Buchanans, Inghrams, Hooks, Hoskinsons, Houlsworths, Sayerses, Siegfrieds, and Van Buskirks. The original buildings have been removed, and today this location is home to Domino's Pizza. (Above, courtesy of the Greene County Historical Society; below, from the Josephine Denny Collection, courtesy of Farley Toothman.)

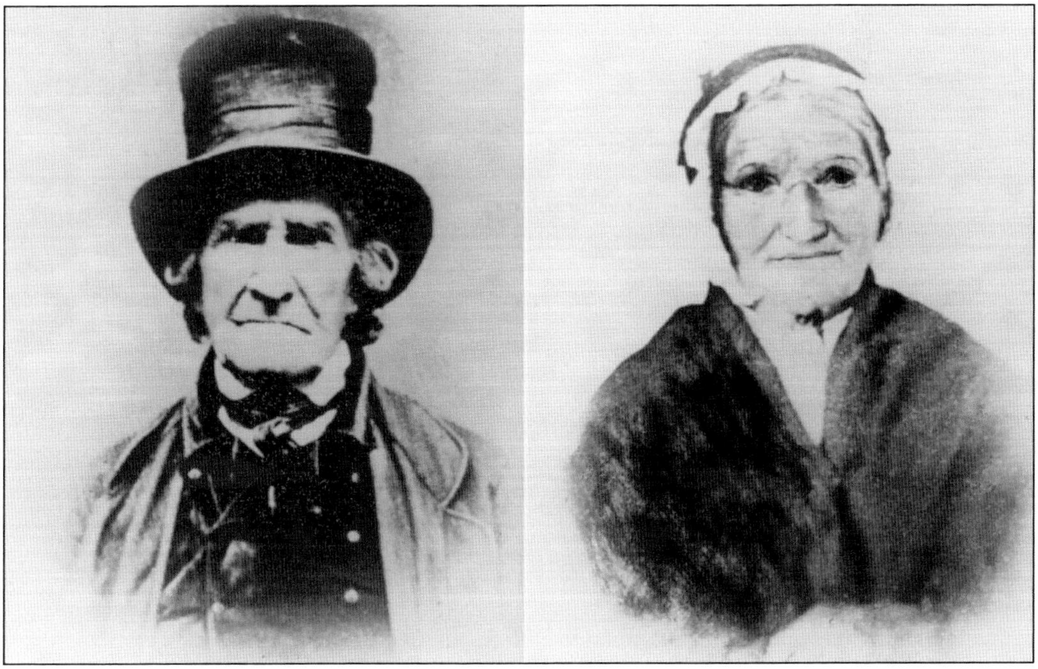

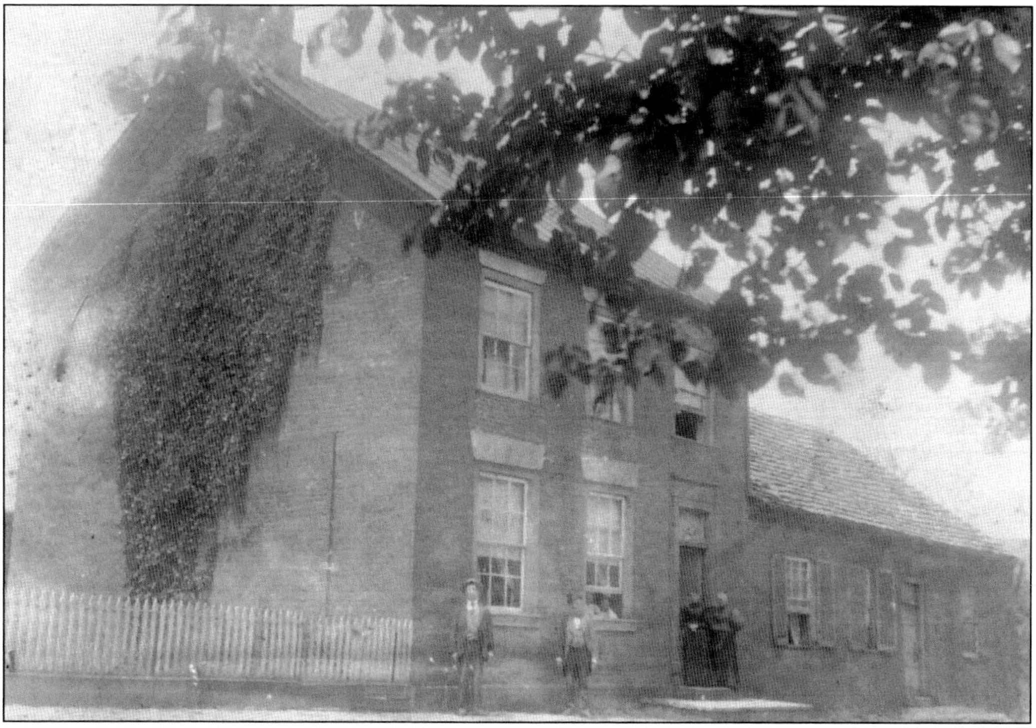

The Robert Adams property had passed to the family of his grandson Henry Clay and Clementine (Rush) Sayers by the time this mid-1890s photograph was taken. Pictured, from left to right, are Chauncey E. Sayers, Henry Clay Sayers Sr., unidentified, Frances Lillian (Scott) Sayers, Ella (Sayers) (Carter) Hirst, and Clementine (Rush) Sayers. (Courtesy of the Greene County Historical Society.)

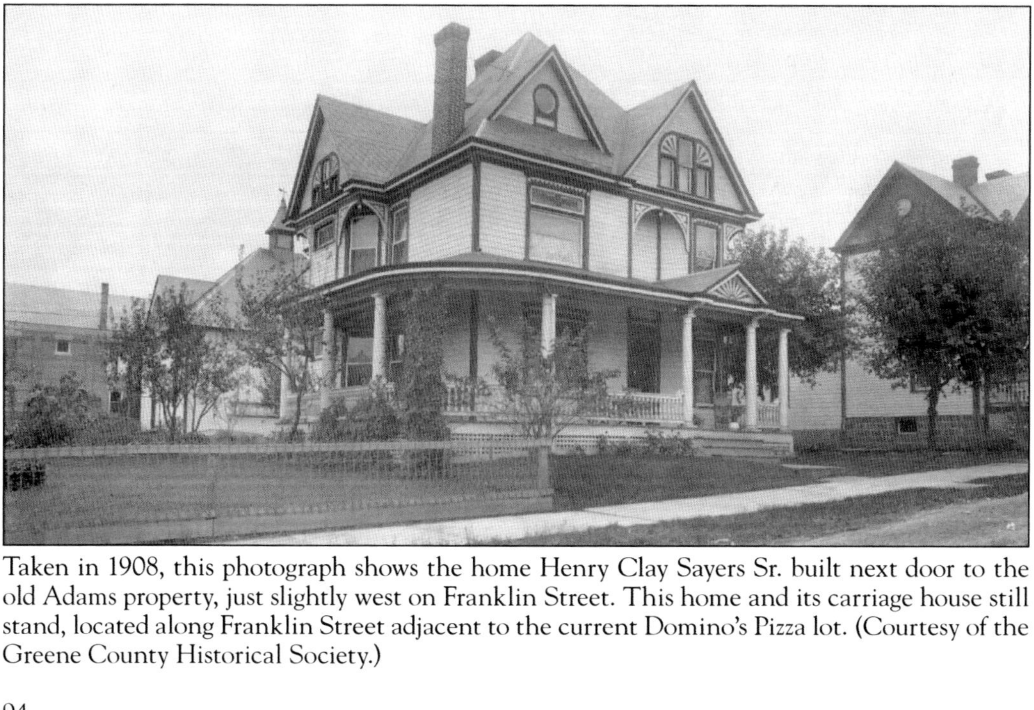

Taken in 1908, this photograph shows the home Henry Clay Sayers Sr. built next door to the old Adams property, just slightly west on Franklin Street. This home and its carriage house still stand, located along Franklin Street adjacent to the current Domino's Pizza lot. (Courtesy of the Greene County Historical Society.)

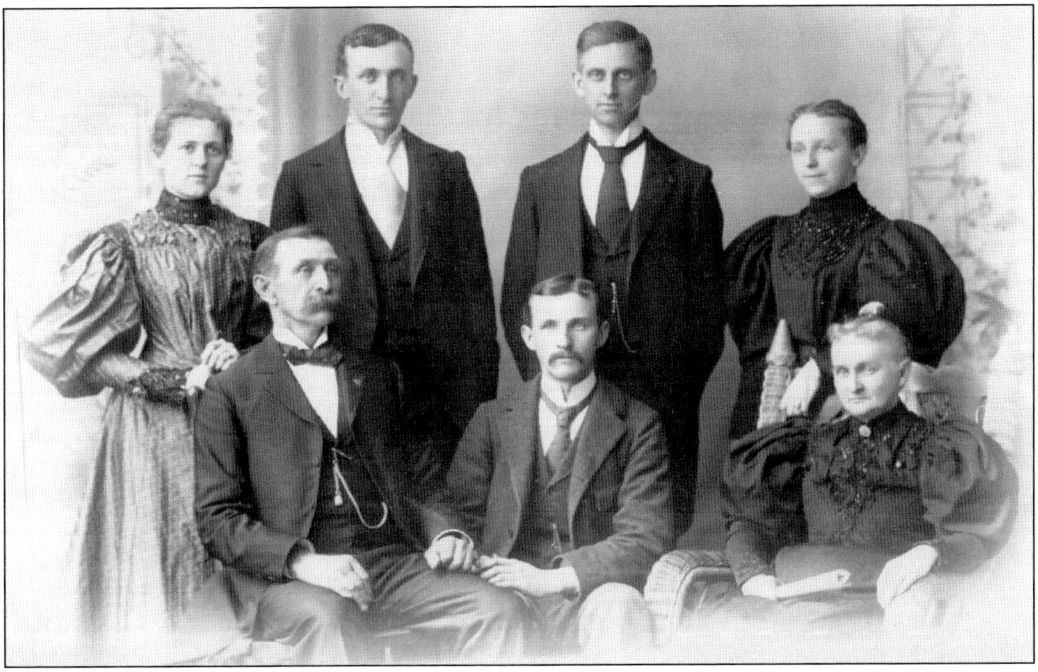

In high fashion, the Sayers family posed for this portrait; from left to right are (first row) Henry Clay Sayers Sr., Chauncey E. Sayers, and Clementine (Rush) Sayers; (second row) Frances Lillian (Scott) Sayers, Henry Clay Sayers Jr., William Porter Carter, and Ella (Sayers) (Carter) Hirst. (Courtesy of the Greene County Historical Society.)

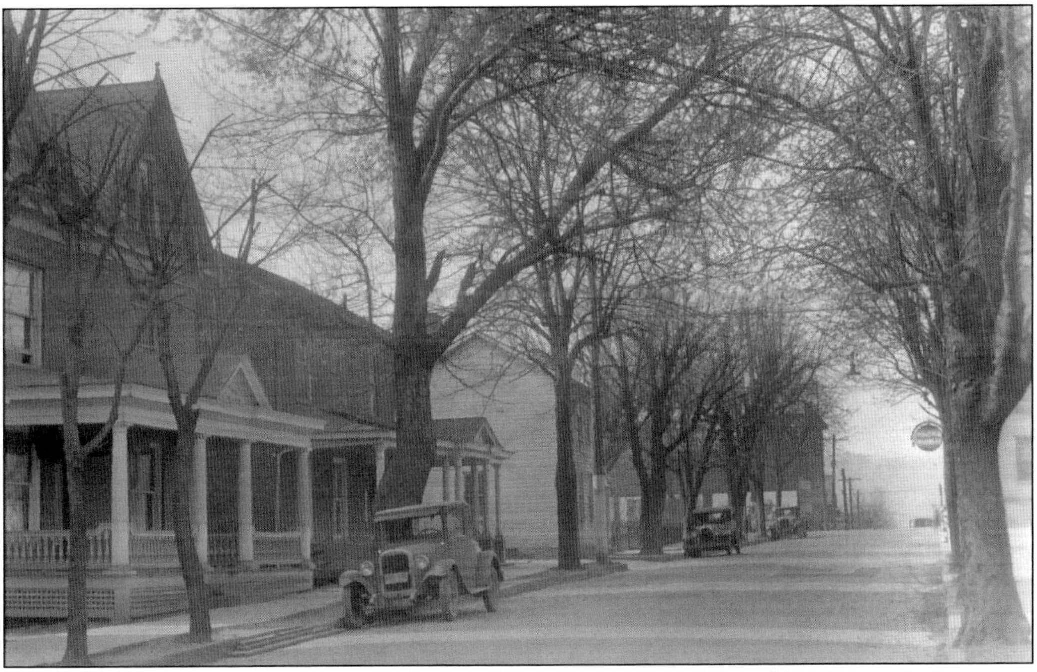

This view looks south on Morris Street from the intersection with Franklin Street; the house on the far left is still in use today. (Photograph by William E.S. Fletcher, courtesy of the Cornerstone Genealogical Society.)

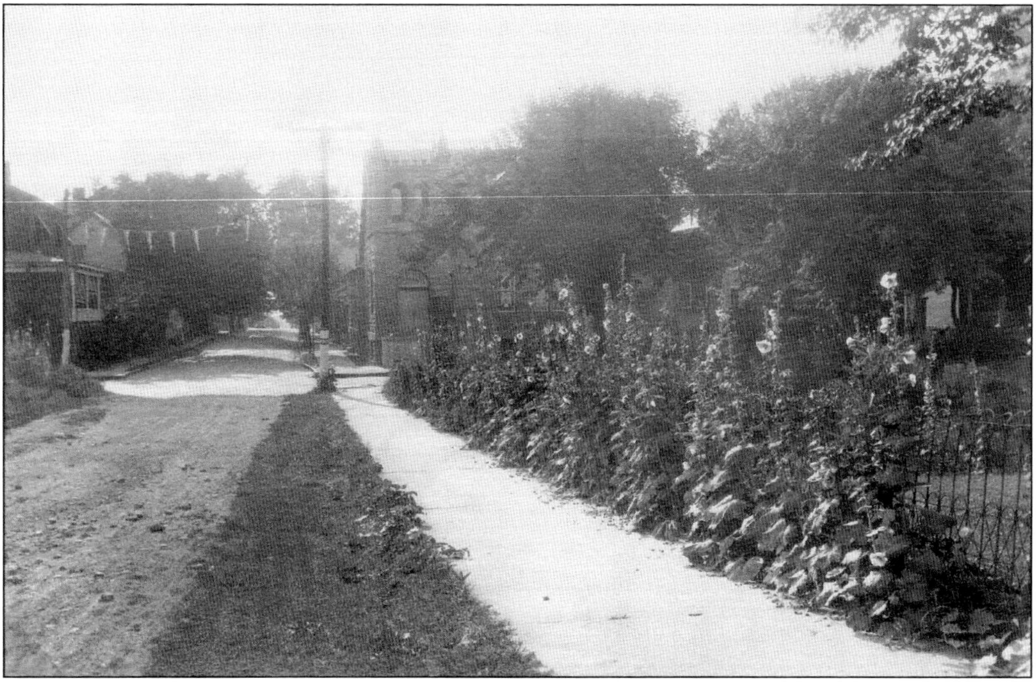

The view in this photograph of Franklin Street looks east toward the Christian church. The lot behind the row of flowers was the longtime home of the Adams and Sayers families, occupied today by Domino's Pizza. (Courtesy of the Greene County Historical Society.)

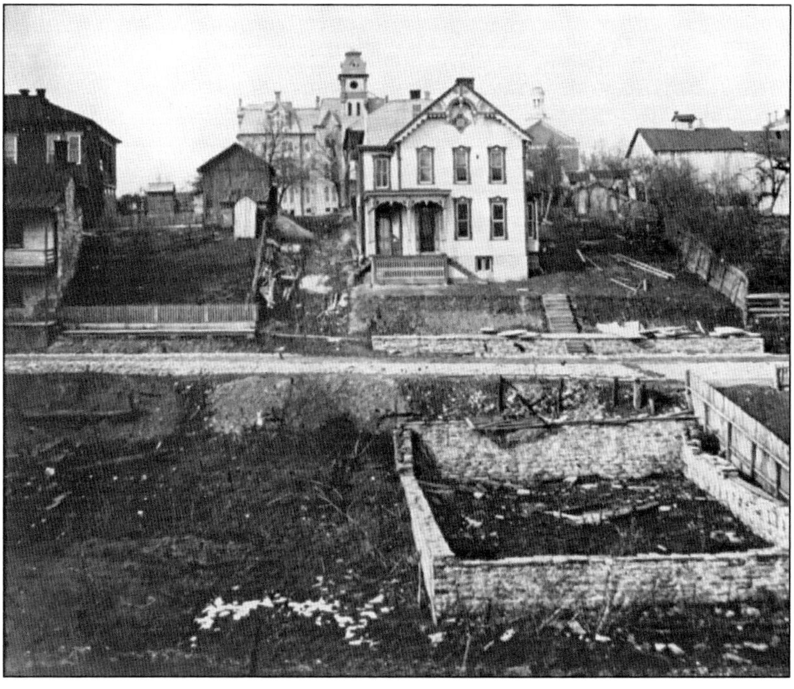

This late-1800s view of Franklin Street shows (far left) the double porch of the stone Amos Piatt house (built 1828), neighbored by the home of Arthur Inghram Cooke (center). In the background are Miller and Hanna Halls on the Waynesburg College campus. (Courtesy of the Greene County Historical Society.)

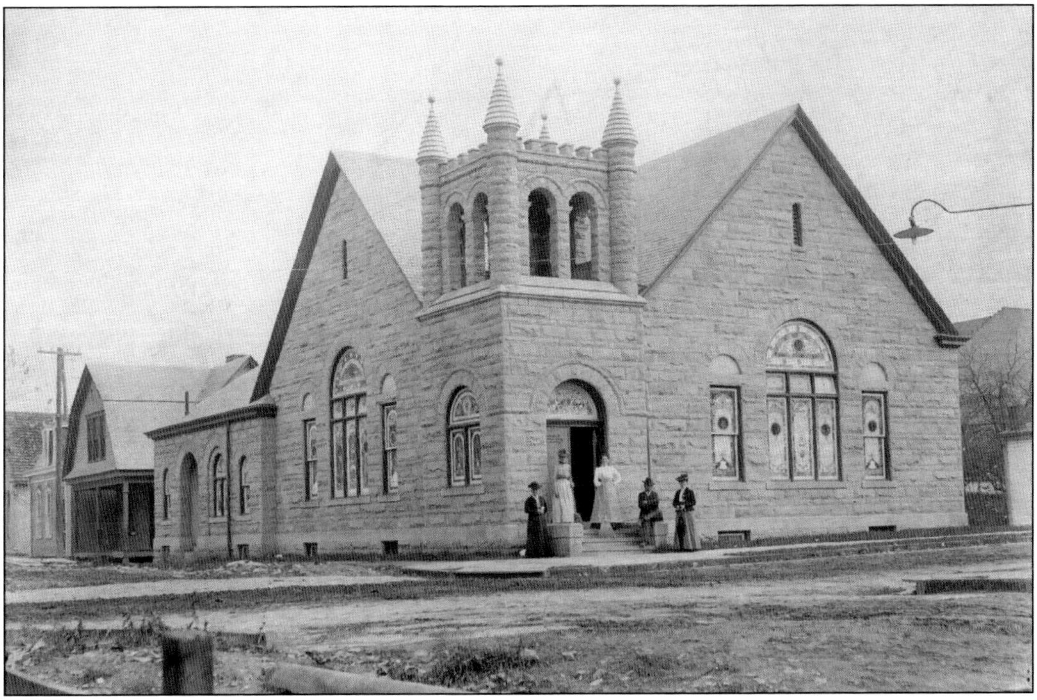

The Christian church is pictured on the corner of Franklin and Morris Streets, before (above) and after (below) the brick pavers were laid. It was dedicated December 15, 1901. The church exterior is constructed of Waynesburg sandstone (bluestone) quarried within five miles of the town. (Above, courtesy of the Greene County Historical Society; below, courtesy of the Waynesburg University Museum.)

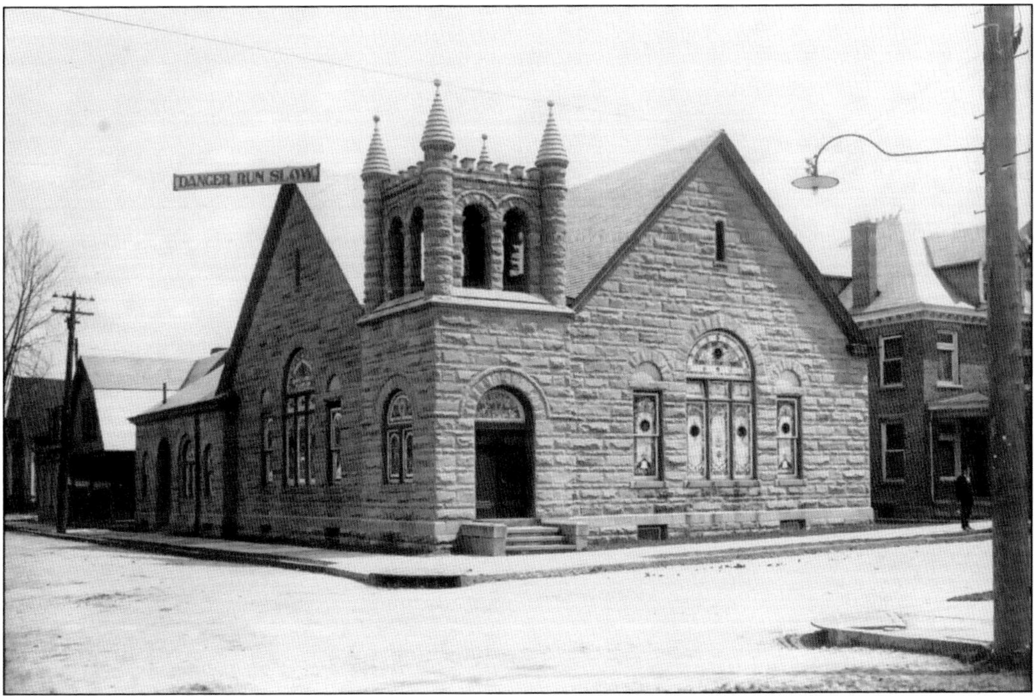

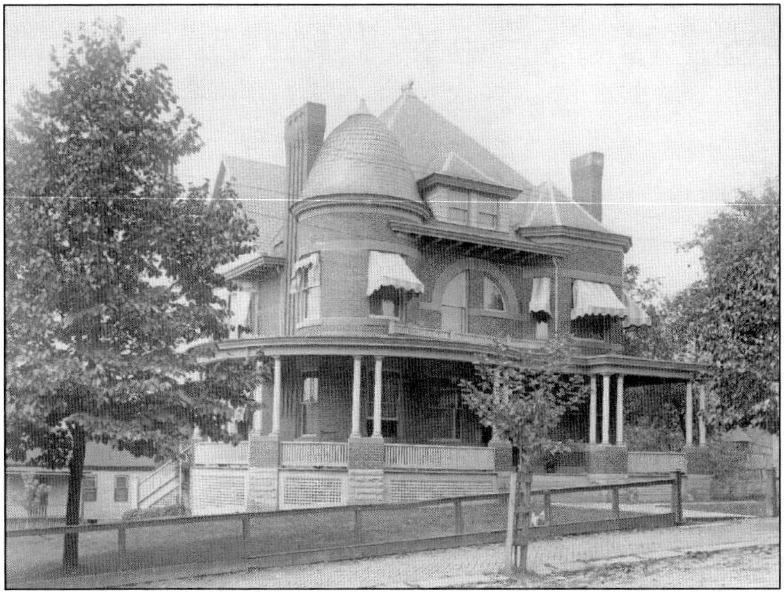

The John T. Rogers family home, later owned by the Albert Sayers family, is on the corner of Morris and College Streets. Today, the house is owned by Waynesburg University and serves as home to the school's president. (Courtesy of the Greene County Historical Society.)

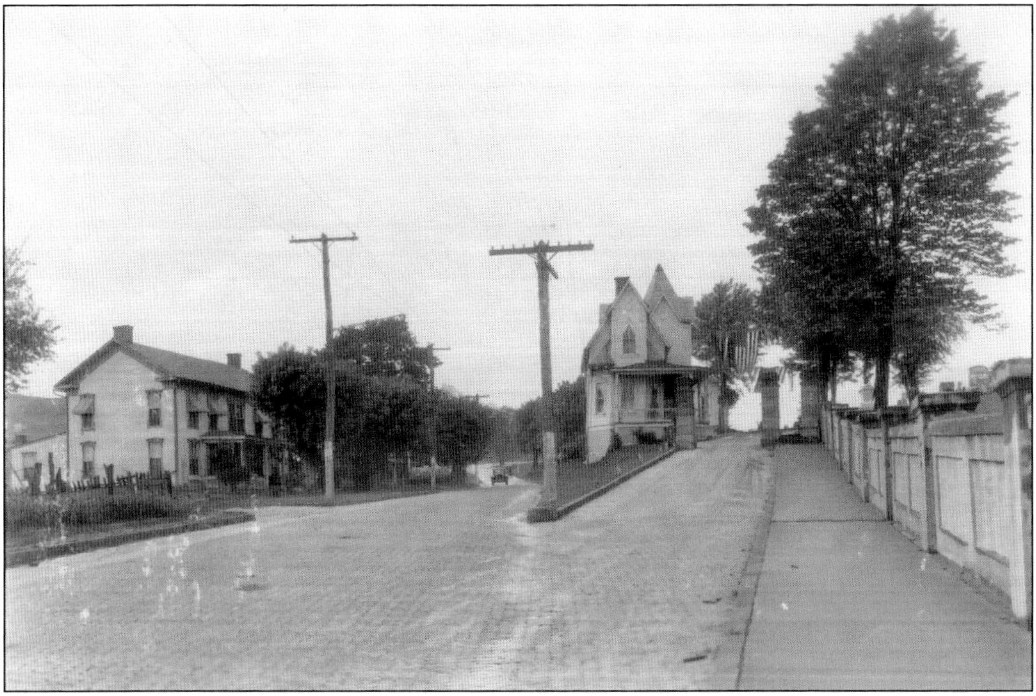

Green Mount Cemetery was established by an act of the General Assembly of the Commonwealth of Pennsylvania on April 15, 1853. Two years later, in 1855, surveying was complete for the original property, and lots were made available for purchase. In 1877, the formed concrete wall and columnar entrance on Morris Street were added. (Courtesy of the Greene County Historical Society.)

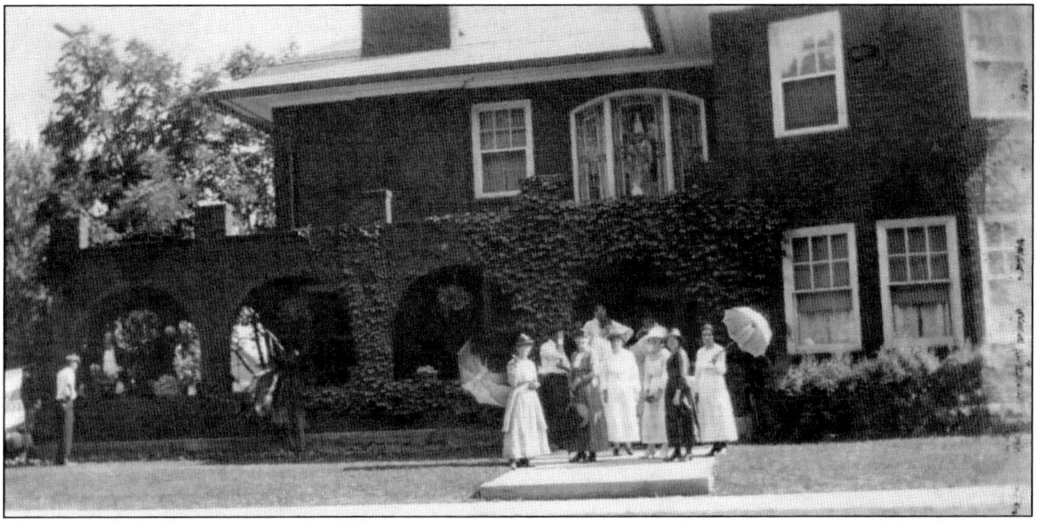

Ladies pose in front of the Robert Ratcliffe and Nancy Annabelle (Jacobs) Headley home on the corner of Wayne and Morris Streets. The house was built by the Headleys in 1906 and later owned by their daughter and son-in-law Grace Edna (Headley) Daugherty and Norval Rogers Daugherty. After the Headley-Daugherty ownership, the house passed to the family of Judge Glenn and Katherine (Throckmorton) Toothman. (Courtesy of Norma Jean Dinsmore.)

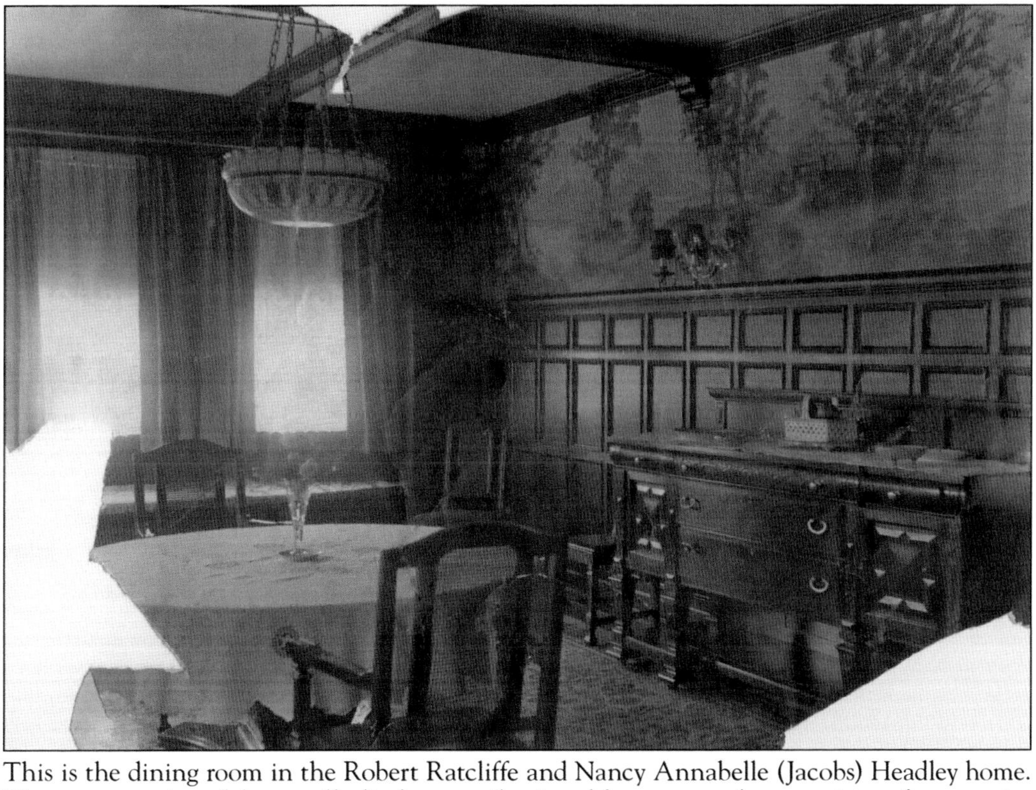

This is the dining room in the Robert Ratcliffe and Nancy Annabelle (Jacobs) Headley home. The upper portion of these walls displays an oil-painted forest scene that transitions from sunrise to sunset. (From the Katherine Jane [Throckmorton] Toothman Collection, courtesy of Glenn Toothman III.).

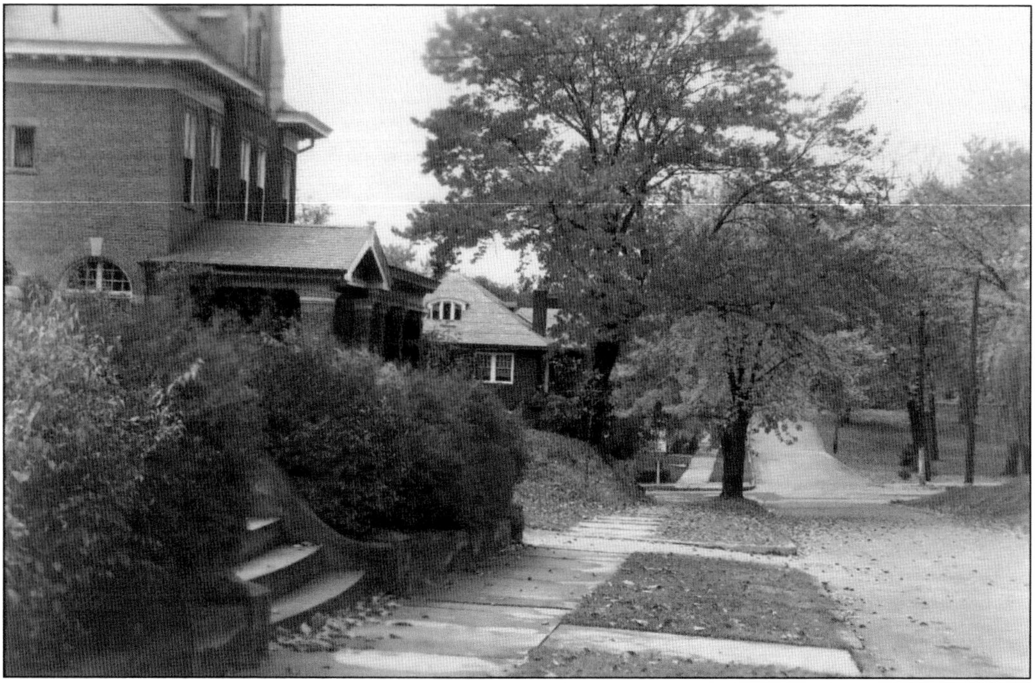

Remodeled in 1915, Sayers Manor (in the left foreground) stands on West Wayne Street, between Morris and Washington Streets. From 1857 to 1891, this was the home of Alfred Brashear and Margaret Kerr (Bell) Miller and their eight children. During much of their lives, College Park was still a part of the cattle-roamed commons. This park was all the distance that separated the Millers from their second home and family, Waynesburg College. Alfred graduated with the first class of men in 1853, then joined the faculty as math professor and ultimately served as president from 1859 to 1899. He met Margaret on campus, where she worked from the opening day as principal of the school's Female Seminary, which, under her leadership, was absorbed by the college, providing a coeducational opportunity for young women to earn bachelor's degrees at Waynesburg as early as 1857. (Both, courtesy of the Greene County Historical Society.)

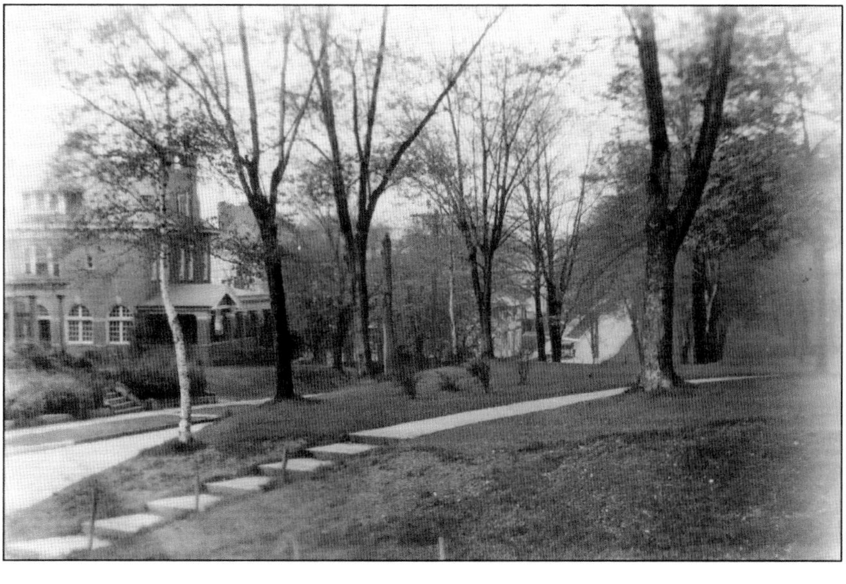

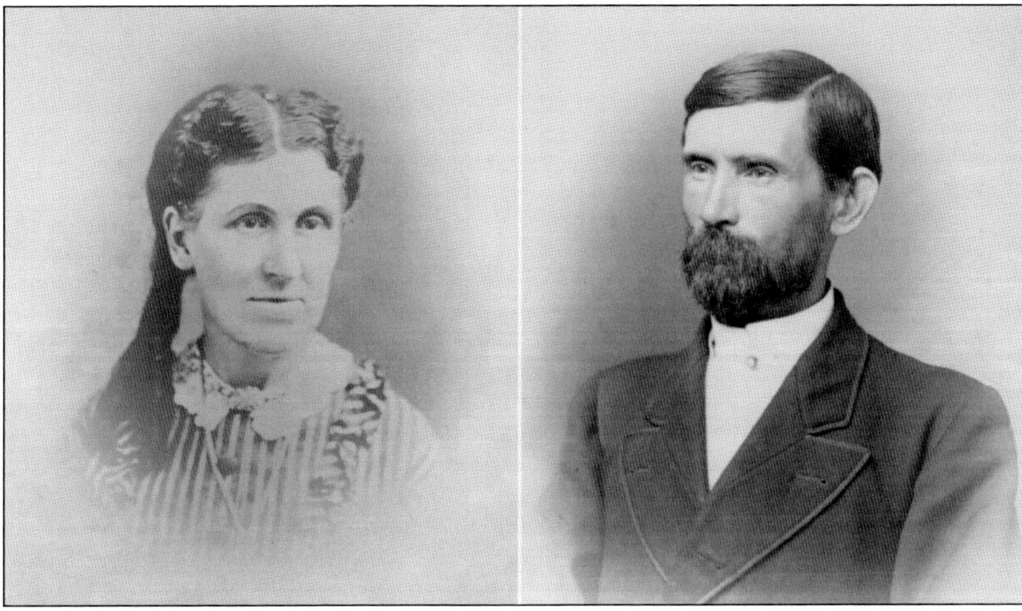

Alfred Brashear and Margaret Kerr (Bell) Miller were a model of marital partnership. While raising their large family, both worked daily, teaching and leading Waynesburg College, as well as laboring together for the social and religious reforms of their day, including abolition and temperance. (Left, photograph by J.H. Rogers; both, from the Robert Silas and Eva Mae [Christie] Merrick Collection, courtesy of Peter Merrick.)

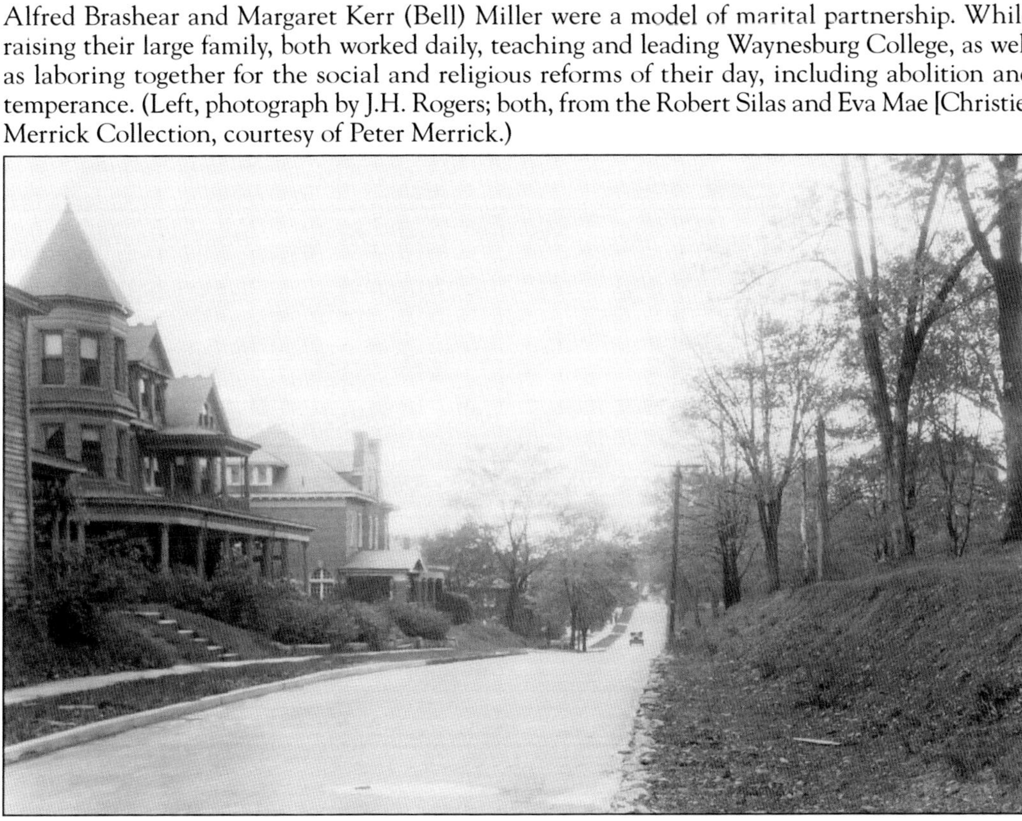

In the foreground next to Sayers Manor is the home built by the Thomas Riley and Bertha (Orndoff) Huffman family. Both houses were demolished by Waynesburg University to allow for the construction of its gymnasium. (Photograph by William E.S. Fletcher, courtesy of the Cornerstone Genealogical Society.)

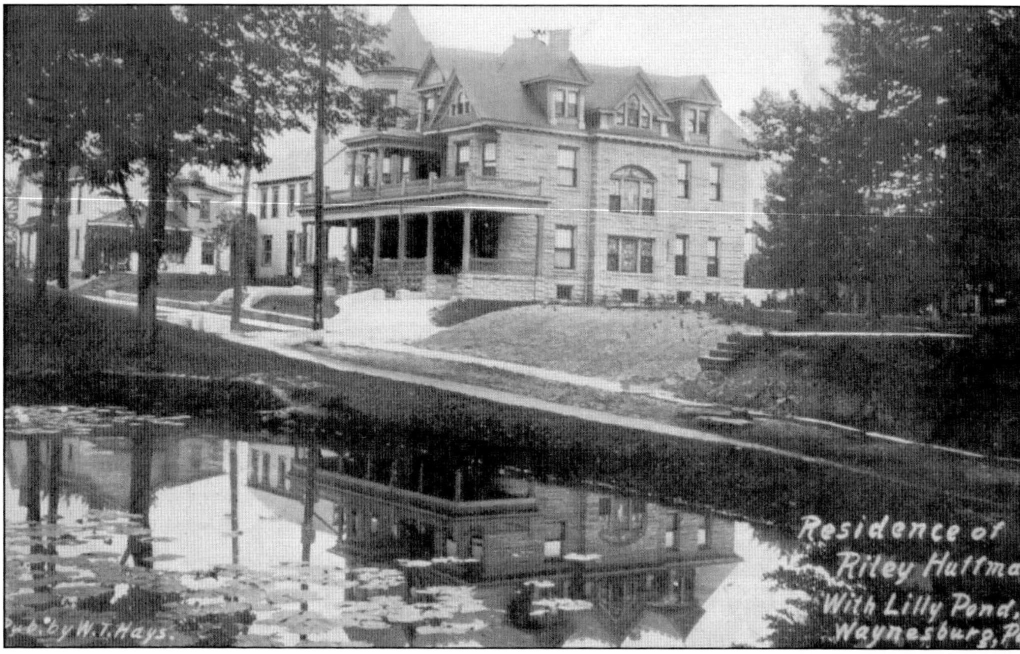

This is another view from College Park of the Thomas Riley Huffman house and neighbors on Wayne Street. The lily pond in the park was affectionately known as "Lake Winetta," for Mary Winetta (Huss) Cooley, whose father, David Rittenhouse Porter Huss, was active in local politics and in the development of the parks. (Photograph by W.T. Hays, from the Walter "Blackie" Markiewich Postcard Collection, courtesy of Brice and Linda Rush.)

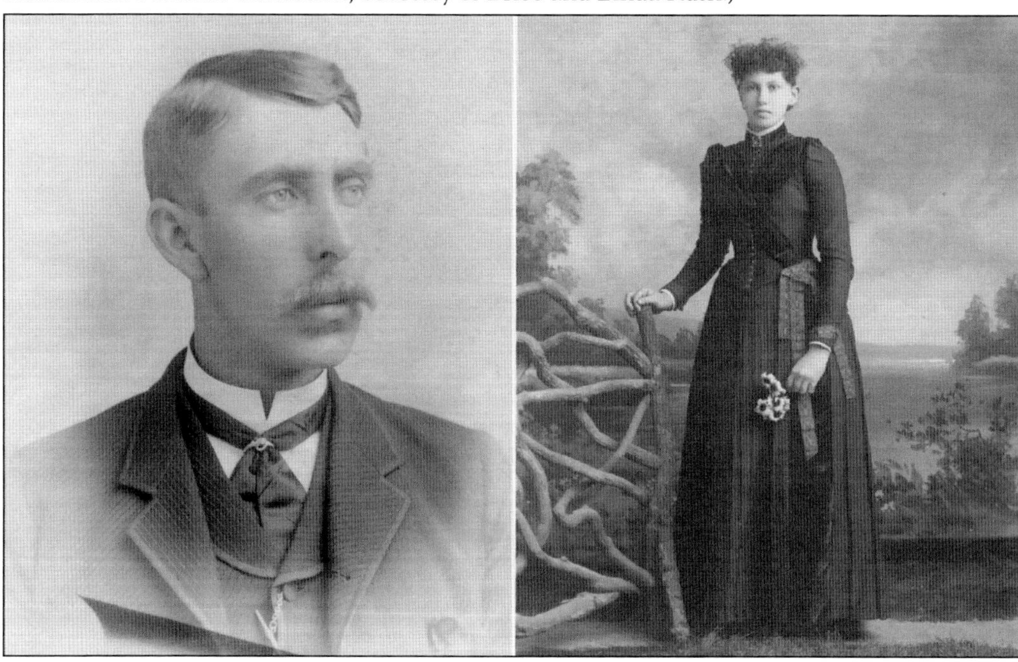

These portraits are of Thomas Riley Huffman and his wife, Bertha (Orndoff) Huffman, whose home overlooked the social activities of College Park. (Photographs by Rogers, courtesy of the Charles Huffman family.)

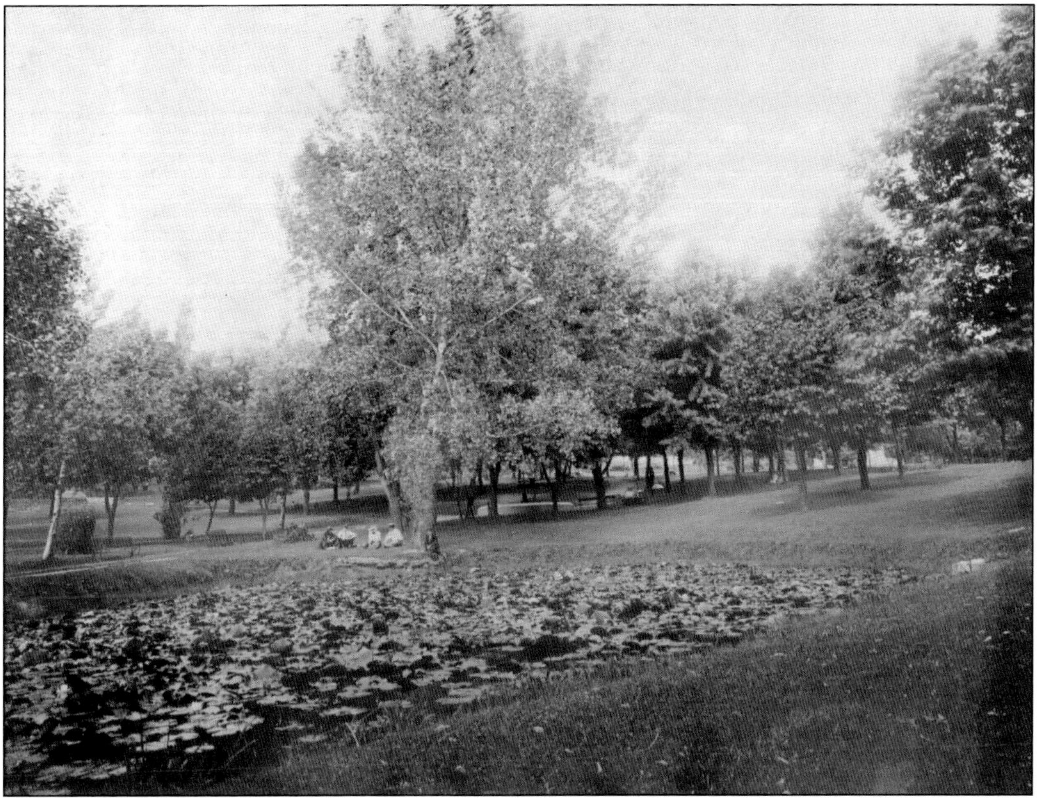

This view of College Park looks across Lake Winetta to the fountain installed in 1894. Mary Winetta (Huss) Cooley was a child during the 1870s when the lily pond named for her was created by Alfred Brashear Miller and his students to use as a reservoir while they dug clay to form the 1,400,012 bricks used in the new college building, Miller Hall. (Photograph by *Waynesburg Semi-Weekly Messenger*, courtesy of Matt W. Cumberledge.)

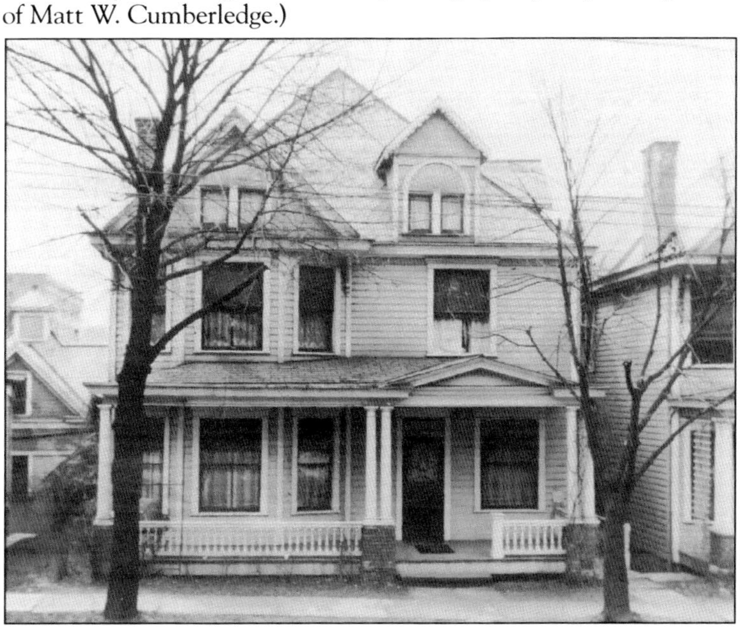

The Anna Rinehart family home, located on Wayne Street, was later the location of Warrior Trail Preschool. Today, this area is the site of the Waynesburg University Center for Research and Economic Development. (Courtesy of the Greene County Historical Society.)

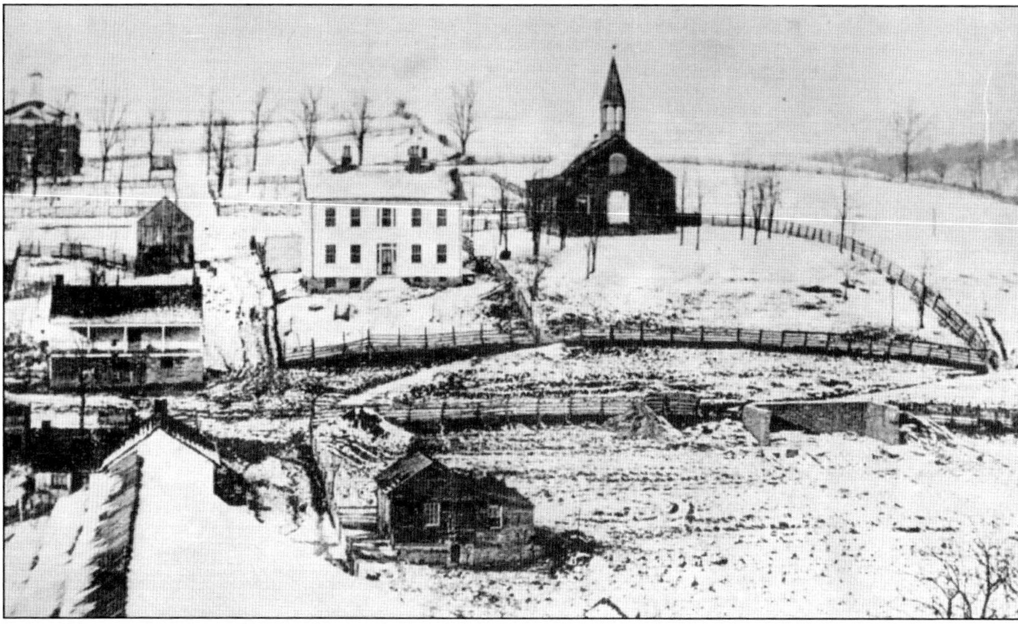

To soldiers returning home from the Civil War, the northern view from High Street looking toward the commons would have appeared much like this. In the upper left is Union School, later known as North Ward, built in 1864. To the right, the old Cumberland Presbyterian Church, also known as the Church on the Hill, was built in 1832 on what became Wayne Street. (Courtesy of the Greene County Historical Society.)

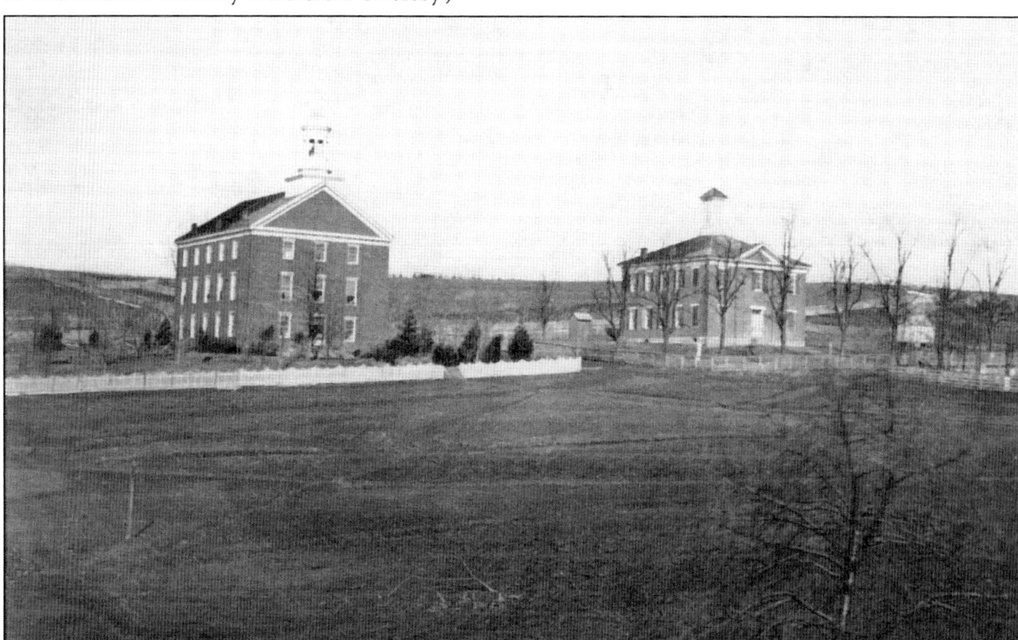

In the 1860s, Hanna Hall (left), built in 1850, and Union School (right), built in 1864, abutted the northern boundary of the commons, where livestock roamed and the Commons Cemetery, though overcrowded, was still in use. The edge of the graveyard can be seen here in front of Union School, where Monument Park is today. (Courtesy of Waynesburg Borough.)

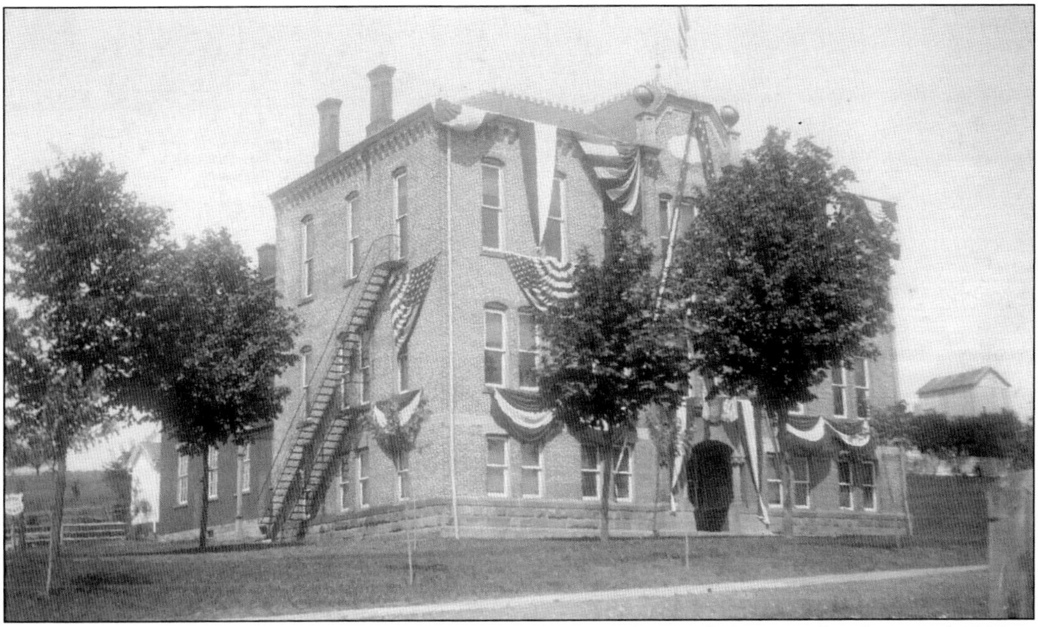

The Waynesburg public school teachers and staff pose in front of Union School around 1898, a time of growth in the public school system. From left to right are (first row) Anne Eliza Hedge, Sarah "Sallie" (Cooke) Sayers, Alpharetta (Bayne) Neven, Helen Margaret Day, Flora (Bridges) Sayers, Louisa Mary (Rinehart) Abell, and Sarah "Sadie" (Babbitt) Butler; (second row) Nora Mae (Summersgill) High, Alice Belle Baer, Nellie Wells Donley, Amanda Louise Hoge, and Ruth (Montgomery) Titus; (third row) Mabel Hammond (Kline) Norris, principal G.P. Gilmer, Music Professor Frank Davis Meanor, Janitor Dawson Adams McCurdy, and Charity Louise "Lou" Teagarden. (Both, courtesy of the Greene County Historical Society.)

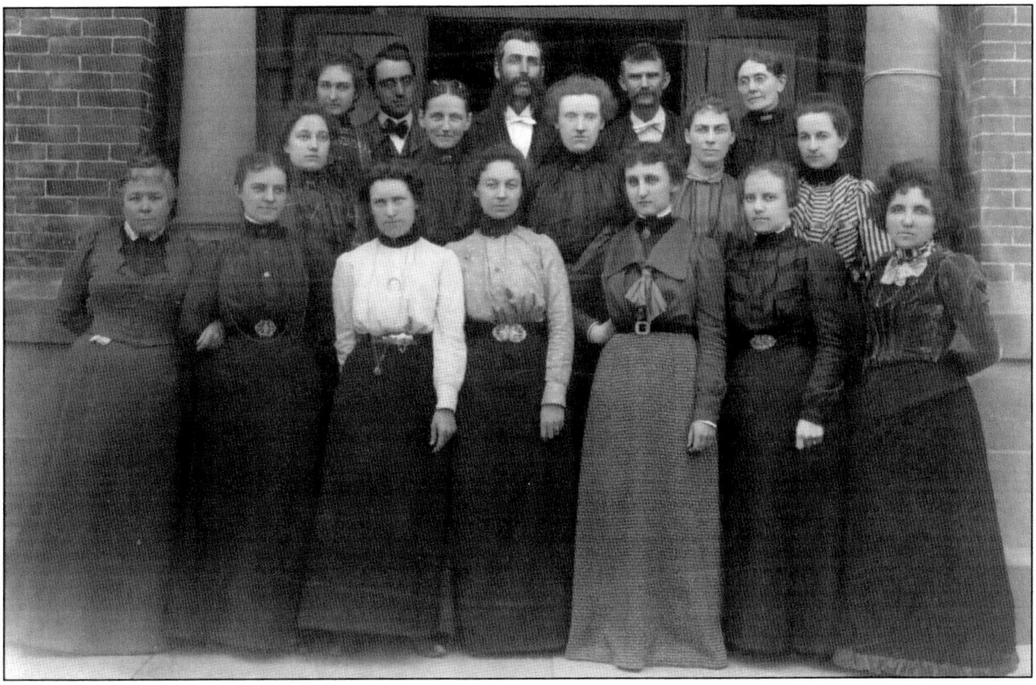

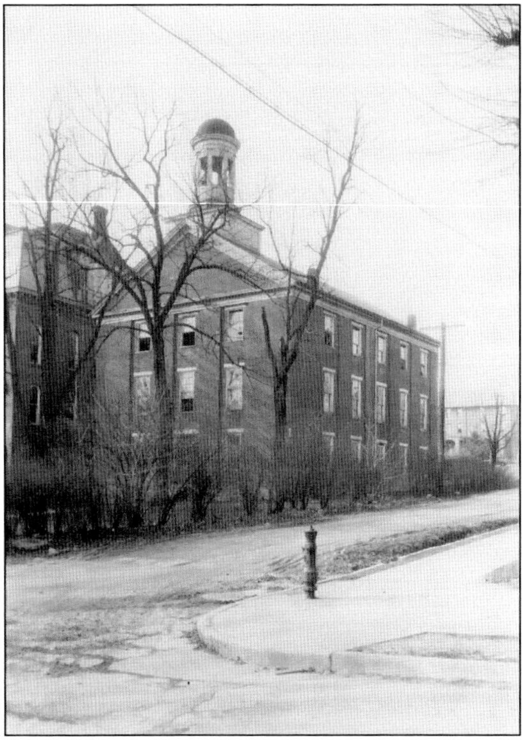

Hanna Hall, built 1850, was the first building on the Waynesburg College campus. It was named in the spring of 1902 after Rev. William Hanna provided a generous gift to allow for significant repairs. (Photograph by William E.S. Fletcher, courtesy of the Cornerstone Genealogical Society.)

The new teachers graduating from Waynesburg College Normal School, class of 1885, pose here with their instructors in front of Hanna Hall. On the far left of the first row sits Waynesburg College president Alfred Brashear Miller, and to his right is Prof. Ezra Degarmo Stewart (father of future Waynesburg College president Paul Rich "Prexy" Stewart). (Courtesy of Candice Lynn Buchanan.)

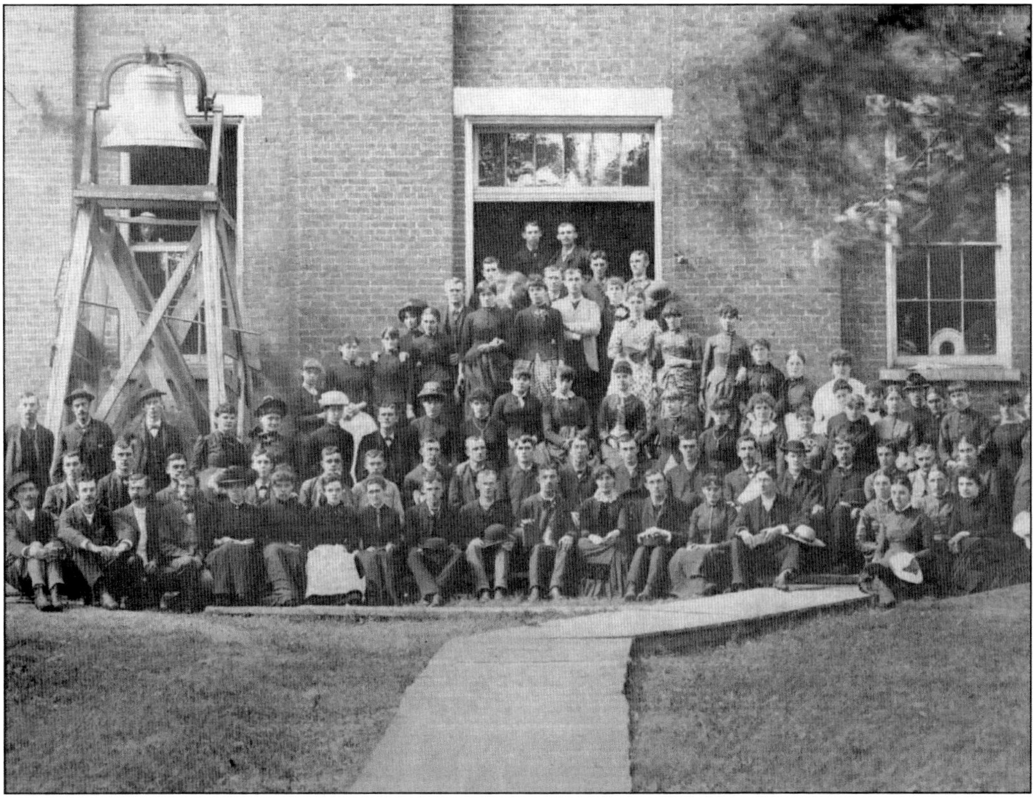

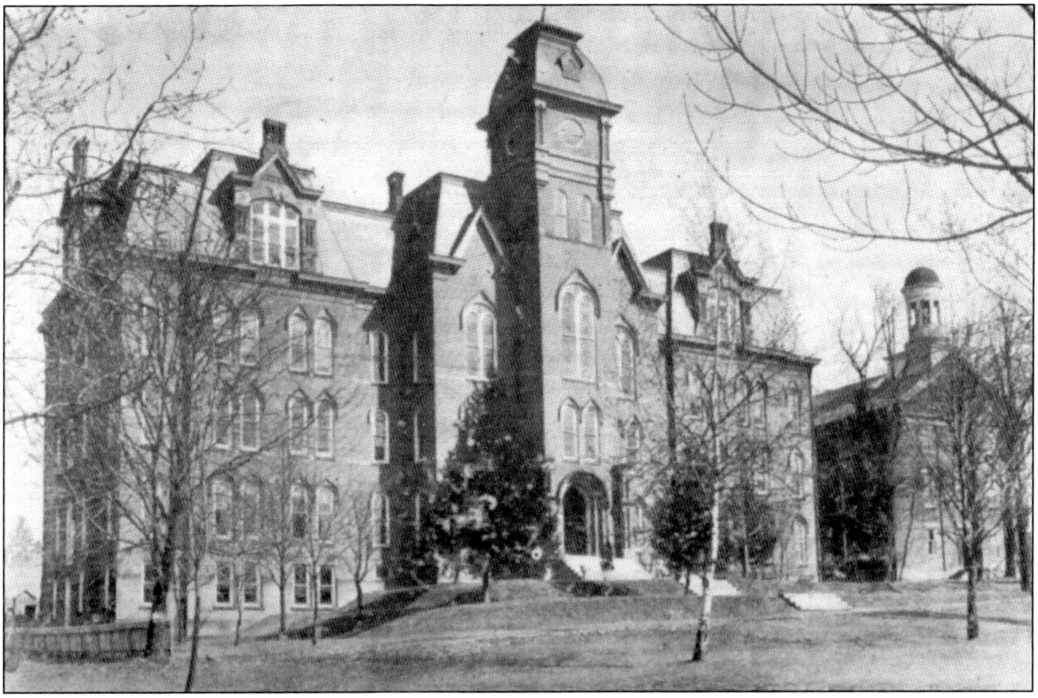

Miller Hall (left) and Hanna Hall on the Waynesburg College campus are seen here. Chimney flues on the roof of Miller Hall in this picture are no longer in place; otherwise, it looks much the same today. (From the Walter "Blackie" Markiewich Postcard Collection, courtesy of Brice and Linda Rush.)

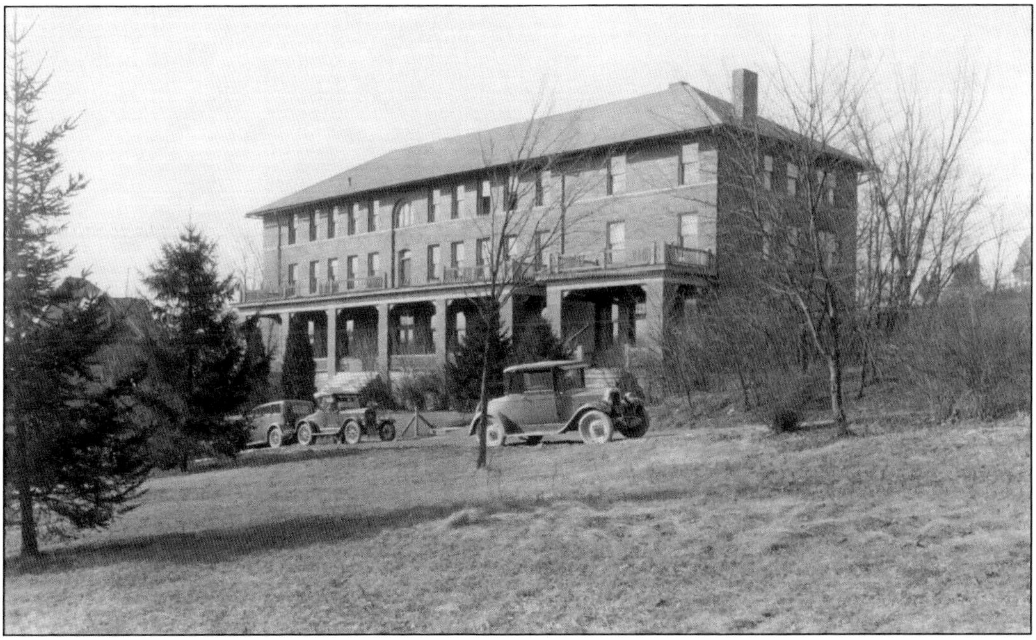

Walton Hall was a Waynesburg College residence hall located approximately where the current parking lot exists when one exits Denny Hall to the east. (Photograph by William E.S. Fletcher, courtesy of the Cornerstone Genealogical Society.)

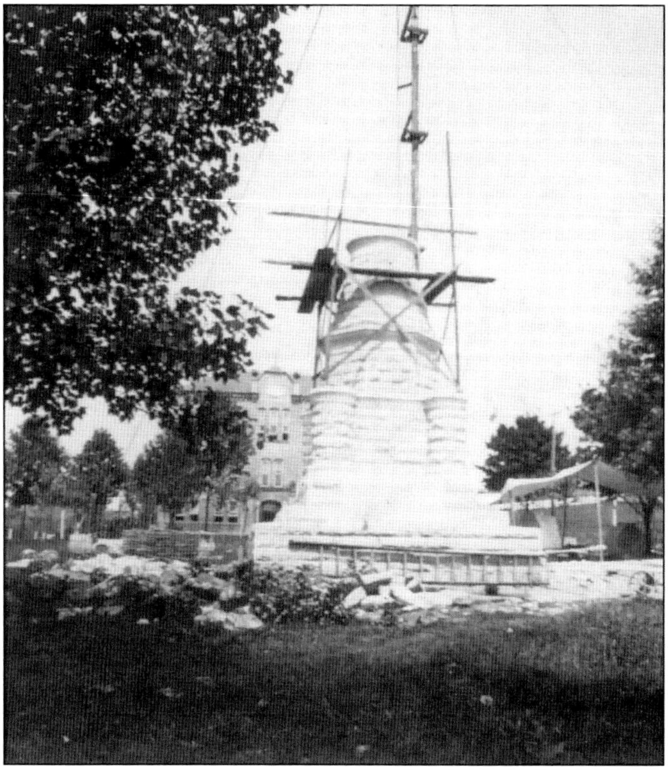

The Soldiers' and Sailors' Monument in Monument Park honors Greene County's Civil War soldiers. Arthur Inghram Rinehart prepared the design for the 65-foot-high feature on a 16-foot-square base, with 7-foot-tall statues at each corner, representing Union veterans from the infantry, the cavalry, the artillery, and the Navy. The final feature in his proposal was a tall shaft that would extend above the base and be topped with a woman, 14 feet in height, holding a wreath of olive branches to represent Lady Liberty. The cornerstone was laid July 4, 1898, and dedication occurred one year later on July 4, 1899. (Left, courtesy of Carl Headlee; below, photograph by *Waynesburg Semi-Weekly Messenger*, courtesy of Matt W. Cumberledge.)

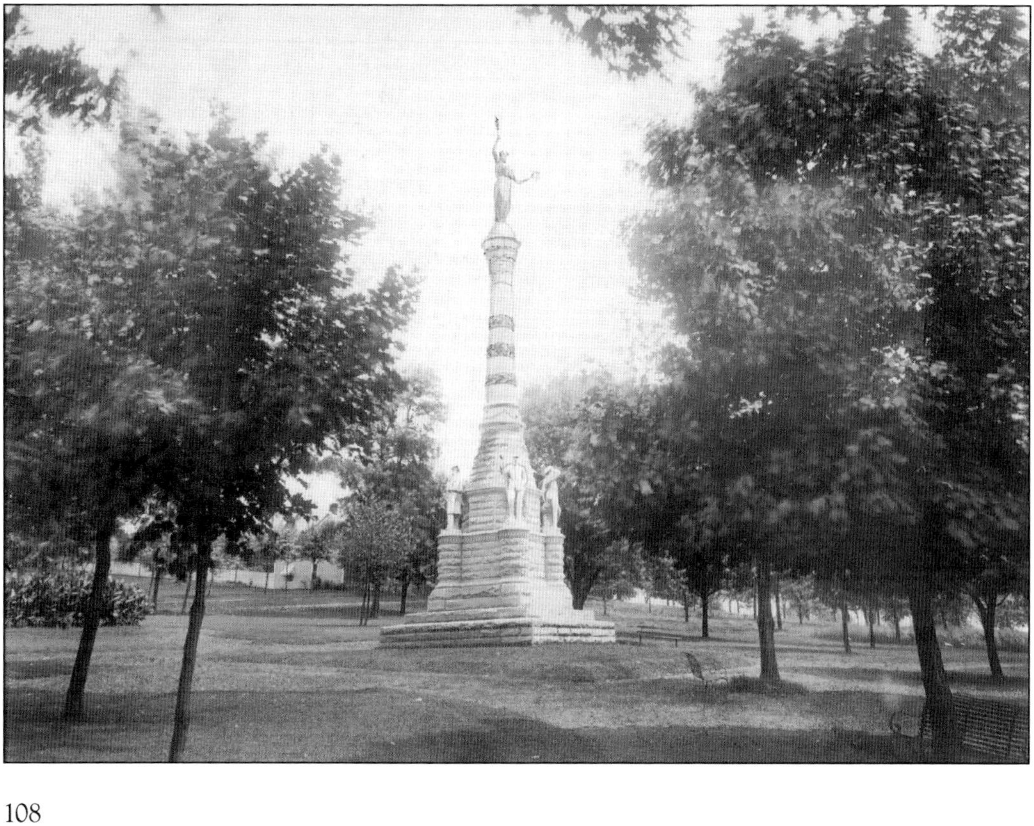

Four

Life on the South Side

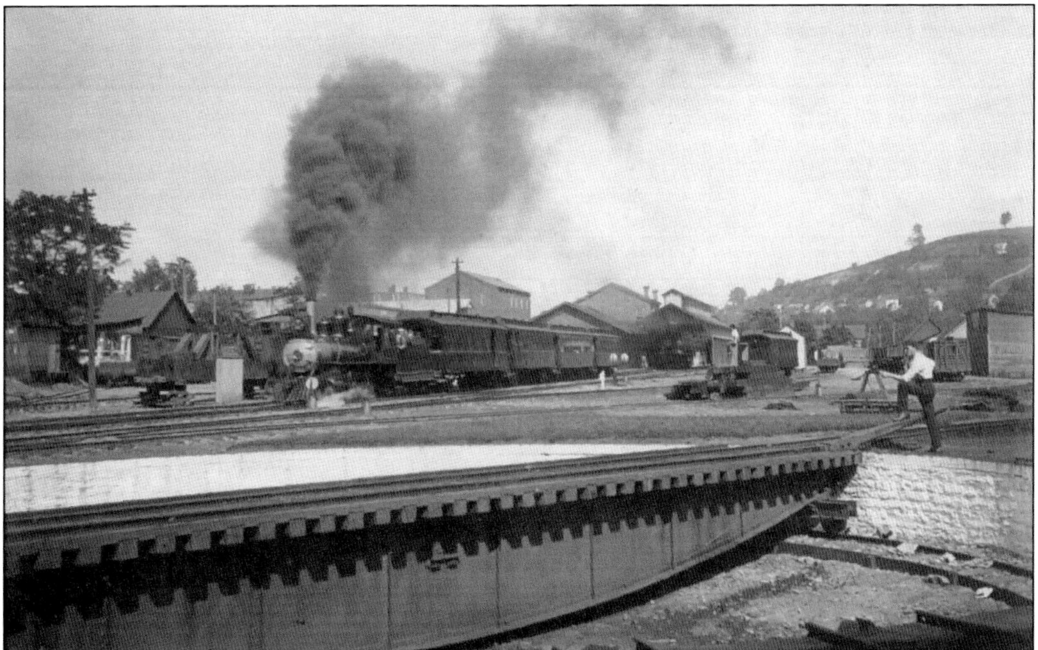

This is a unique view of the Waynesburg & Washington Railroad roundhouse turning table. A handwritten inscription on the back reads, "January 3 1907 / Warm Spring / Round House Turning Table / to Turn Engines around / By Man Power." (Courtesy of the Waynesburg University Museum and James Weinschenker.)

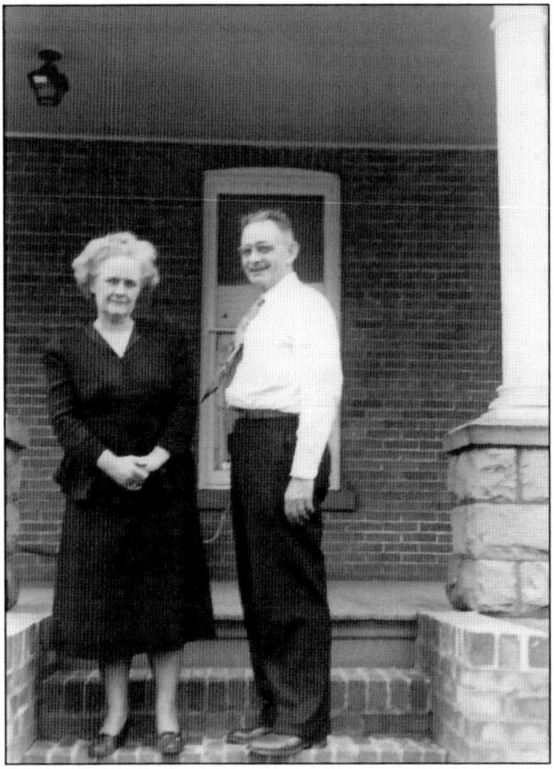

Local historian Howard Louis Leckey Sr. (1892–1951) and his wife, Helen Delilah (Patton) Leckey (1893–1964), stand on the steps of their home at the corner of West Greene and Richhill Streets. Howard was a Waynesburg pharmacist and the author of *The Tenmile Country and Its Pioneer Families: A Genealogical History of the Upper Monongahela Valley.* (Both, courtesy of Candace [Leckey] McPheron.)

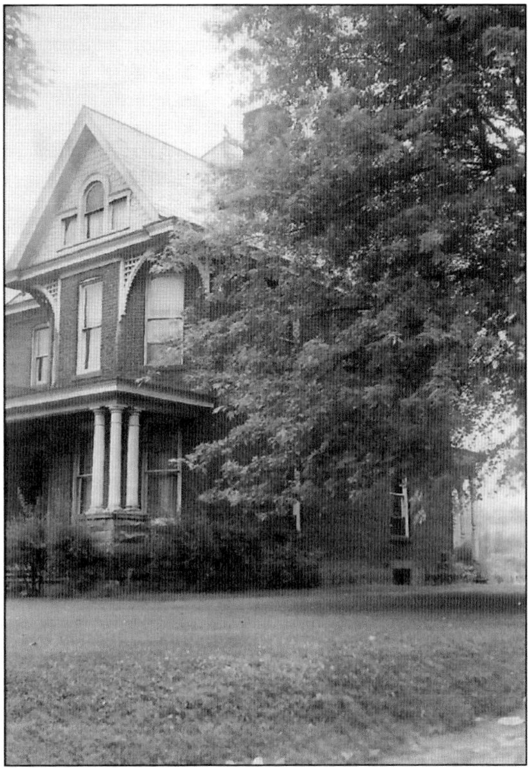

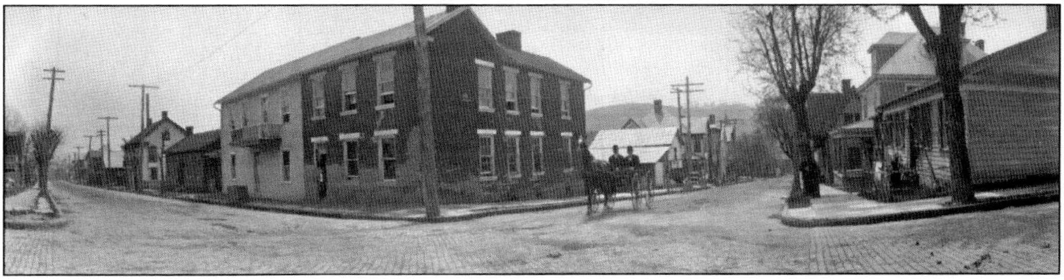

Seen in this view of the intersection at Greene and South Morris Streets, the buildings on the corner at the center of the photograph were later razed, and the current post office was constructed at this location. (Courtesy of the Greene County Historical Society.)

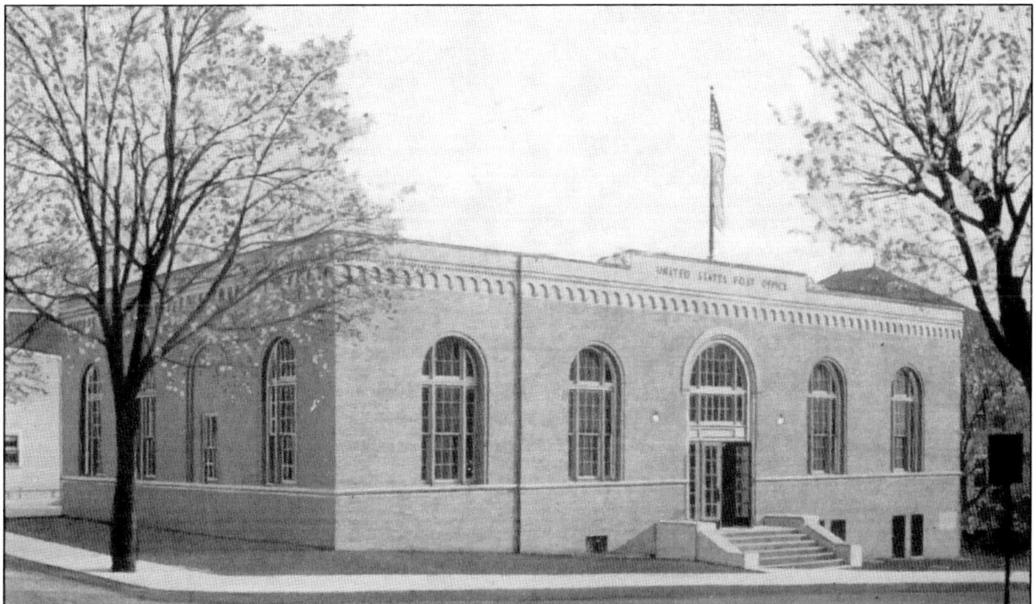

The Waynesburg Post Office, pictured at its present location on the corner of Greene and Morris Streets, was opened June 6, 1931. (From the Walter "Blackie" Markiewich Postcard Collection, courtesy of Brice and Linda Rush.)

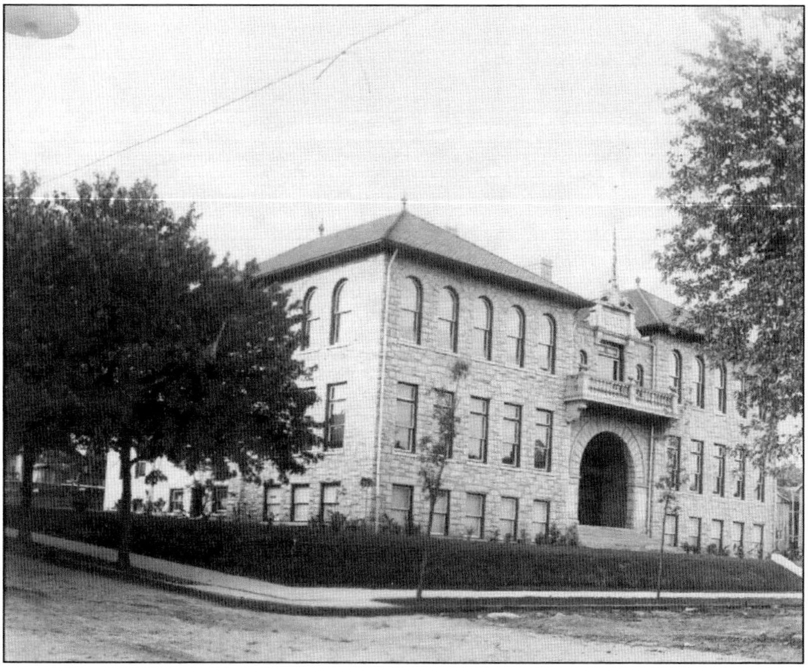

Construction of South Ward School began in August 1900 from locally quarried sandstone. The building was ready for classes to begin in the fall of 1901. Today, the former school is used as apartments. (Courtesy of the Greene County Historical Society.)

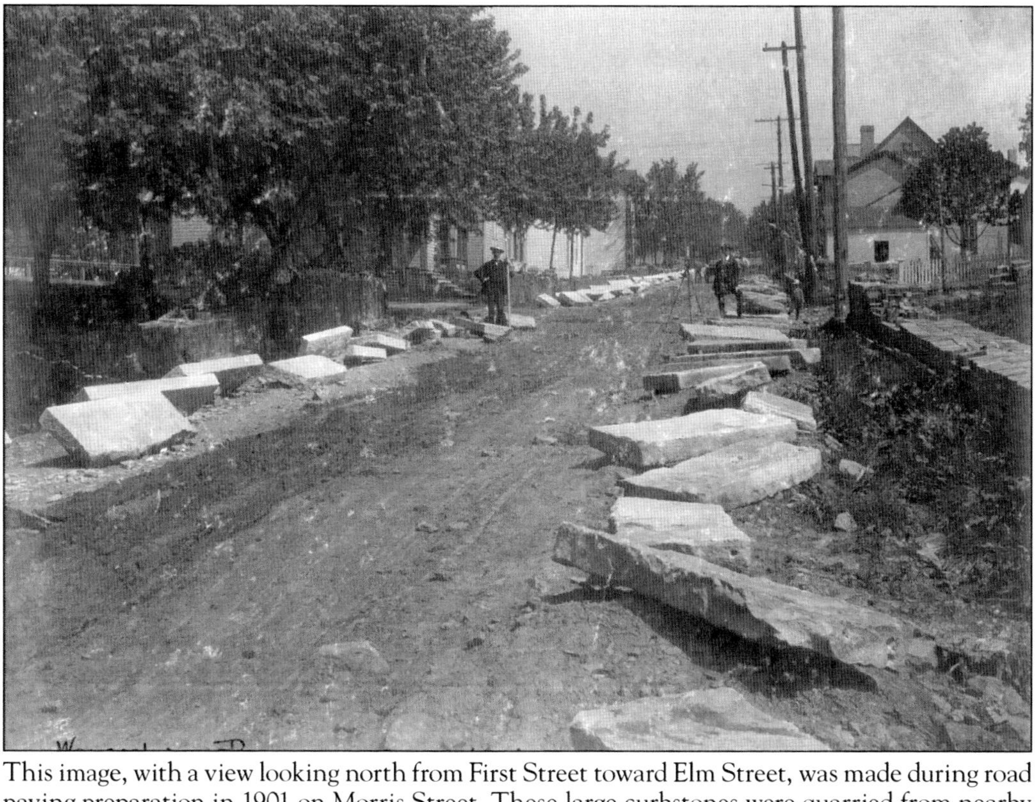

This image, with a view looking north from First Street toward Elm Street, was made during road paving preparation in 1901 on Morris Street. These large curbstones were quarried from nearby locations and delivered along the construction path for installation. (From the George David Jenkins Collection, courtesy of the Greene County Historical Society.)

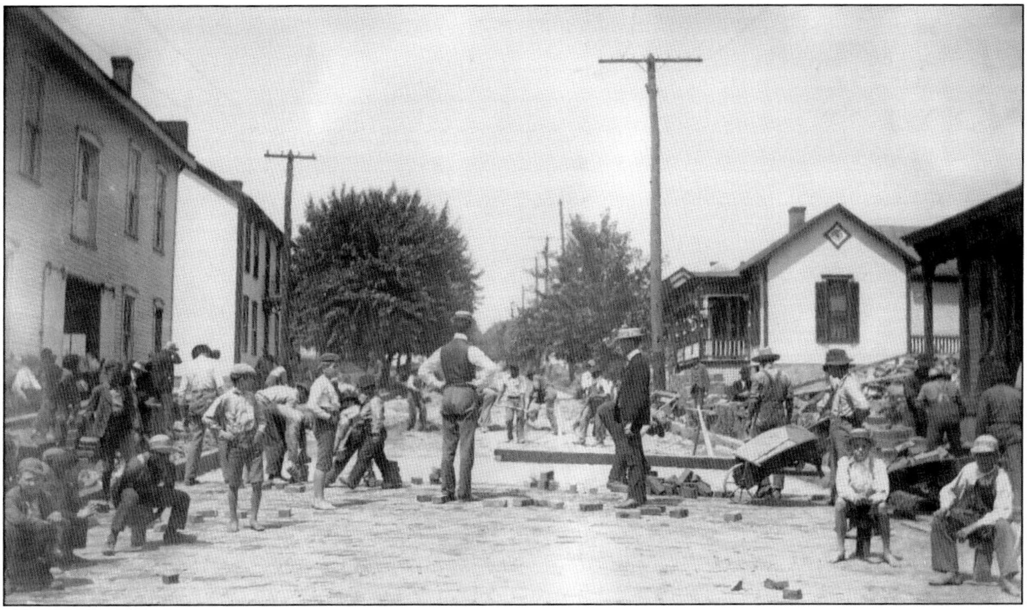

The view in this c. 1901 photograph looks north from Lincoln Street toward Greene Street and shows road paving on Morris Street. Engineer George Jenkins (hands on hips in the center) is seen supervising the work. (From the George David Jenkins Collection, courtesy of the Greene County Historical Society.)

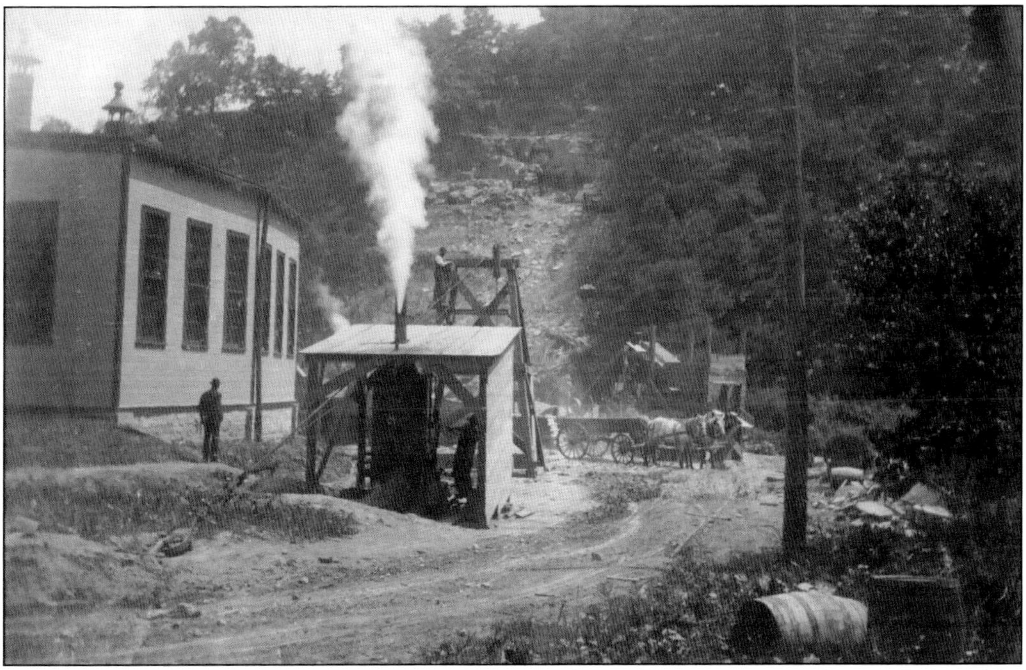

This is a photograph of the stone quarry on Duvall's Hill across Ten Mile Creek from the Waynesburg & Washington Railroad depot in 1901. The stone was conveyed across the creek on a large steel wire to this stone crusher located at the foot of Morris Street. This stone provided both the road and sewer line bases for the town. (From the George David Jenkins Collection, courtesy of the Greene County Historical Society.)

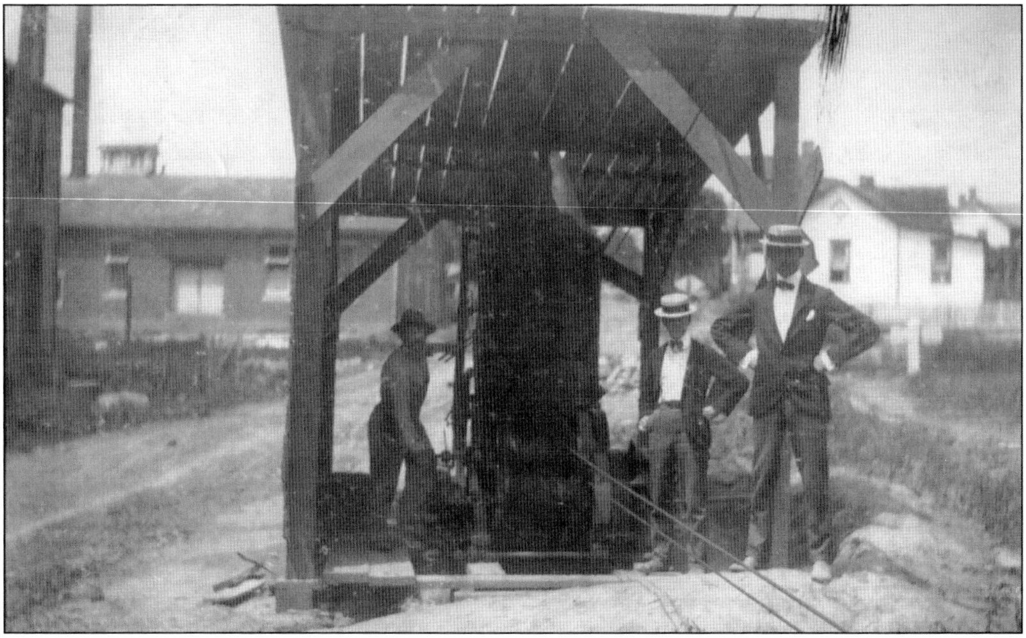

In this 1901 photograph, a hoisting engineer powers the pulley system, which conveys the bulk stone from the quarry across the creek via buckets attached to a large steel wire to the stone crusher located at the foot of Morris Street. (From the George David Jenkins Collection, courtesy of the Greene County Historical Society.)

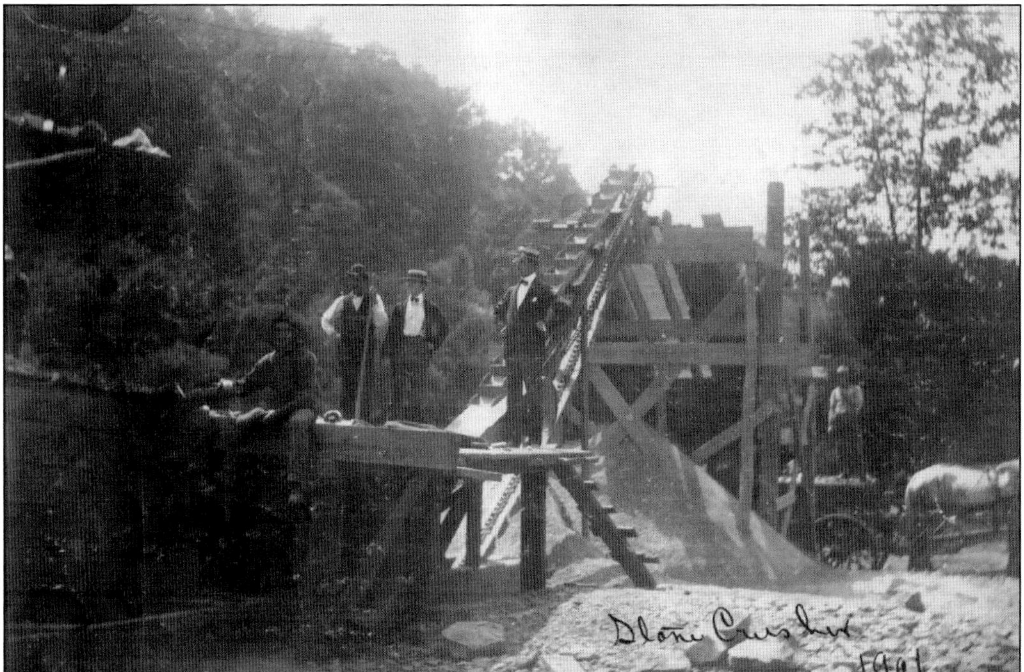

This is a photograph of the stone crusher at the foot of Morris Street in 1901. It served as a temporary work station adjacent to the north side of Ten Mile Creek, where Morris Street begins. (From the George David Jenkins Collection, courtesy of the Greene County Historical Society.)

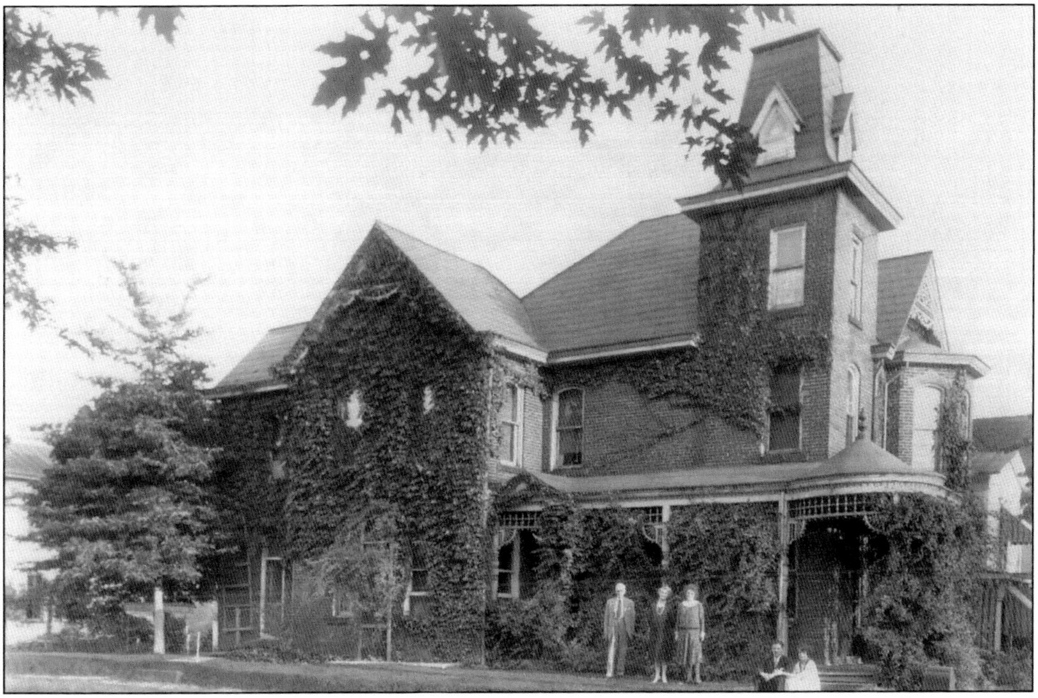

Seen here is the John D. and Caroline (Helphenstine) McKahan family home on the corner of Washington and Elm Streets. Pictured, from left to right, are John D. and Caroline (Helphenstine) McKahan, their daughter Laura (McKahan) Long, Edward Carothers Jr., and Carothers's wife Leah (McKahan) (Carothers) Ellenberger. The home later belonged to Caroline's niece, Caroline (McCormick) (Hurst) Grimm, daughter of Sarah (Helphenstine) McCormick. (Courtesy of the Greene County Historical Society.)

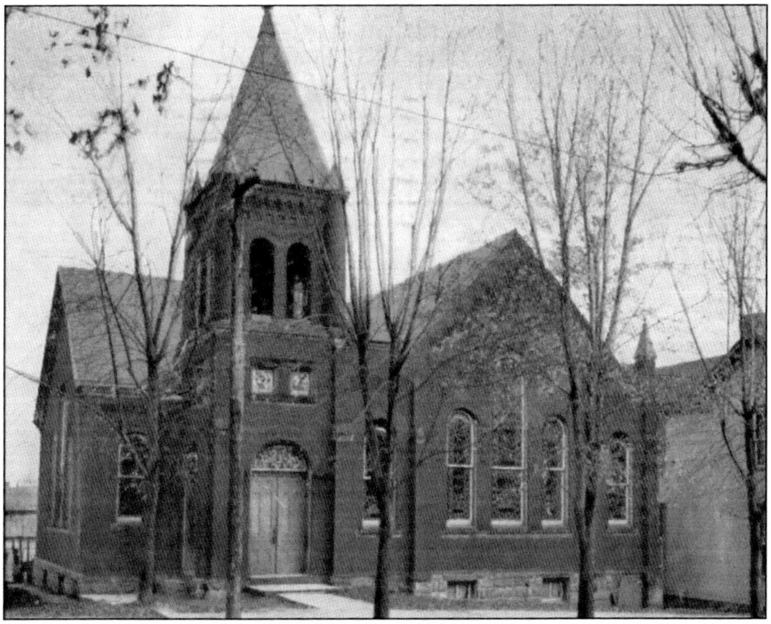

The Methodist Protestant Church on the corner of South and Washington Streets was dedicated on Sunday, July 30, 1893. In honor of the event, news accounts say that no other services were held by community churches; they encouraged all of their members to attend the dedication. (From the Walter "Blackie" Markiewich Postcard Collection, courtesy of Brice and Linda Rush.)

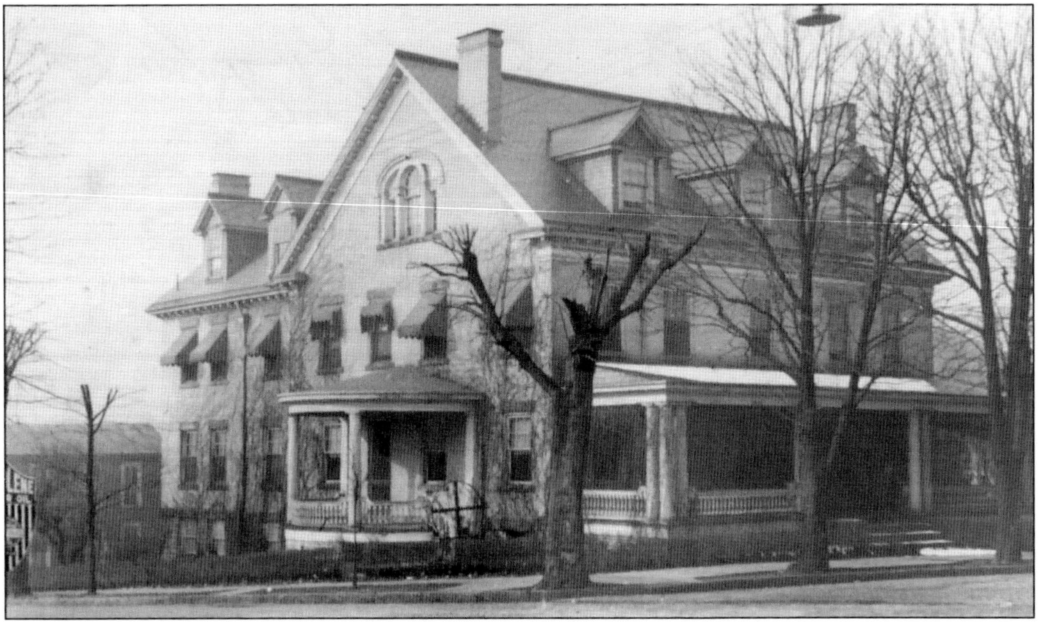

Ivyhurst was the home of Robinson Franklin Downey and his wife, Ella Jean "Jennie" (Wilson) (Lindsey) Downey. It was located on the southwest corner of Greene and Washington Streets, where Community Bank stands today. After Mrs. Downey's death in 1934, the home belonged to Waynesburg College, which housed its music department there until 1967, when Ivyhurst was sold and destroyed to make room for a gas station. (Courtesy of the Waynesburg University Museum.)

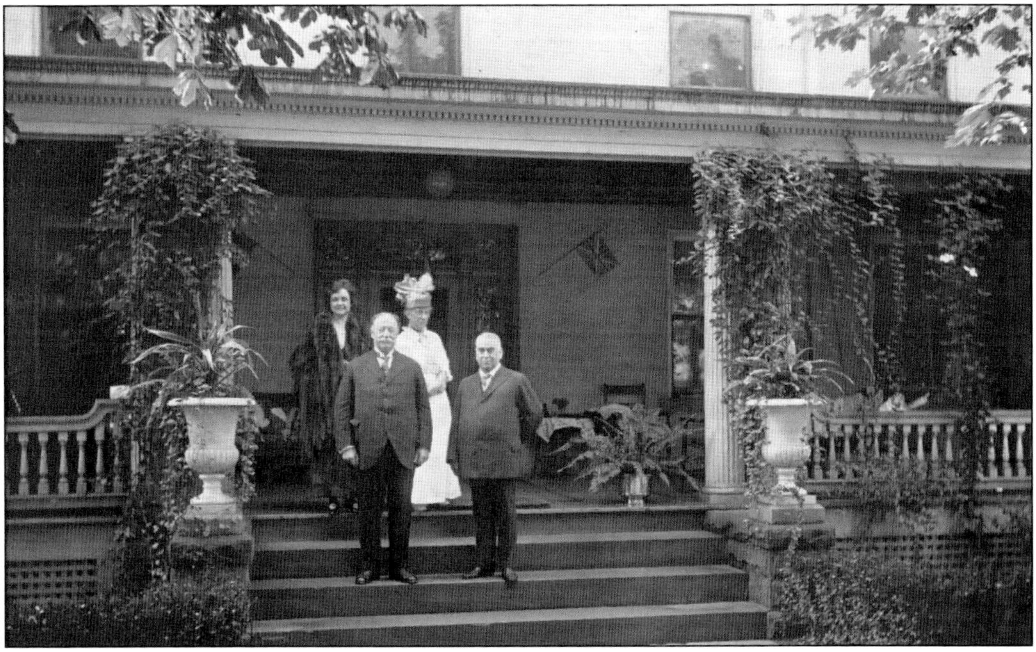

Posing on the steps of Ivyhurst during a presidential visit to Waynesburg on November 4, 1919, are, from left to right, First Lady Helen Louise "Nellie" (Herron) Taft, Pres. William H. Taft, Ella Jean "Jennie" (Wilson) (Lindsey) Downey, and Robinson Franklin Downey. (Courtesy of the Greene County Historical Society.)

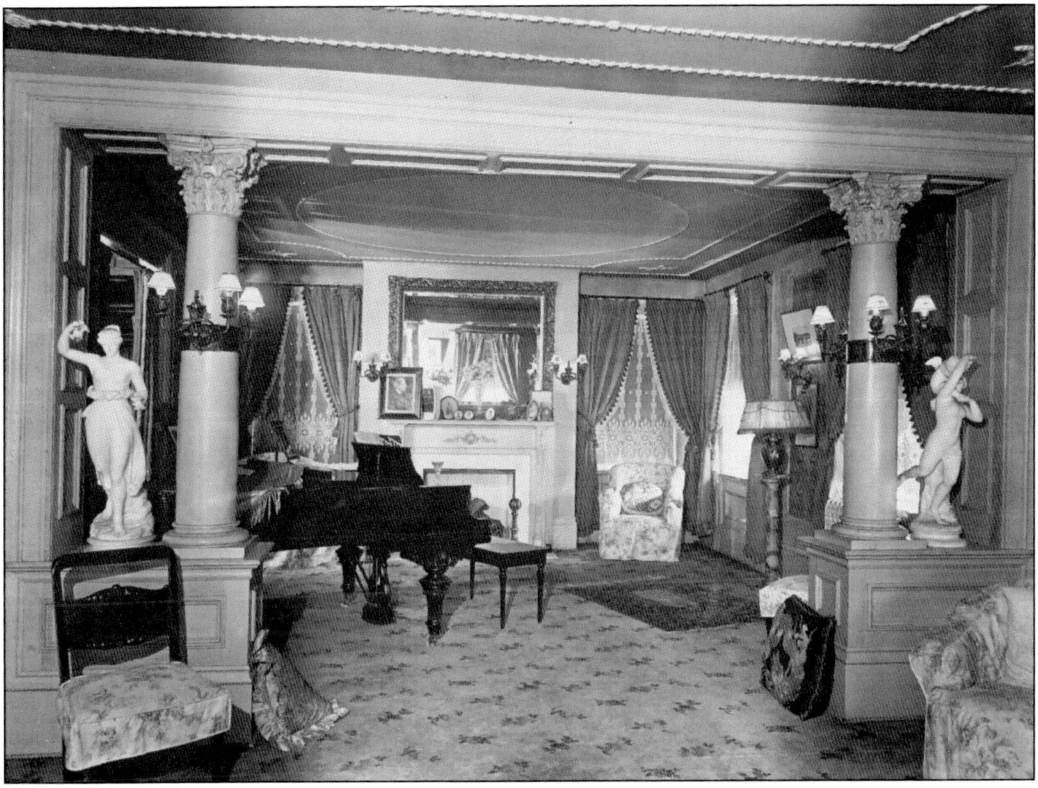

This glimpse inside the ornate rooms of Ivyhurst makes it easy to understand how the Downeys were able to host such socialite guests as Pres. William H. Taft, Woodrow Wilson's vice president Thomas Marshall, politician William Jennings Bryan, and Pres. Calvin Coolidge's wife, Grace Coolidge. Above is a view of the family's music room, and below is a shot of the upstairs hallway. The stained-glass window above the staircase was one of the artifacts to be saved when the house was torn down and is on display at the Waynesburg University Museum. (Both, courtesy of the Greene County Historical Society.)

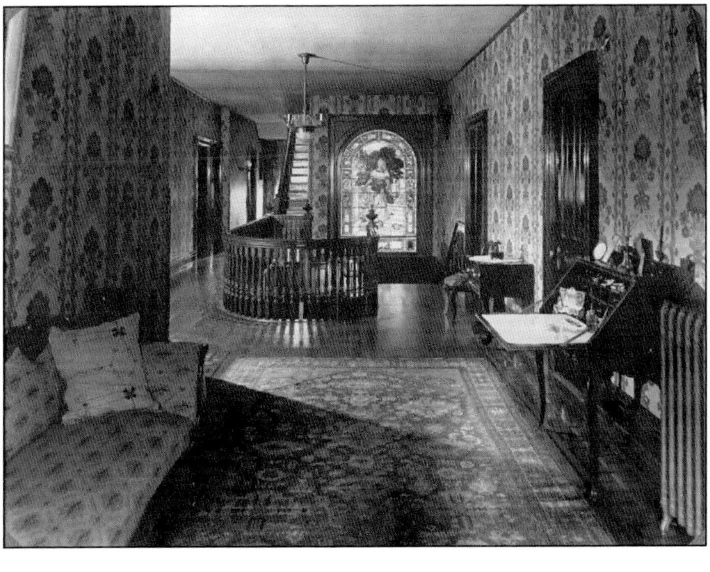

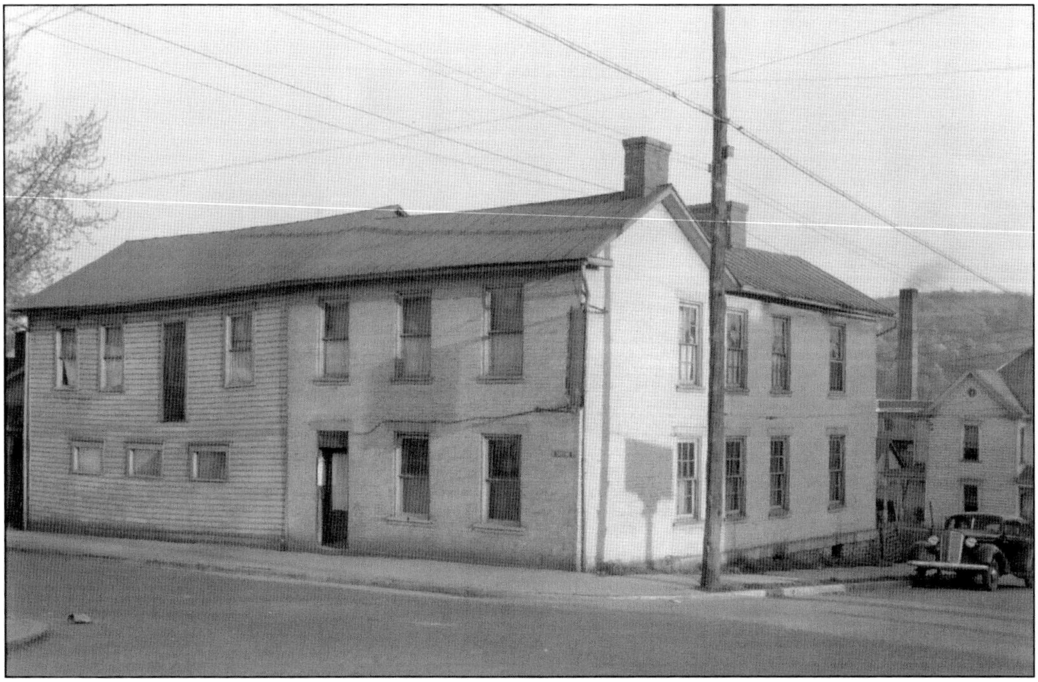

This image shows the former Lemley Hotel at the corner of Greene and Morgan Streets. Today, this corner is the location of the Moose Lodge and the Waynesburg Volunteer Fire Department. (Photograph by William E.S. Fletcher, courtesy of the Cornerstone Genealogical Society.)

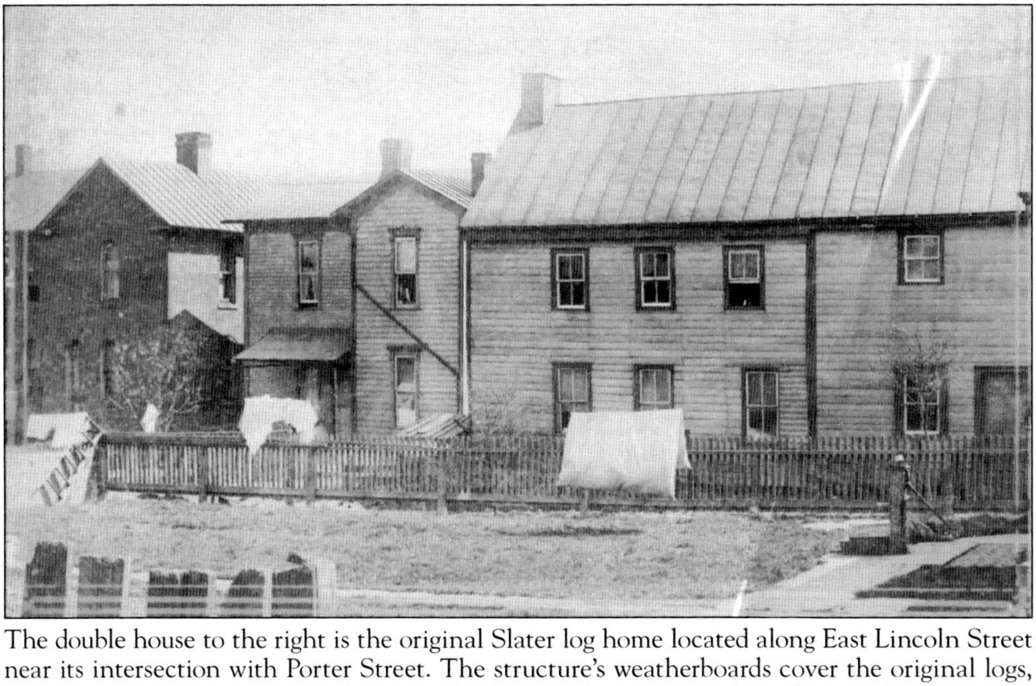

The double house to the right is the original Slater log home located along East Lincoln Street near its intersection with Porter Street. The structure's weatherboards cover the original logs, but the buildings have all since been razed. Thomas Slater was the first white settler on the site of Waynesburg under a Pennsylvania warrant, dated March 1789. (Photograph by J.H. Rogers, courtesy of the Greene County Historical Society.)

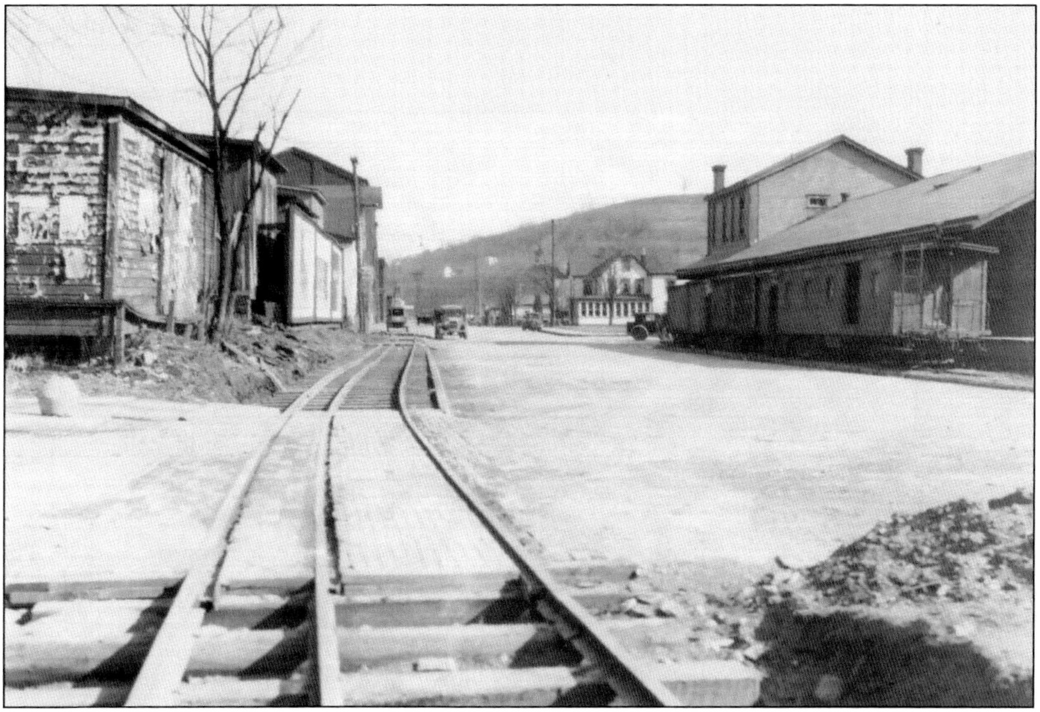

This is a view of First Street, looking east toward Washington and Morgan Streets from Morris Street. To the left are Fairmont Creamery and Waynesburg Milling, and to the right are the Waynesburg & Washington Railroad Station, Joseph Warren Jacobs's home, Joseph Warren Jacobs Birdhouse Company (earlier Henry Moore Jacobs blacksmith shop, later part of Fairmont Creamery), and ice plant. (Courtesy of the Greene County Historical Society.)

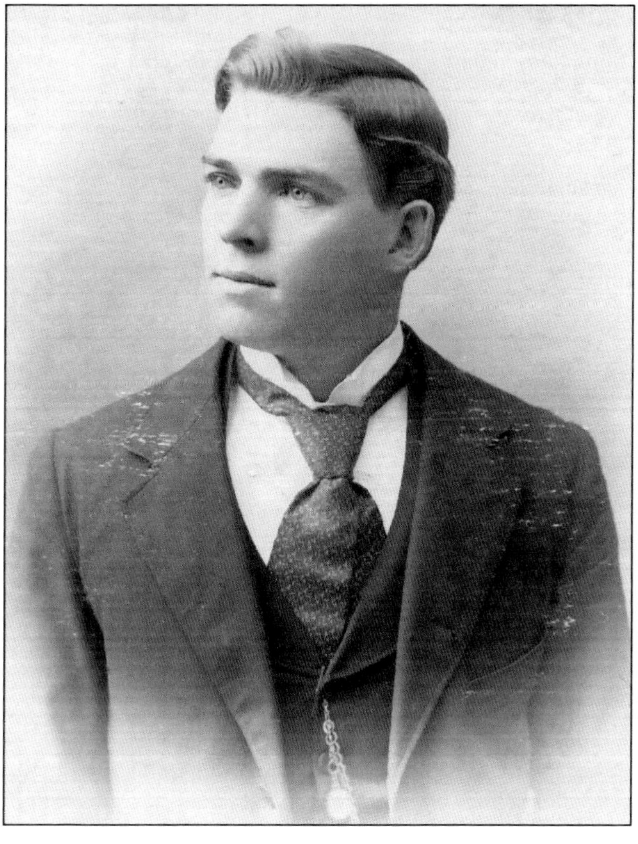

Joseph Warren Jacobs, founder of the Jacobs Birdhouse Company, was an oologist and ornithologist who presented his egg collection at world's fairs and built birdhouses for patrons such as Henry Ford and William Rockefeller. (Photograph by F.S. Hawkins, from the Helen Mae [Jacobs] Fonner Collection, courtesy of George and Anna [Fonner] Blystone.)

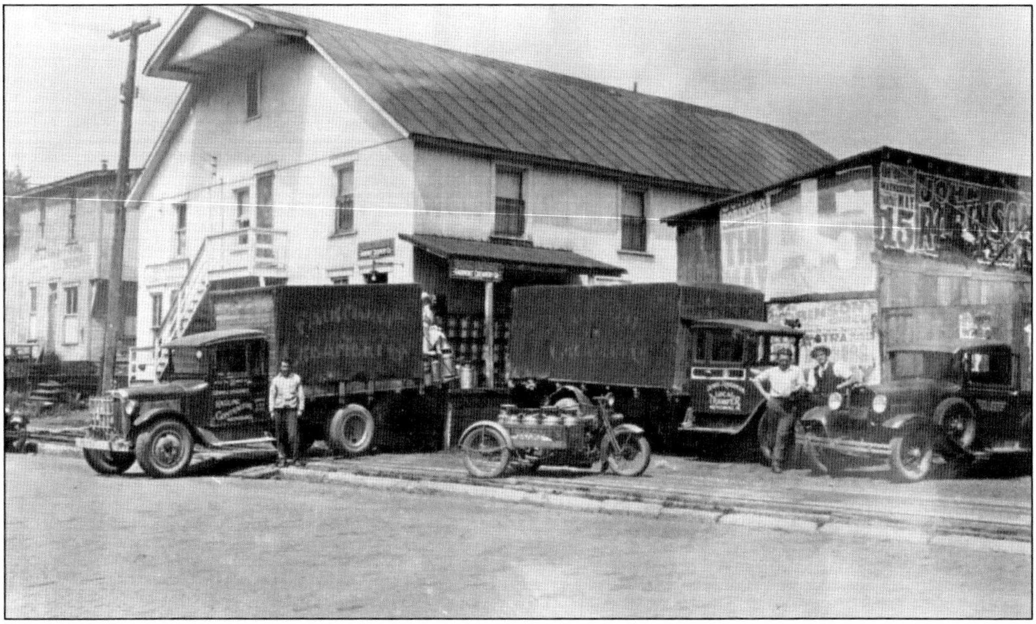

Fairmont Creamery Company was situated on First Street beside Waynesburg Milling and across from the Waynesburg & Washington Railroad. The two men on the far right are Dennis Loughman (left) and Earl Bryan Jacobs. (Courtesy of the Greene County Historical Society.)

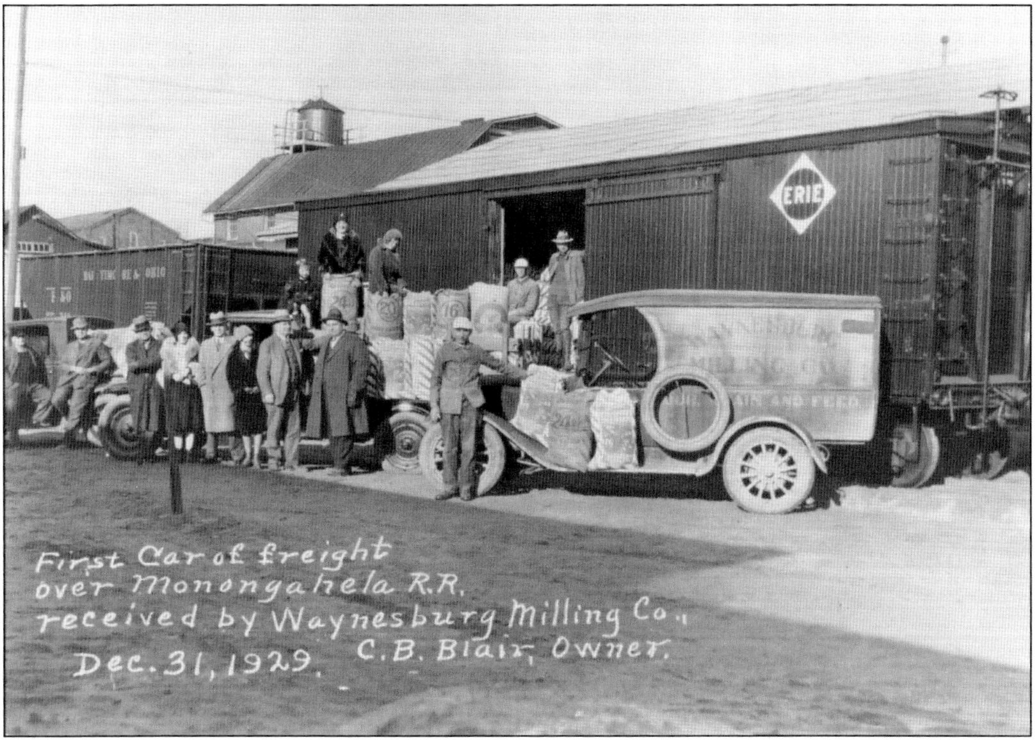

This photograph was taken to celebrate the first car of freight received via the Monongahela Railroad by Waynesburg Milling Company on December 31, 1929. The owner was C.B. Blair. Waynesburg Milling was located on First Street. (Courtesy of the Greene County Historical Society.)

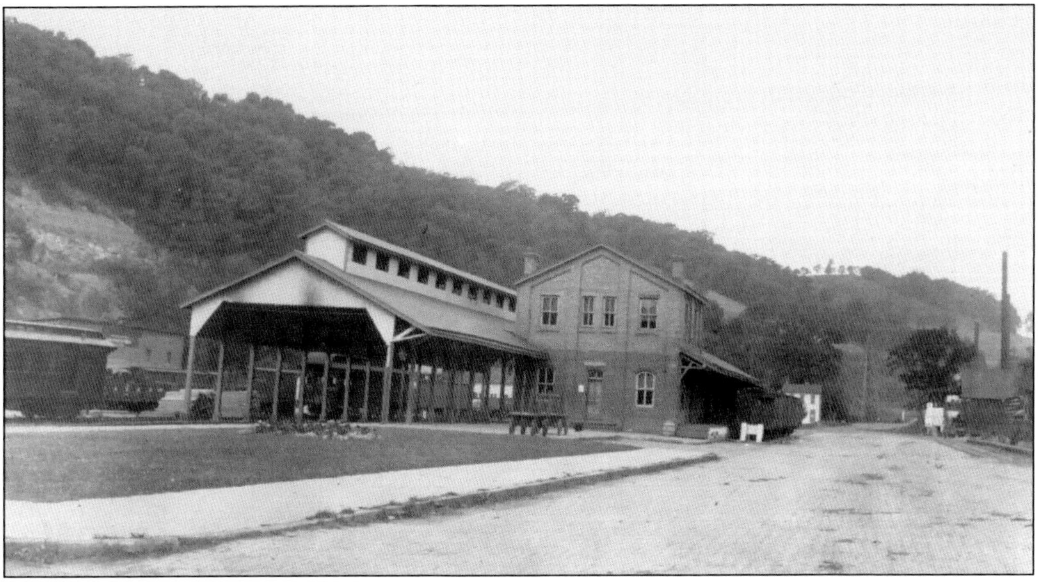

Pictured is the Waynesburg & Washington Railroad depot on First Street. These structures no longer exist; however, the local offices of the Norfolk Southern Railroad are now at this location. (From the Helen Mac [Jacobs] Fonner Collection, courtesy of George and Anna [Fonner] Blystone and James Weinschenker.)

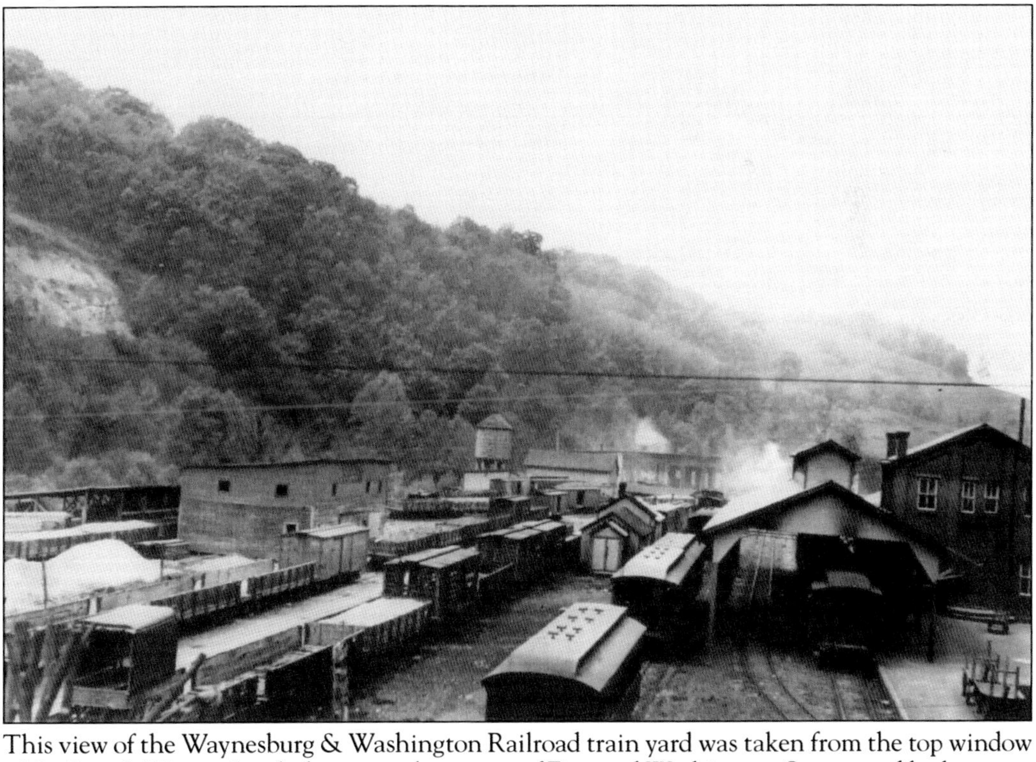

This view of the Waynesburg & Washington Railroad train yard was taken from the top window of the Joseph Warren Jacobs home on the corner of First and Washington Streets and looks across Washington Street. (From the Helen Mae [Jacobs] Fonner Collection, courtesy of George and Anna [Fonner] Blystone, and James Weinschenker.)

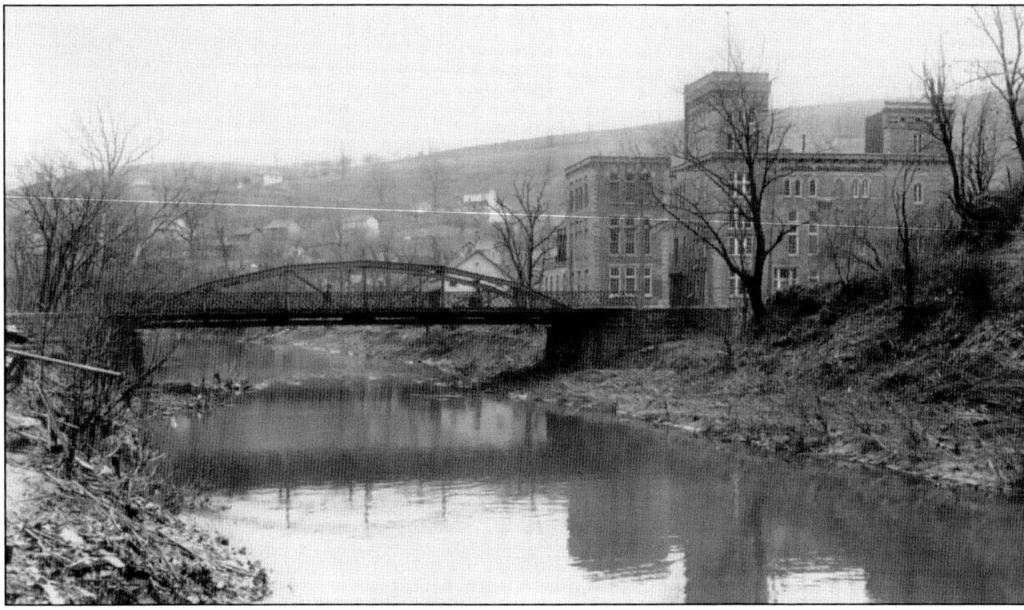

Waynesburg Brewing Company, located along the southern bank of Ten Mile Creek on Morgan Street, was built in 1901–1902. It opened for business in mid-May 1902. (Courtesy of the Waynesburg University Museum.)

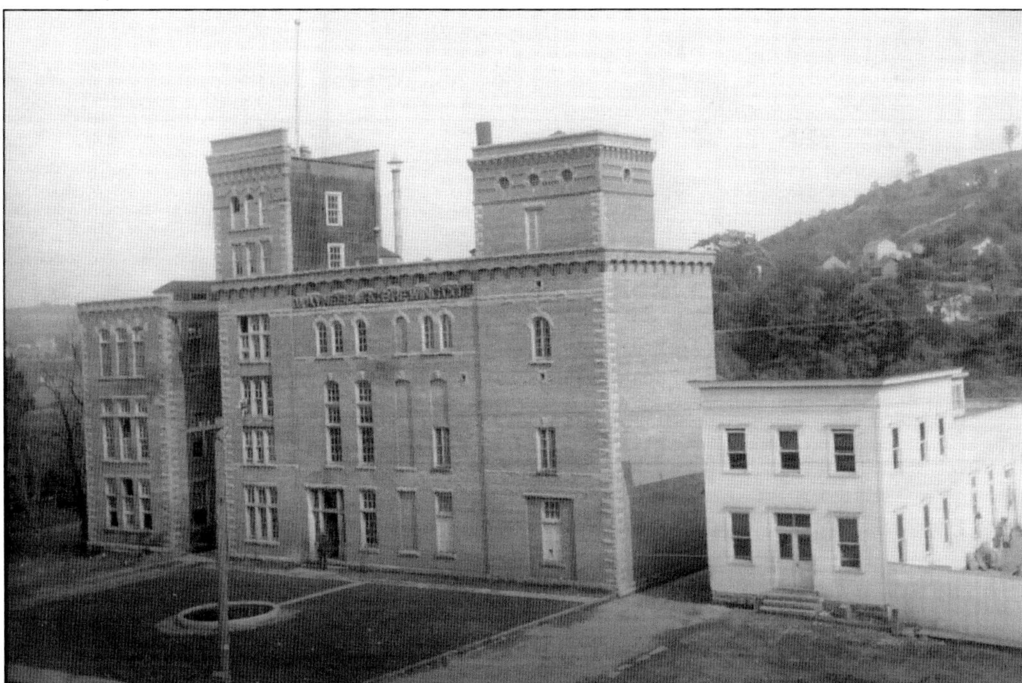

The Waynesburg Brewery's charter to brew beer was issued in November 1900 but was met with outcry from the local temperance supporters. When the brewery opened in 1902, there were no retail outlets for the sale of beer or other alcoholic beverages in Greene County, and it remained that way for years, even in the face of local hotels seeking licenses to accommodate travelers. (Courtesy of Waynesburg Borough.)

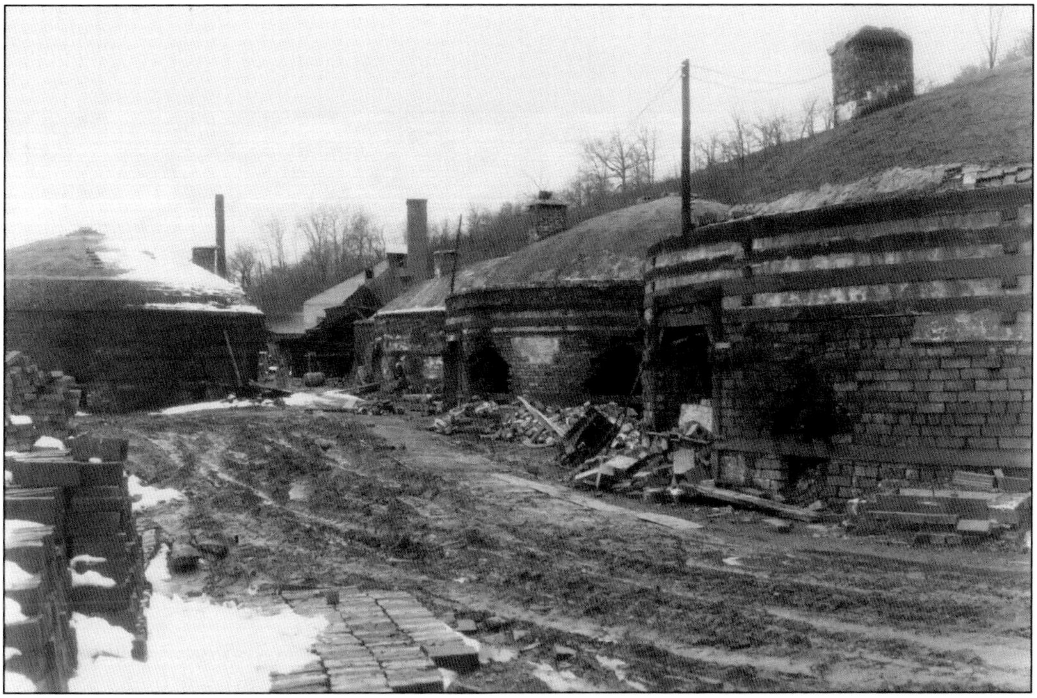

The brick ovens of the Waynesburg Brick and Stone Company were located just south of town and helped supply the local paving projects. (Courtesy of the Greene County Historical Society.)

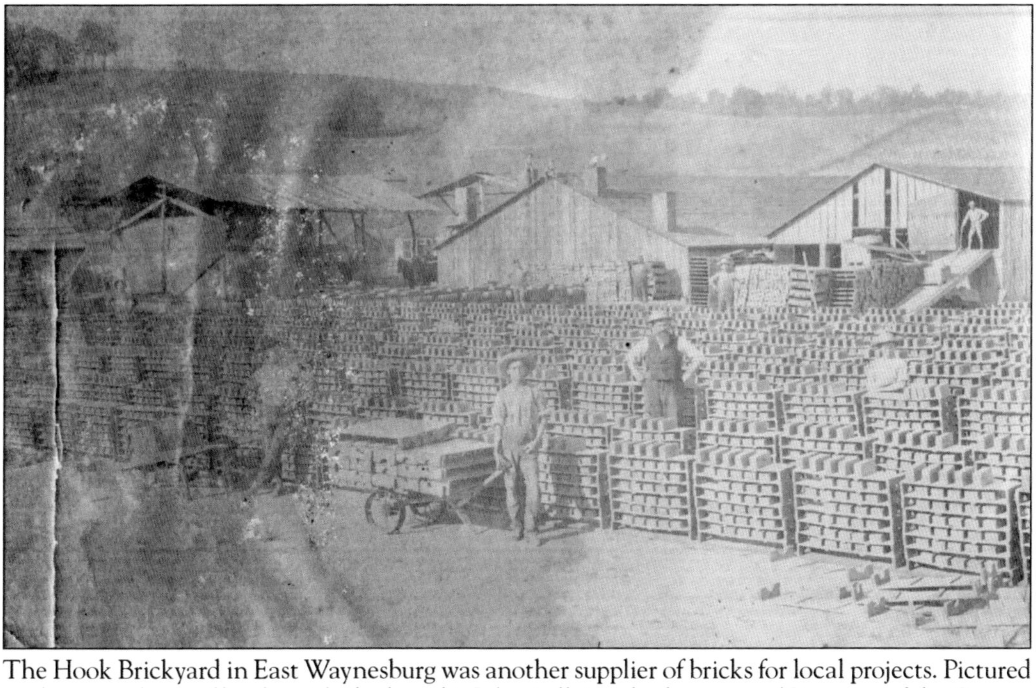

The Hook Brickyard in East Waynesburg was another supplier of bricks for local projects. Pictured in the second row of bricks with the beard is John Polk Hook, the owner. (Courtesy of the Greene County Historical Society.)

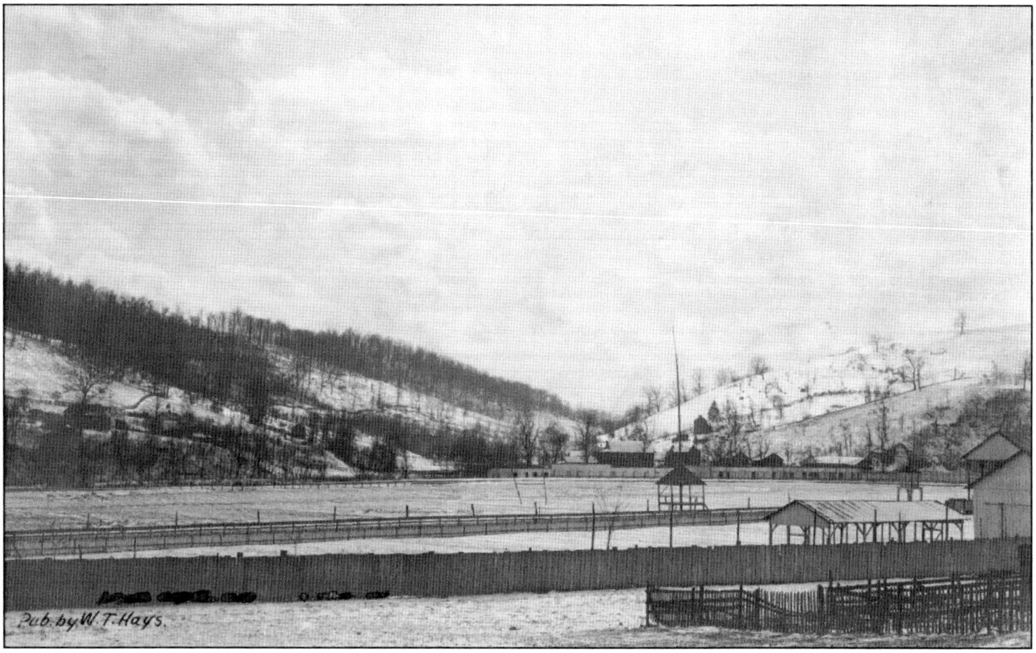

The old Waynesburg Fairgrounds, seen here in 1898, was situated on the south side where the Waynesburg University athletic field is now located. (Photograph by W.T. Hays, courtesy of Waynesburg Borough.)

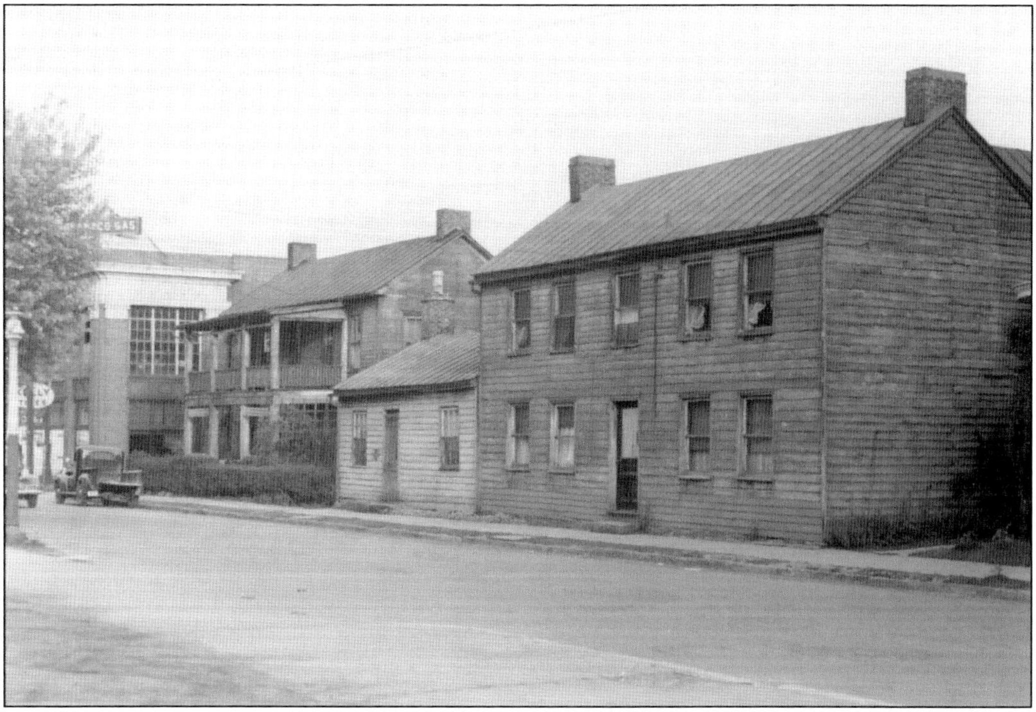

This image, with a view looking east on Greene Street (from Washington Street toward Morgan Street), shows buildings standing near where the current Sunoco gas station exists. (Photograph by William E.S. Fletcher, courtesy of the Cornerstone Genealogical Society.)

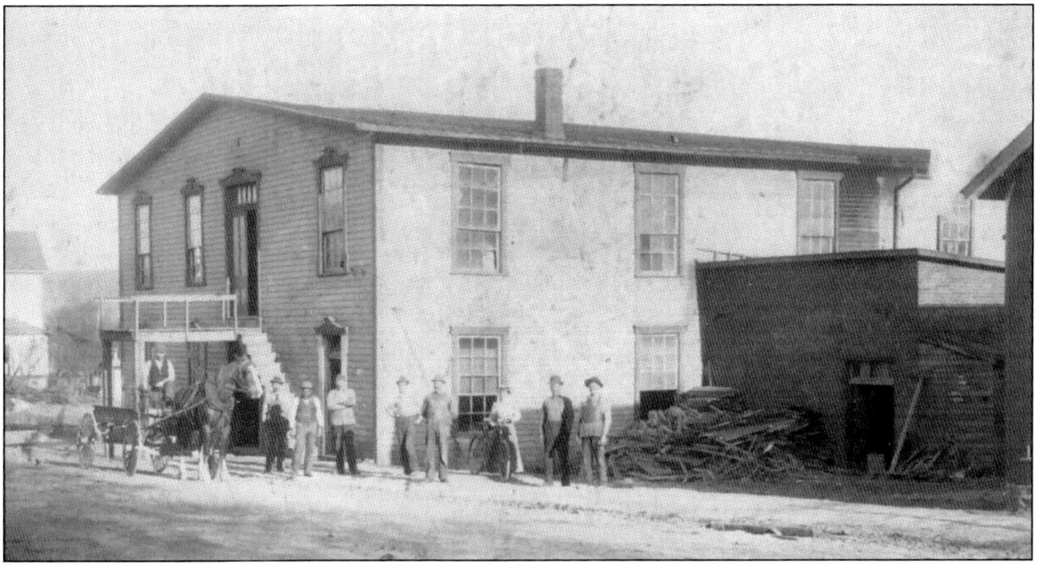

The Elms Brothers Machine Shop was a large planing mill and machine shop at the corner of Greene and Cumberland Streets that supplied services to the booming oil and gas business. It was nearly shut down during the Farmers & Drovers Bank failure; but with help, it survived for many more years. (From the Sarah Virginia [Elms] Simpson Collection, courtesy of Eva Mae [Simpson] Grim and Cicely Stewart-Kunsman.)

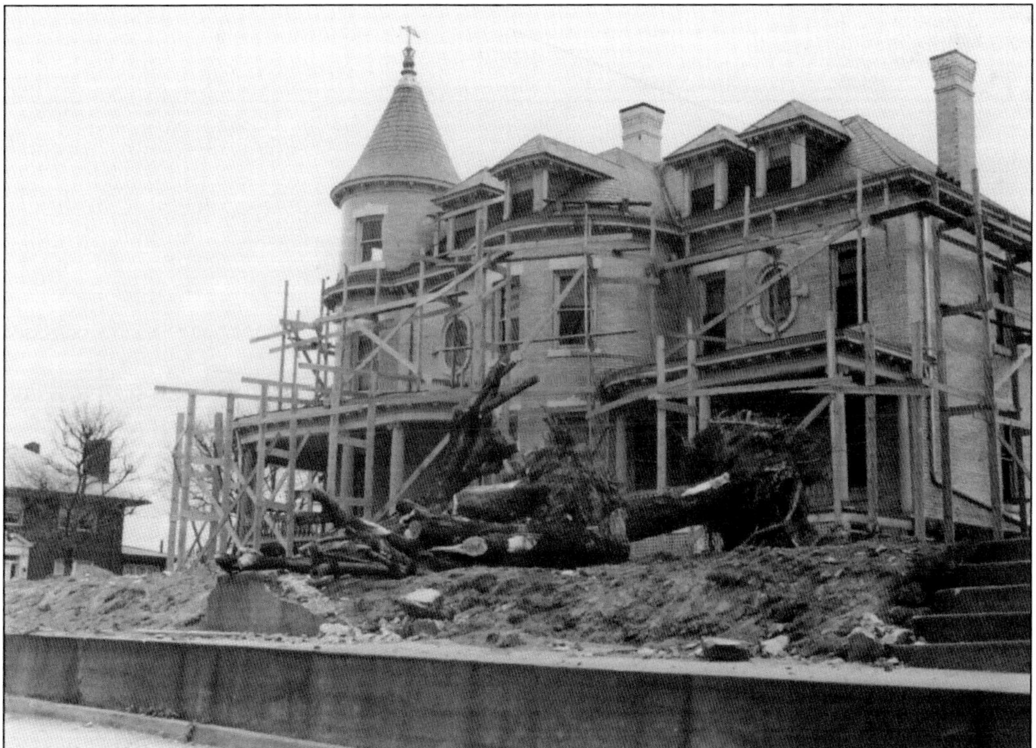

Pictured here is the Freeland house on the corner of Greene and Porter Streets while under construction. (Photograph by William E.S. Fletcher, courtesy of the Cornerstone Genealogical Society.)

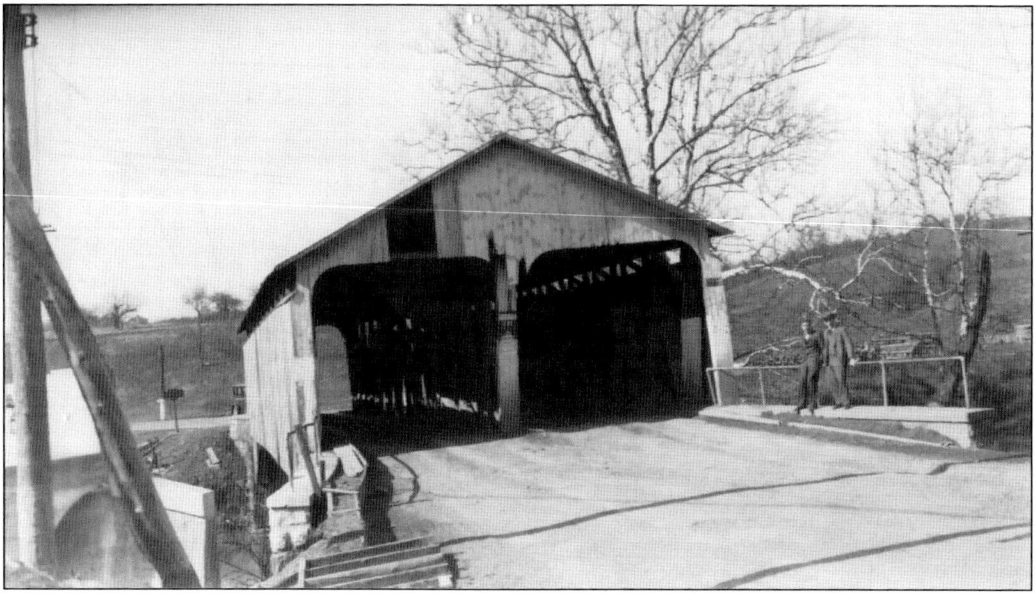

This unique double-lane covered bridge spanned Ten Mile Creek near the current location of Freedom Bridge. The latter was built to replace this wooden structure near the railroad underpass at the confluence of Greene and High Streets on the eastern edge of town. (From the Walter "Blackie" Markiewich Postcard Collection, courtesy of Brice and Linda Rush.)

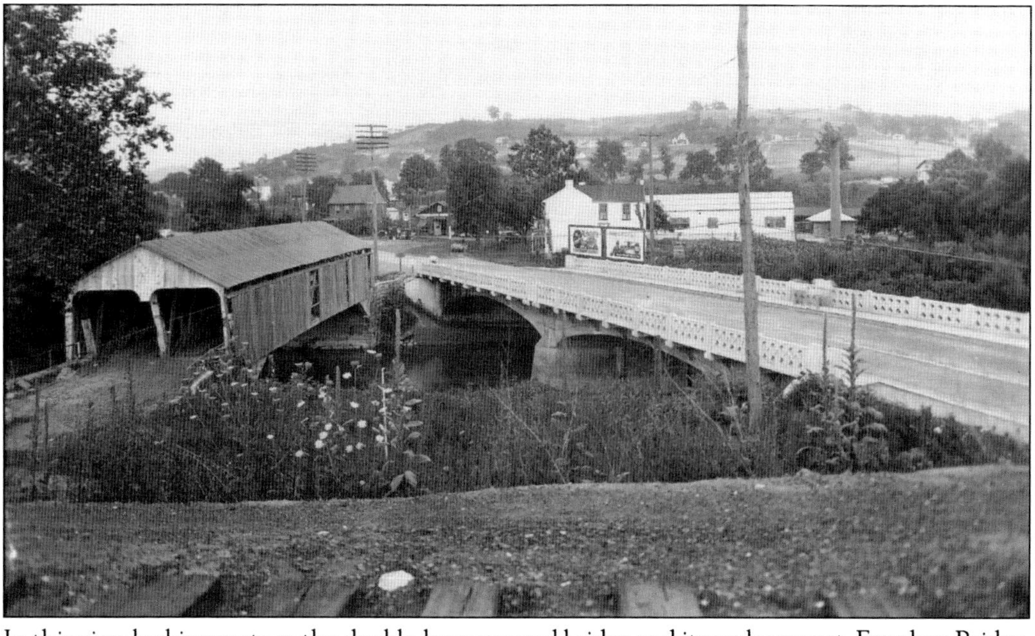

In this view looking east are the double-lane covered bridge and its replacement, Freedom Bridge, built in 1928 on Greene Street. The area on the eastern side of the bridge would later be the location of McDonald's. (Courtesy of the Greene County Historical Society.)

Bibliography

Bates, Samuel P. *History of Greene County, Pennsylvania.* (1888) 1998. Reprint, Mount Vernon, IN: Windmill Publications.

Caldwell, J. A. *Caldwell's Illustrated Combination Centennial Atlas of Greene Co. Pennsylvania.* (1876) 1995. Reprint, Mount Vernon, IN: Windmill Publications.

Dusenberry, William Howard. *Waynesburg College Story, 1849–1974.* Kent, OH: Kent State University Press, 1975.

Fonner, D. Kent. *All Quiet on the Border: The Civil War Era in Greene County, Pennsylvania.* Beach Lake, PA: D. Kent Fonner, 2012.

———. "Failure of the Farmers & Drovers National Bank of Waynesburg, Pennsylvania." *Pennsylvania Magazine of History and Biography* 104 (April 1980).

Hanna, Rev. William. *History of Greene County, PA.* (1882) 1996. Reprint, Apollo, PA: Closson Press.

High, Fred. *Waynesburg Prosperous & Beautiful.* (1906) 1973. Reprint, Parsons, WV: McClain Printing.

Leckey, Howard L. *The Tenmile Country and Its Pioneer Families: A Genealogical History of the Upper Monongahela Valley.* Reprint, Apollo, PA: Closson Press, 1997.

Smith, G. Wayne. *History of Greene County, Pennsylvania.* 2 vols. Waynesburg, PA: Cornerstone Genealogical Society, 1996.

———. *The Waynesburg Commons and Parks.* Waynesburg, PA: Cornerstone Genealogical Society, 2004.

Weinschenker, James D. *Narrow Gauge in Southwestern Pennsylvania: The Waynesburg & Washington Railroad.* Washingtonville, OH: M2FQ Publications, 2003.

Discover Thousands of Local History Books Featuring Millions of Vintage Images

Arcadia Publishing, the leading local history publisher in the United States, is committed to making history accessible and meaningful through publishing books that celebrate and preserve the heritage of America's people and places.

Find more books like this at
www.arcadiapublishing.com

Search for your hometown history, your old stomping grounds, and even your favorite sports team.

Consistent with our mission to preserve history on a local level, this book was printed in South Carolina on American-made paper and manufactured entirely in the United States. Products carrying the accredited Forest Stewardship Council (FSC) label are printed on 100 percent FSC-certified paper.

MADE IN THE USA